How Geek Girls Will Save the Planet

Jennifer Thorpe-Moscon, Ph.D.

2013

© 2013 Jennifer Thorpe-Moscon

Cover by Eric Thorpe-Moscon

ISBN-13: 978-1482786033
ISBN-10: 1482786036

First printing: April 2013

All rights reserved. Any reproduction or other unauthorized use of the material or artwork herein is prohibited without the express written permission of the author.

Printing/manufacturing information for this book may be found on the last page.

Contents

Being a Geek Girl..p. 2

Interviews!
      Computers and Technology........................p. 15
      Math and Science..p. 62
      Gaming..p. 102
      Science Fiction/Fantasy..............................p. 158
      Comics/Manga...p. 241

Being a Geek Girl

"Nerd. Geek. Used to be if you self-identified that way, you'd get thrown into a locker and never have sex. Or worse, whatever that is. But to me and more and more people I know, being a nerd or a geek means having passion, power, intelligence. Being a nerd just means there is something in the world that you care deeply about – be it twelve-sided dice, a favorite sports team, your new laptop, or Knight Rider."

— Olivia Munn, *Suck It, Wonder Woman!: The Misadventures of a Hollywood Geek* (New York: St. Martin's Press, 2010)

"Being a geek is all about being honest about what you enjoy and not being afraid to demonstrate that affection. It means never having to play it cool about how much you like something. It's basically a license to proudly emote on a somewhat childish level rather than behave like a supposed adult. Being a geek is extremely liberating."

— Simon Pegg

If you're anything like me, you were a geek girl before the term existed or was widely known. As a small girl you played with science kits, excelled at math, loved reading and watching fantasy stories, or bested your brothers at Sonic the Hedgehog. As you grew up, maybe you found a group of friends with similar interests. Maybe you didn't, and were always that weird kid who got picked on. Maybe you found other geek girls, or maybe most of your friends were boys. No matter your story, geek girls are united by more than just particular interests – I would argue that geek girls have a unique way of approaching their worlds. Their curiosity, imagination, and drive to learn and explore are unparalleled – and that is why geek girls are destined to rule the world.

The world is beginning to notice. As I write this (true story), there is a commercial on TV for a technology college featuring a woman talking about her love of the subject while assembling a computer. We're not weirdos anymore; we're skilled, intelligent people with a lot to offer. And it is in that spirit that this book is written.

This book begins by giving a brief history of the hidden worlds of geek girls with a review of what life has been like for women in each major area of geekdom: computers and technology, math and science, gaming, sci-fi/fantasy, and comics/manga. One thing that, in my experience, defines most geeks is an equally-powerful interest in things based in reality and things based in fantasy. In fact, as I alluded to before, it is a geek's imagination and creativity that make her the best possible person to solve real-world problems – she can devise a solution that no one else could have invented.

This has been borne out in real-world experiences. Science fiction has, in many cases, predicted later scientific developments. It has inspired real schools of scientific research. As we speak, scientists in laboratories are studying time travel. They are debating it in journals and books. Is it possible? What would be necessary for it to occur? Can the past ever be changed, or is it immutable and we can only interact with it as we were "meant to"? Is there one world or many? These aren't just questions for science fiction authors to explore; they are real questions being addressed in physics labs every day. This is just one example of how the expansive and creative thought processes of geeks make them ideally-suited to real scientific and technological endeavors. It is geeks that will create the world of the future.

Computers and Technology

The term "geek girl" originated with an online magazine, "Geekgirl", run by Rosie Cross in 1993, which is still up and running (http://geekgirl.com.au). As computers and technology grew and became a part of everyday life, geek girls did too. In the early days of computing, there were no educational programs specifically for computers and programming. As one of our interviewees points out, computing companies hired people based on other qualifications that made them suited to the task, such as studies in mathematics or other types of engineering. In these early days before computers were the mainstream, women's difficulty was not so much getting into computing as having a career at all. Societal pressures to be a homemaker were profound. But if a woman beat back that pressure and got an education, in many cases she would not have had trouble getting a job in computing. In fact, there were many women who were instrumental in creating the world of computing as we know it. The first recognized computer programmer was Ada Lovelace, who in 1842 wrote an algorithm for a machine to compute Bernoulli numbers[1]. During World War II, women were enlisted to perform calculations on computers as well as program them for the military and used computers to work on the Manhattan Project. Grace Hopper, widely known as the Mother of COBOL, created the very first compiler for an electronic computer[2]. These are only a few examples; many more women contributed significantly to the development of modern computing.

However, when computers entered into more common usage in the workplace, the idea that computing was "for men" took hold. Between 1984 and 1989, the percentage of Computer Science degrees awarded to women dropped from 37.1% to 29.9%[3]. In the next eight years, the percentage dropped further to 26.7% before plummeting to a depressing less-than-12% in 2010-2011[4]. There are several challenges in overcoming this trend. For starters, the lack of women creates a cycle of increasingly fewer women in the field – women are disinclined to enter

---

[1] Kar, Aditi. "Lady Ada Lovelace and the Analytical Engine." Mathematical Institute, University of Oxford. Web. Accessed 28 March 2013.
<http://people.maths.ox.ac.uk/kar/AdaLovelace.html>
[2] Massachusetts Institute of Technology. "Inventor of the Week Archive: Grace Hopper." *Lemelson-MIT*. MIT, June 2006. Web. Accessed 28 March 2013.
<http://web.mit.edu/invent/iow/hopper.html>
[3] Camp, Tracy. *Women in Computer Science: Reversing the Trend.* Colorado School of Mines, 2001. Web. Accessed 28 March 2013.
<http://www.cs.cmu.edu/~women/resources/aroundTheWeb/hostedPapers/Syllabus-Camp.pdf>
[4] Zwebe, Stuart. *Computing Degree and Enrollment Trends: From the 2010-2011 CRA Taulbee Survey.* The Computing Research Association, 2012. Web. Accessed 28 March 2013.
<http://cra.org/uploads/documents/resources/taulbee/CS_Degree_and_Enrollment_Trends_2010-11.pdf>

into a field where they have few other women with whom to work. It also creates concerns in young girls that computing is not "for me", or that they will be seen negatively by both men and other women for doing something gender atypical. Efforts to specifically encourage women to enter into and advance in computing are double-edged swords. On the one hand, the encouragement can create positive feelings in young women about the field. But on the other hand, it can create the sense that women need "something extra" to succeed, something beyond what men need. This is false, however – such encouragement only creates the peer groups for women that men already have.

What is furthermore damaging is if this encouragement creates stereotype threat in young women. That is, if women are acutely aware of the societal perception that computing is not for them, they may feel intense pressure to disprove that perception – pressure that can result in anxiety that harms their performance. Encouragement of women in computing needs to aspire to make women feel at home in computing rather than invaders in a male world. One step toward this goal would be to make women aware of how instrumental women were in the formation of computing, thereby showing them that they are not invaders. Rather, they have always belonged in computing, and the years in which they have not been included are the oddities.

Mathematics and Science

Similarly, women have always been a factor in the world of math and science. However, math and science have always stacked the deck against women – even the ancient Greeks viewed scientific thought as the province of men. Many women displayed intelligence and creativity in mathematical and scientific thought, but they were rarely recognized for their accomplishments. Those women whose accomplishments were recorded in myth, such as Queen Dido who built Carthage, were ultimately discredited by showing that they were "just weak women" after all – in Dido's case, the tale of her suicide over Aeneas' departure obliterates the importance of her contribution, at least as it is depicted in the literature. While the goddess Athena guided the ways of war, mathematics, and wisdom, real human women could not establish themselves in these endeavors in the public eye.

The Scientific Revolution, beginning with Copernicus, was a turning point for women in math and science. While women at this time were not considered to have equal footing with men, they began to take a far more active and visible role in these endeavors, particularly scientific endeavors based in the home and that furthered homemaker activities, as any pursuit in this arena was considered more acceptable for women[5]. The spread of the Italian thirst for study and knowledge included Italy's relatively greater acceptance of women scholars[6]. That said, the increased exposure of women to science and scientific methods occurred predominantly among the rich. As is often the case, the affluent had greater access to scientific tools, education, and literature, and moreover had the luxury of the time to explore new ideas and write about them. Still, women were often seen as the passive recipients of scientific knowledge rather than active participants in its discovery[7].

Regardless of how they were perceived by men and even other women, some women pushed forth, writing their own scientific reports, translating complicated scientific findings and theories for general consumption, educating themselves when no other means were possible, and mentoring and tutoring other women. Opportunities for women in higher education opened up – very slowly and with much resistance, but they opened nonetheless. Women fought for positions as scientists and, in greater numbers than are usually recognized, as medical doctors[8]. Sadly, even as more women entered into scientific work and education, they were often not recognized for their accomplishments.

---

[5] Watts, Ruth. *Women in Science: A Social and Cultural History.* New York: Routledge, 2007.
[6] Alic, Margaret. *Hypatia's Heritage.* Boston: Beacon Press, 1986.
[7] Watts, Ruth. *Women in Science: A Social and Cultural History.*
[8] Ibid.

Men were neither wholly resistant to nor accepting of women's thirst for scientific knowledge. Many forward-thinking men embraced women into their fields, regarding them as equally capable and a great benefit to science, while others mocked them as though it was humorous that females would play at men's work. Unfortunately this latter idea persists today, though thankfully there are far fewer men in the latter category, proportionally-speaking, now than there once were.

It is the efforts of these women during the Scientific Revolution and since that have opened the door for modern women to mathematics and science. Nonetheless, women have difficulty being acknowledged for their contributions. Cecilia Payne-Gaposchkin discovered of what the universe is composed[9], but to this day has received little recognition for her major accomplishment. But recognized or not, and whether or not the men around them believed that they should pursue scientific knowledge, many women did anyway, thus establishing women as inherently belonging in the scientific world.

Gaming

It is a curious thing that gaming was ever regarded as a man's world. Today women comprise almost half of all gamers, including roleplaying games, video games, and computer/online games. In part, this misperception of gaming is due to the fact that games have long been marketed toward men – but not even men in their diversity and complexity, men as simplistic horny warhounds. Women appearing in games have long been mostly naked and buxomy, their characters having little in terms of personality or development. Yet this marketing strategy increasingly falls flat with both genders – I personally can't even think of a single man who buys or plays a game because there is a voluptuous female character in it (they like boobs, but tend to devote their interest to

---

[9] She is an Astronomer. "Cecilia Payne-Gaposchkin (1900 - 1979)." She is an Astronomer, 2013. Web. Accessed 28 March 2013. <http://www.sheisanastronomer.org/index.php/history/cecilia-payne-gaposchkin>

the real thing). Thus, the strategy has changed somewhat in recent years, as strong female protagonists can be found in some games including first-person shooters and tournament-type games. Female game creators have taken the reins in some instances and developed games that appeal to women as well as men. We can hope that as more women enter game creation – and many more are – there will be more games that either consider women's interests specifically or, as many women in fact prefer, are truly gender-neutral.

  It is not simply the games themselves that have engendered this belief that gaming is a "man's world". Some male gamers hold negative attitudes toward female gamers, in part in response to a history of marginalization of gamers in general. Male gamers, looked upon as weird or dorky by the non-gaming world, may be helping themselves to feel better about themselves by looking down upon female gamers. In saying that girls don't belong in gaming, they establish gaming as their world, something they can own that others cannot access, to which only they are privileged. It is a world in which they can act out their fantasies, ones that they might want to hide from girlfriends and girl friends. Moreover, simply in creating a derogated outgroup, they can feel positively by comparison about their ingroup. This may come across as nasty, and it is, but it is an outgrowth of normal human categorization processes and the need to defend one's own identity. However, as gaming becomes more and more mainstream, it is likely that male gamers will have no need to do this and therefore will be more accepting of women in their games. In addition, the more gender equality we see in society as a whole, the more males may feel as comfortable displaying their gaming fantasies in front of women as they are in front of other men. As it stands, today far fewer male gamers hold these sorts of negative attitudes about female gamers than once did, and most welcome women into their games.

  MMOs (massively multiplayer online games) and other RPGs (roleplaying games) have actually been some of the most progressive in this area, primarily because they offer the opportunity for women to create their own characters. The player's guides for many games have been adapted to include sample descriptions of both male and female characters that are equally powerful and diverse. While some gaming groups may exclude women, and certainly the stereotype that women do not enjoy gaming persists, this is changing too as more women seek out gaming groups and men find that they enjoy what their female players bring to the table. Even on a cultural level this stereotype is being destroyed. One example is the television program "The Big Bang Theory". In some of the show's episodes, the nerdy male characters are viewed through the eyes of the "normal" Penny. In a lot of ways we as the audience are expected to identify with Penny and laugh not with but at the male geeks and their "odd" ways. We get a few glimpses early on of a female nerd, Leslie Winkle, but she is not part of the main cast. However, later episodes introduce the equally-nerdy female characters of Bernadette and Amy and even find Penny becoming addicted to the MMO Age of Conan. While Penny's relationship with the game in that episode is decidedly unhealthy, it shatters the belief that "normal" girls don't enjoy gaming.

Science Fiction and Fantasy

The arenas of science fiction and fantasy may have been those in which women have been the most readily embraced. Since these genres were not as institutionalized as science itself, women were not discouraged from them as pervasively. The first female science fiction writer may have been Lady Margaret Cavendish, the Duchess of Newcastle. In 1666 she published "The Description of a New World, Called the Blazing World". This was over 150 years before Mary Shelley, the woman commonly thought of as responsible for launching the science fiction genre itself.

Early pulp magazines eagerly accepted science fiction writing by women at rates far higher than is generally recognized – some magazines had as high as 40% female authorship[10]. Before 1965, there were at least

---

[10] Davin, Eric Leif. *Partners in wonder: women and the birth of science fiction, 1926-1965*. United States of America: Lexington Books, 2006.

203 female science fiction authors who published under their own names – not, as is commonly believed, under a male pseudonym[11]. That is not to say that there was no bias against women, bias that persists particularly in the fields of hard science fiction, action-adventure fantasy, and epic fantasy, but simply to suggest that it has not been as pervasive as is often believed. Moreover, an examination of letters written to pulp magazines suggests that female readership was high, as many letters by women were published. These letters indicated that much of the hostility toward women who enjoyed science fiction was directed at them from those outside of the field, those who did not themselves enjoy science fiction. Any hostility from within the field was relatively minimal, and when it appeared, it was readily shut down by sharp female fans[12].

Additionally, there is reason to believe that women's relative scarcity in the field of science fiction was not due to overt sexism by those within the field, but rather the sexism inherent in society that imposed constraints on women not imposed upon men – motherhood and domestic duties[13]. Indeed, it is society's continued assertion that motherhood is the most important – in many cases the only important – role for women that has kept women from pursuing other lines of work. In addition, the fact that the responsibilities of parenting usually fall disproportionately on the woman has enabled men to pursue lines of work that women have not had the time to pursue. "Unfortunately, unlike men, wives don't have wives to take the daily burdens of life from them so that they may become creative geniuses."[14] It will be no surprise to most geek girls – smart, creative, ambitious women – that a lack of equality in one area of life spills over to every other area, and this is true no matter which geeky career field one might pursue.

---

[11] Ibid.
[12] Ibid.
[13] Ibid.
[14] Ibid.

Comics and Manga

Though women have been a minority in comic book writing, illustrating, and publishing, they were present from the beginning. In mainstream comics, some of these women illustrated comics that involved children[15], a theme that society found quite acceptable for them to address. More daring cartoonists addressed the theme of suffrage in their comics, notably early feminist Nell Brinkley, whose attractive female characters exemplified the modern (at the time) American woman and the themes that concerned her[16]. Indeed, women cartoonists incorporated the themes of their times into comics just as men did – they had to, lest their comics become outdated. Still, many early female cartoonists left their professions to pursue marriage and motherhood as yet again a disproportionate focus on these roles for women pressured them in ways that men were not pressured.

Not all women, however, relegated themselves to only drawing children or carefree flappers, nor to abandoning their careers for housewifery. Dale Messick created Brenda Starr, the first popular, strong, action-oriented female character, and encountered much backlash from men in the industry. In creating Brenda, she was trespassing on "male territory" and paving the way for all of the female action heroines to come. Her work and resistance to this backlash is the reason that strong female characters have a home in comics today. But to create such an action-oriented character she had to change her name, something authors of lighter comics did not have to do – she was born Dalia, not Dale[17].

During wartime in World War II, female cartoonists became more prevalent and strong female characters, such as aviators or other warrior

---

[15] Robbins, Trina. *The Great Women Cartoonists.* New York: Watson-Guptill Publications, 2001.
[16] Ibid.
[17] Severo, Richard. "Dale Messick, Cartoonist Who Created Brenda Starr, Dies at 98." *Arts.* New York Times, 7 April 2005. Web. Accessed 28 March 2013. <http://www.nytimes.com/2005/04/07/arts/07cnd-messick.html?_r=0>

women, appeared with some regularity. After the war, however, women largely left action strips and returned to either homemaking, drawing more "gender-acceptable" strips about romance or teens and other youth, or both. Finally, when comics entered a slump in the late 1950s, of the major publishers only Marvel and DC survived, both of which were directed toward young men with a focus on superheroes. In the slump's inevitable firings, women were the first to go, and few remained in the slump's wake.[18] In Japan as well, manga was predominantly created by men.

In response, women created worlds of underground comics. They had to create their own niche; women had a difficult time establishing themselves within male-created alternative comic books partly due to explicit gender-based exclusion and partly due to the mature female-relevant themes they wished to address. It is for these reasons that the underground and independent comix market has included many all-women publications – written, illustrated, and published entirely by women. The number of these has steadily increased, with many addressing feminist themes and even reintroducing women warriors. There are now more female cartoonists than ever before, but most publish in independent publications, self-published comics, or small presses[19]. In these worlds, there are no restrictions on the topics women can address, and as such their comics run the gamut.

At the same time, women in Japan in the late 1960s emerged into the world of manga. Hagio Moto, Riyoko Ikeda, Yumiko Oshima, Keiko Takemiya, and Ryoko Yamagishi, later called the Year 24 Group, joined forces to mark the first major female debut into the genre[20]. Their work included themes such as romance and superheroines targeted toward women and girls. While much of manga was for a long time targeted toward one gender or the other, it has gained worldwide popularity with

---

[18] Robbins, Trina. *The Great Women Cartoonists.*
[19] Ibid.
[20] WikiProject Anime and Manga. *Anime and Manga.* California: Wikimedia Foundation, 2011. Digital file.

both genders, including themes of personal development, suffering, and heroism.

Women have recently become established in the high ranks of even mainstream comics and a force in darker, mature-themed books. One notable example of this is Karen Berger, who in 1993 was given her own DC Comics imprint to manage – Vertigo – thanks to her success with darker-themed stories including The Sandman. Indeed, graphic novels in general are one arena in which women have made enormous strides.

By 2010, geek girls were given the ultimate in formal recognition in the world of comics – a panel all our own at San Diego Comic-Con entitled "Geek Girls Exist". Since then, in October 2011, we even had our own conference, GeekGirlCon. At the 2012 New York Comic-Con, the Sunday program included many panels devoted entirely to women. Also in 2012, a group of entrepreneurial women published "Womanthology: Heroic", a collection of comics written by over 140 women, the proceeds of which go to charity. Since then, IDW picked up Womanthology for a 5-issue series that will be compiled into a graphic novel called "Womanthology: Space"[21].

In all geeky fields, things are improving for women, and those who have found success want to pass it on. Recently, some toys have been developed to encourage young girls to learn science and engineering, have confidence in those areas, and have fun with them. One toy is GoldieBlox by Debbie Sterling, designed to provide engineering education via a female role model who is smart, is relatable, and loves engineering (http://www.goldieblox.com/). Pilot testing showed that girls found GoldieBlox highly engaging and both liked and wanted to be like Goldie[22]. Lynn Liben at Penn State will be studying the effect the toy has

---

[21] Womanthology, IDW. Web. Accessed 28 March 2013. <http://womanthology.blogspot.com>

[22] Isaacson, Betsy. "Can GoldieBlox, AKA Legos For Girls, Entice More Girls To Be Engineers?" *Women in Tech*. The Huffington Post, 21 September 2012. Web. Accessed 28 March 2013. <http://www.huffingtonpost.com/2012/09/20/goldieblox-legos-for-girls_n_1901488.html>

on girls over the next few years. Another set of toys is provided by Nancy B's Science Club, offering products such as a microscope, binoculars, a telescope, and accompanying activity books that are designed to teach scientific skills (nancybscienceclub.com). While these toys may be used by both girls and boys, by featuring a female leading the child through the tasks, they teach children to see women as inherently belonging and capable in the STEM world. Geek girls no longer languish in the shadows; we are front and center.

In every area of geekdom, there have always been women passionately striving, creating, and building, whether or not these women ever received any media or other public attention. In this book, I interview many well-known women including some from each area of geekdom about their fields – asking them how they fell in love with the world of geeks and how they established themselves within it, as well as about any sexism they encountered in so doing. To what extent did they have to overcome implicit or explicit sexism to succeed? Were they encouraged, ignored, or even actively discouraged? Each woman's story is unique, each having experienced a different path to success. Some do not fit neatly into one category, as their work has spanned different geek genres, but in the interest of simplicity I have categorized them according to the area for which they are most known (a tough call at times) – do not, however, take that as a sign that it is the only area! I am grateful to these women for participating in this book and contributing their voices. I hope that you will find their stories as inspiring as I did.

Interviews: Computers and Technology

Ruzena Bajcsy..p. 16
Anita Jones..p. 19
Susan Landau..p. 23
Barbara Liskov..p. 27
Jo Ellen Moore..p. 31
Evi Nemeth..p. 34
Rosalind Picard...p. 38
Ellen Spertus...p. 44
Telle Whitney...p. 47
Jennifer Widom..p. 50
Nicole Zeckner..p. 53
Lixia Zhang...p. 57

Ruzena Bajcsy

Dr. Ruzena Bajcsy is Professor of Electrical Engineering and Computer Science and Director Emerita of CITRIS (the Center for Information Technology Research in the Interest of Society) at the University of California, Berkeley. Previously, she was head of the National Science Foundation's Computer and Information Science and Engineering Directorate. Dr. Bajcsy actually holds two doctorates, one in electrical engineering and one in computer science. She has received several awards, including the Association for Computing Machinery (ACM)/Association for the Advancement of Artificial Intelligence Allen Newell Award, the ACM Distinguished Service Award, the Computing Research Associates Distinguished Service Award, and the Benjamin Franklin Medal in Computer and Cognitive Science. The latter was in recognition of her work on robotic perception and innovations in the analysis of medical images.

How did your passion for robotics and machine perception develop?

I always wanted to be an engineer following in my father's footsteps, and robotics was a natural incentive towards understanding people and machines.

What is the most exciting project on which you and your students are currently working?

We are trying to understand the physics (kinematics and dynamics) of human motion using robotic and control theoretic models.

What do you envision as the future of your line of research – particularly, in what ways do you most hope it will have a positive impact on people's lives?

The future is how to understand and predict the behavior and interaction between machines and people. How to design prosthesis, how to design walking chairs, how to design living spaces for elderly people.

What was the environment like for women in computing in the early years of your career?

Not so good, there was a great deal of suspicion what women can do in engineering.

How has it changed since then?

Considerably! I think there is more acceptance that women are as smart as men. There is more acceptance that women can hold their place in science and engineering. If there still is a lack of women proportionally being in the field of science and engineering, it is a cultural bias that may come from family, and from peers that inhibit girls and women from getting into these fields.

What advice would you offer girls and women interested in a career in computer science?

Do not be afraid; you can do it, and there are many jobs waiting for you.

How do you think we can encourage more women to get involved in STEM fields, generally, and change the perception of these fields as being inappropriate for women?

It is hard to say. Statistics points to the fact that girls do as well as boys in math or sometimes even better until they come to middle school.

At that point girls need encouragement from family and teachers to offset the peer pressure. We also need much more promotion of women in STEM fields, showing that they are normal human beings, feminine, mothers, etc.

Anita Jones

Dr. Anita Jones is a computer scientist and former Director of Defense Research and Engineering for the U.S. Department of Defense. In 1981 she and her husband founded Tartan Laboratories, a compiler technology company. She is University Professor emerita at the University of Virginia and a member of the MIT Corporation, the National Academy of Engineering, and the Council on Foreign Relations. In 2004, Dr. Jones received the Augusta Ada Lovelace Award from the Association of Women in Computing, and has also received the Department of Defense Award for Distinguished Public Service, the Computing Research Association's Service Award, and the Air Force Meritorious Civilian Service Award. She has a seamount (a mountain rising from the ocean seafloor that does not reach to the water's surface) in the North Pacific Ocean named after her by the U.S. Navy (it is located at 51° 25′ N and 159° 10′ W).

Dr. Jones: I don't feel "geeky" in the least. I feel empowered! I have an engineering education (in computer science) and experience that comes from many years in the field. I know how to create things that society wants and needs. I know how to analyze and reason so that I can make sound decisions. An engineering education – in any field of education – empowers one – man or woman – to go out and make a difference. If that is "geeky", let's have more geeks.

How did your passion for computer science develop? How did you know that computer science was the career for you?

When I was choosing a career (after getting an undergraduate degree in math and a master's in English literature), I decided that I wanted to be involved with something that would be fast-paced, something that would change society during my lifetime. And the very best choice at that time was computer science!

What inspired you and your husband to found Tartan Laboratories?

We, like many researchers in universities, had an entrepreneurial bent. Tartan exploited some software research achievements of my husband. We decided to take the small company route to move those ideas into practices. And that was the beginning of Tartan.

As Director of Defense Research and Engineering for the U.S. Department of Defense, what would you say were your most rewarding activities? What were the most challenging aspects of the position?

The most rewarding activity was to oversee the funding of some of the best new research ideas, to fund stunningly brilliant researchers and developers both inside and outside the department. People and ideas – the best ones – are a national treasure, and it was an honor to be in a position to move both forward.

One challenge was to protect the DoD science and technology budget from major cuts. I was DDR&E at a time when the DoD was in the final years of a decade-long 40% cut in budget. Forty percent! There were budget limitation issues on every front. The science and technology (S&T) budget is discretionary, and each year during my tenure as DDR&E, one or another service expressed a desire to make major reductions in the S&T budget with the assurance that it would be "put back" in out-years. But, as any researcher can tell you, stable funding across many years is absolutely needed to make major advancement. Unstable budgets torpedo the advancement of research. So, when the DoD was internally building their budget, I had the responsibility, and some authority, to ensure that draconian cuts in the S&T budget were not made. Mostly, I succeeded.

However, when I lost in the budget preparation exercises inside the Pentagon, often the House and Senate Armed Services Committees came to the rescue and "put the money back", because they – in a bi-partisan way – believed that the investment in research and technology was absolutely crucial to the military's future capability. So, while it was a difficult time, all around me were people who shared a belief in the criticality of what we were doing.

What is the most exciting project on which you are currently working?

Let me change that to most "important". I am deeply concerned about the rapid growth of postdocs in the conduct of research. First, there was astronomic growth in the life sciences, and now we see a smaller, but exploding, increase in my field of computer science. Postdocs are just out of their Ph.D. degree experience and are at the height of their intellectual powers. Postdocs are "training positions for people who might not need more training"; typically underpaid, often not independent positions, but assistants to their advisor; often not well mentored; and transient workers forced to move at the time that some are having and rearing small children because postdocs are not permanent positions. Postdocs need better treatment – across the board. I am attempting to raise the conscience of my computer science community to improve the lot of postdocs.

Have you encountered any sexism in your career? If so, how have you overcome it? What advice would you offer girls and women interested in a career in computer science? How do you think we can encourage more women to get involved in STEM fields, generally, and change the perception of these fields as being inappropriate for women?

Some, but not a lot. I think that engineering is an especially good area for women. It is, by its very nature, creative. Engineers invent – to solve society's problems. Women are natural nurturers. They have an innate need to help society.

Second, engineering honors sound reasoning and good design. It does not really matter if the best argument is made by a man, woman, or purple-spotted dog. Usually – well, not quite always, but usually – the best argument "wins". I have seen more discrimination in fields where reasoning and argumentation is somewhat more subjective, such as law and banking. So, I think that engineering is one of the better fields for women.

Susan Landau

Dr. Susan Landau works in the areas of cybersecurity, privacy, and public policy. As a student, her project on odd perfect numbers won a finalist position in the Westinghouse Science Talent Search. Later in her career, she introduced the first algorithm for deciding which nested radicals can be denested, which is now known as Landau's algorithm. Dr. Landau was a Distinguished Engineer at Sun Microsystems and has been a faculty member at the University of Massachusetts at Amherst and at Wesleyan University. She has held visiting positions at Harvard, Cornell, Yale, and the Mathematical Sciences Research Institute. She maintains the ResearcHers Email list, a forum for female computer science researchers, and an online bibliography of women's writing in computer science. In 2008 she was awarded the Anita Borg Institute Women of Vision Award for Social Impact, and in 2011 was inducted as a Fellow of the Association for Computing Machinery. She is a 2012 Guggenheim Fellow.

How did your passion for mathematics develop? How did you decide to pursue computer science as a career?

In sixth grade I was in the first class of my school to be in a middle school. I remember doodling in math class – squares and rectangles and figuring out which rectangle of a given perimeter had the largest area – and having a teacher who was enthusiastic about my doing so. I was on the junior math team in 7th grade, in high school, and I went to the National Science Foundation program in math for high school students. There the model was to find patterns, make conjectures, and prove things. I ended up teaching there. That, and my education at Bronx High School of Science (a New York City public high school emphasizing science and math), locked me into mathematics.

I went to graduate school wanting to do computational algebra, but got pulled over to computer science by the algorithms work, group and graph theory algorithms at the time. I did my Ph.D. thesis on computing methods, determining whether a Galois group is solvable quickly.

What made you decide to create and maintain the ResearcHers E-mail list?

There is an organization called the Computing Research Association Committee on the Status of Women in Computing Research (CRA-W). I went to a workshop of theirs; they had been doing things for academic women, but there was no way to link women in government and industry labs. There is lots of research going on there! CRA-W gathered women from those areas and asked us what things we thought needed doing; one was this list, and I said sure, I'll do it.

What positive effects have you seen for female computer scientists as a result of having this forum?

It's been a low volume list. One interesting communication occurred when I was at a conference a few years ago. A speaker mentioned his mother not being able to do something on the computer, implying that it was because she was a woman. Later on at lunch another person asked me how to deal with that subtle sexism. I asked colleagues on the list and got back a series of responses. Sometimes questions are sent out, and sometimes announcements of meetings are sent. There is a professors' list related to specifically academic issues regarding being a woman, for example getting tenure.

Have you encountered any sexism while pursuing your career? If so, how did you overcome it?

Of course! I encountered it in high school when I got asked if I was the cheerleader of the math team, and I replied no, I was the captain. I encountered it in college when I wasn't taken seriously. I encountered it in graduate school, where professors expected that women would drop out to get married and have babies. I deal with it in different ways, sometimes with humor, sometimes with anger, sometimes with sadness. Things are better than thirty years ago, but there is still plenty [of sexism]. These days it's easier because I'm in a senior position. But there was one incident a few years ago, when I was concerned why I hadn't been considered for something. A colleague told me, "You're missing a certain chromosome!" That wasn't good, but on the other hand at least it wasn't because of my work.

It's hard – you have to have a lot of grit and determination. It helps to have a support network. Things like the Association for Women in Mathematics or CRA-W or workshops CRA-W or AWM run are important. Getting an education in a supportive environment, going to institutions supportive of women scientists. Having friends when you get knocked down to pick you up and tell you to go back in – these things are important.

What projects are you working on now? What excites you the most?

I have been working on surveillance issues; I moved from straight math to algebraic algorithms, which are close to cryptography, to issues related to surveillance and public policy. I published a book two years ago, my second book, on wiretapping and how it doesn't make us more secure, called "Surveillance or Security? The Risks Posed by New Wiretapping Technologies". These are odd things for a mathematician to be doing! I've also been writing law review pieces related to legal aspects of surveillance. I write as a technologist, but if you want to have an impact, you have to write to the communities that have an impact. I've done briefings in Congress as well, which is probably unusual for a scientist.

What advice would you offer girls and women interested in a career in computer science or related fields?

Go to a university that's supportive of women. Take courses in computer science and outside computer science. Learn to write and speak well. Find interesting internships. Make friends in computer science because the going always gets rough and it's good to have support. Always ask yourself why you're doing what you're doing and why you get pleasure from pursuing that, and make sure you keep doing that.

How do you think we can encourage more women to get involved in STEM fields, generally?

I would like science to be cool. Better science toys for young kids, better education in science from K-12. I'm glad that there is a math museum open in Manhattan now; there are many more science museums now than when I was a child.

Those are ideas for everyone... as for women, I'm currently organizing a computer security workshop for women because numbers have been so poor in that field for women and underrepresented minorities. I don't know the answer; the numbers vary for each field. Once a field gets to one-third women, it gets more comfortable for women, but getting to that third is hard. There are no easy answers.

Barbara Liskov

Dr. Barbara Liskov was one of the first women to receive a Ph.D. in computer science, in her case from Stanford University. Dr. Liskov's foundational work includes the design of the programming languages CLU, a language that featured methods for defining and using abstract data types, and Argus, the first high-level language supporting distributed programs. These languages were important precursors to object-oriented programming. Perhaps most notably, Dr. Liskov developed the Liskov substitution principle, also known as strong behavioral subtyping, in which objects of a declared subtype should behave as objects of the type are expected to behave.

Dr. Liskov has won many awards for her research, including the John von Neumann Medal for "fundamental contributions to programming languages, programming methodology, and distributed systems", the 2008 Turing Award from the ACM, the 2007 ACM SIGSOFT Impact Paper Award for "Abstraction Mechanisms in CLU", the 2007 ACM SIGPLAN Programming Languages Lifetime Achievement Award, and the 1996 Society of Women Engineers Achievement Award. She is currently the Ford Professor of Engineering in the MIT School of Engineering's Electrical Engineering and Computer Science department. She leads the Programming Methodology Group, a research group "dedicated to research in distributed systems, object oriented databases, programming languages, and software design" (from the group's website, http://www.pmg.lcs.mit.edu/).

How did your passion for computers and programming develop?

I got into computer science by accident. When I graduated from UC Berkeley in 1961 with a degree in math, I decided to work rather than continue with graduate school. I looked for a job in mathematics but wasn't able to find anything interesting. Instead, I accepted a job as a programmer, at the Mitre Corporation, even though I had no background, because it sounded more interesting.

My first day at Mitre I was handed a Fortran manual and asked to write a program to solve a little problem. I discovered that I really enjoyed programming and that I was also good at it. And this is where my career in Computer Science began.

I was always interested in math and science from a very young age. I took all the advanced courses offered at my high school even though I felt that this wasn't something a girl was expected to do. And when I took the pre-calculus class (which was the most advanced math course offered at that time) I was the only girl in that class.

I continued this interest at college. There was never any doubt that I was going to end up majoring in science or math. I started out as a physics major but switched to math when I realized I liked it better. I was one of very few girls pursuing a math major. Often I was the only girl in a class, or sometimes there was one other girl. I don't recall any incidents where I was subjected to prejudice, although I also don't recall any times when I was welcomed.

Please discuss why you found the Liskov Substitution Principle to be so important in programming and what made you think about codifying it.

I invented the Liskov Substitution Principle (LSP) in the mid-1980s. I had been asked to give a keynote address at OOPSLA, the main conference concerned with research on object-oriented languages. I took this opportunity to read the literature in that field and I discovered that classes were being used for type hierarchy in addition to inheritance. I thought the notion of type hierarchy was interesting but not well understood: people didn't understand what rules should be followed to determine whether one type could be considered a subtype of another. I invented LSP to address this issue.

LSP is very important for object-oriented programs because it allows a programmer to reason about the correctness of a program by considering only the declared types of the program variables. When the program runs these variables might refer to objects belonging to subtypes of their declared type, but that won't matter if LSP is obeyed. For example if a program is written to operate on an array, the programmer can reason about its correctness assuming the argument is an array, even though that argument object might belong to some subtype of array. Thus it extends the most important benefit of modularity, which is the ability to reason about the use of a module from its specification, to object-oriented programs.

What is the most exciting project on which you and your students are currently working?

My most recent students have been working in the area of distributed systems. We have been inventing ways to improve the performance and the security of these systems. For example, we have developed a system called Aeolus that makes it easier for the developer of an application to protect the confidentiality of user information.

What was the environment like for women in computing in the early years of your career? How has it changed since then? What advice would you offer girls and women interested in a career in computer programming? How do you think we can encourage more women to get involved in STEM fields, generally, and change the perception of these fields as being inappropriate for women?

When I got into computer science there was no undergraduate major to prepare you for work in this field. As a result companies were hiring people on spec, hoping that they would have the needed ability. This is how I was hired. And a substantial number of these people were women -- a higher proportion than now.

However, I believe that the reason the percentage of women has declined has nothing to do with the work. Computer science is a field that many women are very good at and find very interesting. However, this point isn't well understood by young girls, especially girls in high school and earlier. Instead, girls often decide they don't want to go into this field, since it seems nerdy or perhaps they think that being good in math and science isn't acceptable for girls.

I think this is very unfortunate because the work is very interesting and there are amazing opportunities.

I think that the perception about nerdiness applies mainly to computer science and perhaps to some extent to engineering disciplines. As far as computer science is concerned, it partly comes from computer games, which tend to be more interesting for boys than girls. But it also comes from popular notions of what it is like to do this kind of work.

I think the problem with STEM fields in general is a societal one. This means it is very hard for educational institutions to make much progress here. I do think though that the kinds of outreach efforts that are being made are helpful. MIT has a number of these. For example we run a summer program for girls to provide them with a better understanding of what engineering is. Other universities typically have similar programs.

My advice for young women is to think about what you enjoy doing and what you are good at. And then just do it. Don't let stereotypes dissuade you. This is basically the same thing I did. When I was young women weren't supposed to have careers like mine and they weren't supposed to be interested in math and science. But I did it anyway and it turned out to be a very good choice.

Jo Ellen Moore

Dr. Jo Ellen Moore is Professor of Computer Management and Information Systems at Southern Illinois University. Dr. Moore's research, building on both her industry and academic experience, has focused on management within the technological world, incorporating findings on human behavior and psychology. Her work has illuminated some of the causes of and solutions for employee burnout and turnover in technological fields and has revealed secrets of how to effectively manage projects and their teams. She has been quoted on employee burnout in The Boston Globe, Omaha World-Herald, Computerworld, and Harvard Management Update. She has done extensive research on interactions between geeks and non-geeks in the workplace and the implications of geeks wearing the label proudly, rather than with shame.

As she discusses below, her career has taken many twists and turns, a great example of a geek who could not be limited to one interest or field of study. She has received the "Most Developmental Associate Editor" award for 2007 from MIS Quarterly. Her recent work includes an exploration of "prestigious stigma" in the case of the technology geek – the notion that geeks wear their stigma with pride, and this has implications for their interactions with others in the workplace.

How did you decide to pursue computer programming initially?

I didn't. All I decided on was to major in math. And the reason I decided to major in math was because I realized it was the homework I always pulled out first in high school, the only homework I enjoyed doing.

I wasn't sure what I would do with my math major; I just knew I didn't want to teach (more on that in a moment ;-)). As I was nearing graduation, I saw job openings in computer programming and had a little programming in my math major so applied and that's how I got started in information systems and technology.

Your career has taken some twists and turns – can you talk about the path that you followed to get where you are today? What inspired you to change direction, ultimately focusing on organizational behavior and project management within the technological world?

I was really good at programming, and enjoyed it. I was so good at programming that I was promoted all the way to management before the age of 25. I was really bad at management, and hated it.

While human behavior was the bane of my existence as a manager, at the same time I was intrigued by it. This spurred my interest in psychology and led me to begin work on a master's in psychology, eventually leaving my job to go to graduate school full-time at Illinois State University.

As I was finishing up my master's thesis, I accepted an opportunity to teach applied computer science at ISU. To my surprise, I found I truly enjoyed teaching college students! I stayed in this non-tenure track teaching position at ISU for several years, then decided to "make it official" and go for my Ph.D. I was fortunate to be accepted into the Organizational Behavior doctoral program at Indiana University, completing my Ph.D. in 1997 and then taking a tenure-line position here at Southern Illinois University Edwardsville. My job here has been a perfect match to my interests in teaching as well as research.

In addition to your own career, you have mentored other women interested in technology careers. Have you experienced any sexism or seen it experienced by those you mentored? If so, how did you and/or they overcome it?

I have been extremely fortunate, both in my industry positions and academic positions, to have not encountered bias due to gender. I realize, though, that my mindset and attitude may contribute to this. I am about THE WORK. My focus is on completing the task or project at hand. In my experience, if you work hard and do good work, you will be promoted for the WORKING PROFESSIONAL that you are. I see myself as gender-neutral in the workplace, in that it doesn't occur to me whether the person I'm talking with is male or female, and that's how I want to be viewed in return. I believe YOUR OWN hard work and strong focus on the task or project at hand is your most effective tool to fend off sexism.

What research projects are you working on now? Which ones excite you the most?

Right now, I am working on a study examining ways in which individuals handle dissatisfying elements of their work environment and ways in which managers can help. My research always builds on organizational behavior theory and research, and is always poking at issues that pertain to IT professionals. If it isn't something important to IT folks, then you won't find me researching it. IT workers are still "my people" :-)

What advice would you offer girls and women interested in a career in computer programming, management, and/or technology? How do you think we can encourage more women to get involved in STEM fields, generally?

Advice to females interested in IT, go for it! I honestly believe IT is one of the most gender-neutral fields there is. And traits commonly associated with females (e.g., communication skills) are highly valued in IT today, especially in project leader and manager roles.

To encourage more women to enter STEM fields, I think we need all females to have the opportunity to dabble in these areas. Our loss is females who would be great in these fields but are not exposed to them and therefore do not find their way to them.

Evi Nemeth

Dr. Evi Nemeth is a computer scientist, engineer, teacher, and author. Before venturing into computer science, Dr. Nemeth studied mathematics. Her expertise is in networks and system administration. She is the lead author of the UNIX System Administration Handbook, the Linux Administration Handbook, and most recently the UNIX and Linux System Administration Handbook. Her work formed the foundation of modern network cryptography. With Steve Wozniak, she established the Woz scholarship program that has provided funding to bright undergraduates. Dr. Nemeth has made efforts to bring Internet technology to the developing world.

What inspired you to study mathematics, and how did that lead to you becoming interested in computer system administration?

My high school math teacher, Mr. Evans, made me like math and since it was the only subject I consistently got As in, I chose it as a college major. For grad school, I had met a professor, Ron Mullin, at my teaching job at Florida Atlantic University. He was on sabbatical and we worked together for a year on his research issues. When Florida Atlantic wanted a terminal degree for all faculty, Ron suggested that I go to Waterloo for grad school since I had already done about half the research needed. So I did. When I graduated from Waterloo (1971) there were few jobs in mathematics but computer science was the coming thing. Since I had worked with computers all through undergrad, I just re-labeled myself and applied for positions where they wanted math and computer science. At the time there were few schools with computer science degrees. At my first permanent job at SUNY (State University of New York) Utica, we got an NSF equipment grant, purchased a DEC PDP 11/45, and ran Bell Labs UNIX – first version 6 and later version 7. Taking care of that machine introduced me to computer system administration.

Can you discuss how you came to discover the inadequacies in the Diffie-Hellman trap, and what that has meant for modern network cryptography?

The real brains to the Diffie-Hellman work was Ron Mullin, my Ph.D. advisor. I provided the computing power thanks to the HEP supercomputer company in Denver who donated their test floor and an engineer to my efforts every night. I adapted code to the HEP, rewrote parts in assembler to make them go faster, and commuted 35 miles to the factory test floor every night to run code to solve the discrete log problem for the key length that the Diffie-Hellman exchange used. We made a table of values and their logs for each number in the finite field. Then extracting the key took only seconds on a PC (slow in those days) and since this was the mechanism being used in financial systems transferring gobs of money here and there the key length was re-evaluated and increased substantially. HP was actually making a hardware chip to implement the key exchange and scrapped it. A software company was selling software to do it and continued to sell the software long after we had broken the key exchange.

You have mentored many young students – what inspired you to take such an active role in their education and development, including developing the Woz scholarship program?

When I joined the faculty at the University of Colorado in Boulder, I saw faculty totally concentrating on grad students for their projects and saw the undergrads and younger students as an untapped resource. So I found the good ones who were always in the lab, always helping others, and hired them to run the undergrad lab in the CS department. The only rule was that if they installed some new and wonderful thing in the lab they weren't allowed to sleep until it either worked or they had backed it out. In the beginning I couldn't pay them except with a login on the research machines that were running UNIX. When Woz visited the Dean of Engineering he heard about my kids running the research machines and donated money that I turned into the Woz scholarship, which paid undergrad in-state tuition and wages for working in the lab to a few Woz-scholars each semester. I found working with undergrads better than grad students who often had wives and deadlines and other distractions whereas undergrads had infinite energy.

Have you encountered any sexism while pursuing your career? If so, how did you overcome it? Have you noticed any changes in the acceptance and encouragement of women in computer science over the course of your career?

I never experienced sexist prejudice in my job. I think if you do your job well you will be judged for your performance, not your gender or color. But don't forget, I worked mostly in a university environment where there is hopefully less politics and prejudice.

I think the enrollments of women in Colorado's undergraduate computer science program are decreasing and have been for the last 10 years at least. The department has modified the curriculum in the hope of attracting more students, especially women.

What advice would you offer girls and women interested in a career in computer science or related fields? How do you think we can encourage more women to get involved in STEM fields, generally?

The broadening of what is called computer science to include many of the softer graphic arts and design realms, together with the high employment rates in IT, might spark more interest from women. Any student not sure about an IT career might consider taking an internship or volunteer somewhere to get a feel for the types of jobs that are available in IT. Then if you major in computer science in college, you can focus your attention on courses that would best prepare you for that job you saw as an intern.

Be sure to take courses like technical writing along with your geeky classes.

Wasn't sure what STEM meant, but Wikipedia knew! I think the problem happens in middle school. That's when girls seem to get turned off math and science or, if not turned off it, made fun of if they like it. I wonder if it would help to make middle schools unisex so all the boy/girl aggravation of the hormone stuff happens outside school. Not sure this would help, but it might.

I wonder if a math camp based on materials like in the "Breaking Away from the Math Book" series (Andrzej Ehrenfeucht and Patricia Baggett) could re-awaken math/science interest in girls [author's note: this book series contains creative projects for young children designed to increase confidence and interest in math].

Rosalind Picard

Dr. Rosalind (Roz) Picard is founder and director of the Affective Computing Research Group at the Massachusetts Institute of Technology (MIT) Media Laboratory, co-director of the Things That Think Consortium, and leader of the new and growing Autism & Communication Technology Initiative at MIT. She is co-founder, chief scientist, and director of Affectiva, Inc., where she and others make technology to measure and communicate emotion.

Dr. Picard's work spans the areas of multidimensional signal modeling, computer vision, pattern recognition, machine learning, human-computer interaction, and affective computing. She has used her research to develop innovative technology, holding multiple patents for new sensors, algorithms, and systems for sensing, recognizing, and responding respectfully to human affective information. Her work's applications extend to autism communication, human and machine learning, health behavior change, marketing, advertising, customer service, and human-computer interaction. Dr. Picard has consulted for companies such as Apple, AT&T, BT, HP, i.Robot, and Motorola.

How did your passion for computer science develop?

I didn't take the usual computer science path; I took the electrical engineering path. I liked math and I liked learning. I was curious about how technology worked and I heard that you could make a good living doing that. I wanted to go out and invent things – I became most interested in electrical engineering at Georgia Tech when I heard that it was the hardest program.

I did not actually study computer science per se; I had to take computer programming courses in the CS department as part of my engineering degree. At the time CS was more about programming than building cool technology. Now computer technology has moved into everyday life and people who study either engineering or computer science get to work on the cool stuff. The work I've been doing isn't traditional computer science or engineering; it sits at the boundary of where these meet pretty much every other application area involving people.

What inspired you to conduct research modeling vision and learning? What have been the most exciting or surprising findings that you uncovered?

I've been doing this a long time, so there have been a lot! There were two recent pretty cool findings.

One was that we were trying to figure out how to measure emotions other than just asking people. What people report, it turns out, can be different than what's going on physiologically. A person might report, for example, being happy, but his or her body is physiologically depressed. There are two things going on: an awareness of emotions that are happening and an ability to communicate them. We started to develop technologies that would measure voice and facial expressions to capture more of what's going on, and help communicate these.

Through this research, we learned that when people are using computer agents to tutor them, one of the biggest predictors of whether they learned the material was confusion. It was surprising, but confusion – provided it was eventually resolved – predicted learning. The right amount of confusion helps engage you and increase attention.

Another surprise came with people who couldn't talk about their feelings. Alexithymic people are often unable to understand their own feelings or put them into words. A lot of people are alexithymic, and some have autism as well. We were wondering why these people sometimes have meltdowns that seem to come from nowhere. We got to know people who have this problem and fall on the autism spectrum. They told us that, in fact, they see others as not understanding their feelings! In many cases the body expressions they exhibit don't reflect what's going on internally.

What's interesting are real-world emotions in real life, so we decided to build technology that could be worn and sense emotional information, such as a camera at your desk, a wristband while walking... we put sensors in a lot of stuff, including steering wheels, socks, telephones, and computer mice. One of our undergraduates a few years ago asked to take home a pair of sensors to try on his autistic brother. I said sure, no one was using these over break. I looked at the data he collected on the computer and it looked mostly normal. But then it came to one afternoon – he was wearing the sensors on his left and right wrists, which usually look the same in their activity readings – and suddenly one side went up extraordinarily high and the other not at all. I thought that it must be broken; the readings shouldn't go up that high – and both sides should read similarly. I asked the student what had happened; he said he would check the diary. He came back and said "that reading was right before he had a massive seizure." I showed the data to someone who studies epilepsy, and we conducted a study on kids with epilepsy whose seizures were not being reduced adequately by medication. We found that grand mal seizures reliably produced a huge spike measured by the wristband. Partial seizures also showed a significant response. It turns out that we had a seizure detector, that the seizure reaches deep into the emotional sectors of the brain, and we could read it out on the wrist. This was not something we ever dreamed of proposing to find; we would have been laughed out of MIT if we said we could find electrical events deep in the brain with a band on the wrist.

We found another huge surprise that relates to something in the brain often found to be present when people died after a seizure. Sometimes (fortunately it's rare) people have a short seizure, which doesn't seem particularly severe, and afterward they seem fine and go to bed, and they never wake up. For most of those who died while their brain waves were observed, it turned out that the brain waves were flat for a long time after the seizure had ended. We found that the higher the spike on our wristband, the longer the brain waves were flat. What this means is now we want to get the wristband built with an alert system so that guardians can tell, then, that if they see a big spike, they might want to give the person a shot that could potentially save his or her life. It's something that doctors are keen to look at now. Suddenly here I am talking to doctors and epilepsy experts, trying to work with them to see if we might be able to help people with a very serious condition.

This was not the typical engineering path but you go where the data and findings lead you, and if it's important, then you help bring it to market. Once you have computer technology and science skills, you become a systems thinker and you can bring that logic to any system in life – including business. Systems thinking prepares you well for almost everything. Just studying business tends to give you only a business career. With training in computer science or engineering you have powerful tools that serve many different kinds of careers.

I still on occasion write the random program, but mostly have teams implementing them.

Another surprising finding was in my work with facial expressions. Usually people think that a smile means someone is happy, for example. I was interested in expressions in real world interactions. We found that in 90% of times when people got frustrated in real world interactions, they smiled, the same smile that people identify as the true smile of happiness. We haven't figured out why they do this; they certainly are not happy. Measuring the dynamics of the smile, not just its final "peak" appearance, we can teach computers to discern if the user is smiling out of delight or frustration. If we want people and technology to get along better, technology has to do a better job of understanding if it's frustrating or pleasing its user. We can improve that relationship. We've built a computer that's better than people at telling the difference between happy and frustrated smiles.

There are surprises every day; I like to build things we can use and take outside and try out. It becomes more fun when you're wearing a new thing and understanding a thing about yourself that no one has ever seen before.

Why is it important or useful to give emotional capabilities to computers?

Importance depends on the use. One use is computers as technology to help people understand themselves better – measuring, say, what parts of my life cause me the most stress? Or what parts of online learning cause the student the most boredom or confusion? These emotional tools can be used to measure an audience, or we can use them personally to better understand ourselves. Another use is the computer as a software agent or robot, where it needs to do a task with you and observe if it's doing things that confuse or frustrate you, much like if you and I are collaborating; if I see you're frustrated I'll pause and give you a moment.

In the first case, affective technology is like a tool we employ to learn more about ourselves. In the latter case, affective technology helps an automated system to be more emotionally intelligent.

Have you experienced any sexism during your career? If so, how did you overcome it?

It's absolutely there. I think I've seen it the most – it's subtle – as "underexpectation". A guy and I would be hired at the same time and with the same background, and be told that they expect him to succeed but not me. They give women less work and underestimate what women can do. They expect less and pay less. Women's papers are accepted less often. For a long time I wouldn't put my first name on papers; I'd put my initials so they wouldn't think about gender when reviewing my papers, because a study had shown that the exact same work, submitted with a male name and with a female name, got accepted for publication more when it had the male name. Especially in computer science, archetypical success stories are guys. Until women succeed in high profile areas, and get recognized and trumped up as much as men, then people will think it's a man's world. People think of men like Mark Zuckerberg as brilliant founders of technology companies and don't have a female example.

What advice would you offer girls and women interested in a career in computing? How do you think we can encourage more women to get involved in STEM fields, generally?

You don't have to fit the mold of whatever you think you're supposed to be. Find what you love doing and find a way to do it. It is tricky; the more feminine you are the less people take you seriously; I hope that's changing. I've been in a room full of men, and they seemed more comfortable if I wore slacks and a collared blouse than a dress. I did it to fit in; I didn't have to do it, but I did it to make people around me more comfortable with me. The more you appear to be a sex symbol, the less seriously they'll take you. The more you look like them, the more they'll take you seriously. Most women who succeed tend to succeed big; they overachieve. The women we have at Media Lab are amazing, really stars. Definitely at the top – people don't give them any easy breaks; they are there and they earned it.

Ellen Spertus

Dr. Ellen Spertus is a Professor of Computer Science at Mills College and a senior research scientist at Google. She has worked for Microsoft and was featured in the New York Times as one of the computer scientists who might change the face of the computer industry.

Dr. Spertus' work has included mobile apps. She is one of the creators of App Inventor for Android, creating a user-friendly development environment enabling people who are not computer scientists to write such apps. She has also done work examining reasons for the underrepresentation of women in computer science. In the past her work has included contributing features to a social network and creating software to automatically recognize insulting or abusive email, applying natural-language processing and machine-learning techniques in so doing.

Dr. Spertus' awards include the 2007 Women Who Dare Award from Girls Inc. of the Island City, being one of the 2002 ABCNews.com Top Ten Wired Women, being rated the 2001 Sexiest Geek Alive, and the 1992 MIT EECS Department Meritorious Service Award.

How did your passion for computers and computer science develop?

My father loved computers and brought home terminals that connected through the phone line to the mainframe at work in the mid-70s, and I learned to program from him and my big brother. Once personal computers became available, we had an Apple II+, then an IBM PC.

Can you talk a bit about your research on the interface of computer technology and gender issues? What inspired you to conduct research in this area? What have been your most prominent findings?

I don't think I do research on the interface of computer technology and gender issues. I have written about issues that girls and women face in becoming computer scientists. As an undergraduate at MIT, I wanted to understand why there were so few other women who loved computer science. I took a course "Women and Computing" from Prof. Sherry Turkle and began doing research on the subject. I ended up writing a 100-page report, Why Are There So Few Female Computer Scientists?, which got widely distributed and led to more opportunities to work in the area.

Have you encountered any sexism while pursuing your career? If so, how did you overcome it?

I have not faced overt sexism. I think the advantages I've had through my upper-middle-class family background outweigh any negatives from being female. Of course, every woman in technology encounters men who say (without any evidence) that she or another woman got her position because she is female. My biggest barriers (which did not interfere with my success) were internal psychological ones, feeling that being a computer scientist made me less feminine, and vice versa. Such messages are pervasive in our culture and were much more so when I was growing up. (I was born in 1968.)

What projects are you working on now? Which ones excite you the most?

I am currently in transition. The past project that excited me the most was App Inventor for Android, an online programming environment that makes it easier for beginners to write mobile phone apps. I was part of the team who created it, I developed a course around it (Technology for a Better World), and I co-authored a book about it. It was very gratifying to see people, young and old, become excited about computing and realize that programming was something they could do. I was also pleased to see it used by programs that specifically aimed to bring underrepresented groups into computing, such as The Technovation Challenge, Youth Radio, and Youth APPLab.

What advice would you offer girls and women interested in a career in computer programming and technology?

Computer science is like magic. Where else can you put together words to make powerful entities do your bidding? Programming is spell-casting, and robotics is transfiguration – animating lifeless silicon. Whatever your other interests – biology, education, art, you name it – learning to program will increase your ability to pursue it. If you're worried that boys/men won't like you if you are good at computer science, don't be. The silver lining of the uneven gender ratio in computer science means that any woman interested in men can be the belle of the ball.

How do you think we can encourage more women to get involved in STEM fields, generally?

I wish I knew. I am hopeful about educational programs that expose girls to computer science and show how it can be applied to a variety of fields and to improving people's lives.

Telle Whitney

Dr. Telle Whitney is a computer scientist and CEO and President of the Anita Borg Institute for Women and Technology. She held senior technical management positions with Malleable Technologies and Actel Corporation and serves on the advisory boards of Caltech's Information Science and Technology, the California Institute for Telecommunications and Information Technology, and Illuminate Ventures. She co-founded the Grace Hopper Celebration of Women in Computing with Anita Borg in 1994, joined the Anita Borg Institute in 2002, co-founded the National Center for Women and Information Technology (NCWIT) in 2004, and is also a member of the Forbes Executive Women's Board.

In 2008, Dr. Whitney received the Women's Venture Fund Highest Leaf Award. In 2009, she received the ACM Distinguished Service Award, received the Marie Pistilli Women in Electronic Design Automation Achievement Award, and was named one of San Jose Business Journal's Top 100 Women of Influence. In 2011, Fast Company named her one of the Most Influential Women in Technology.

How did you become interested in computer science? How did you know that it was the career for you?

When I was an undergraduate at the University of Utah, I was unsure on my major. I took an Interest Inventory test and Computer Programming came up at the top. I then took a programming course (Cobol) and loved it. I switched my major.

You have a long history of promoting women's involvement in computing, including founding the Grace Hopper Celebration of Women in Computing Conference with Anita Borg, being President and CEO of the Anita Borg Institute for Women and Technology, co-founding the National Center for Women and Information Technology, and being a member of the Forbes Executive Women's Board. Can you talk about some of the initiatives you have spearheaded to try to change the culture of technology for women and open doors for women to get involved?

At the Anita Borg Institute, we work both with women and with organizations. Women are involved in a number of our programs, including GHC and WoV, as well. Our work with women provides professional development, inspiration and connections with others.

We have increased our work on Moving the Needle in the last few years. These initiatives include:

Top Company for Technical Women Award — a chance for organizations to receive confidential feedback on their women in the workforce numbers, both total percentage and rate of change.

Top Company for Technical Women workshop — designed for people inside of organizations that want to change the culture for women, this workshop features best-in-class initiatives from organizations that have created change.

Technical Executive Forum — a small invitation-only group of C-level executives who share issues and initiatives as well as listen to research on moving the needle. We also include a session with larger working groups from our partner organizations.

Have you encountered any sexism while pursuing your career? If so, how did you overcome it?

Certainly I have encountered many thoughtless comments from my colleagues and supervisors over the years that didn't understand that they were unintentionally putting me into a category. For the vast majority of my career, I respond by remaining focused on the business issue, whatever it is, and ignoring the senseless comments.

What projects are you working on now? What excites you the most?

I am particularly excited about two efforts right now: (1) our increasing focus on Moving the Needle, as described above, and (2) our expansion internationally. We recently held our third annual conference in India, and expect to increase our global participation.

What advice would you offer girls and women interested in a career in computer science or related fields? How do you think we can encourage more women to get involved in STEM fields, generally?

A significant number of the jobs of the future sit at the boundary between Computer Science and other disciplines, including Medicine, Environment, etc. I think these fields, especially Computer Science and Engineering, are where the largest number of jobs are.

Jennifer Widom

Dr. Jennifer Widom is the Fletcher Jones Professor and Chair of the Computer Science Department at Stanford University and a member of the National Academy of Engineering. Her research focuses on nontraditional data management, including the use of humans to improve computer data processing. She has received several awards including the 2007 ACM SIGMOD Edgar F. Codd Innovations Award and the 2005 "Test of Time" Paper Award from the ACM SIGMOD International Conference on Management of Data for her paper "View Maintenance in a Warehousing Environment" with Y. Zhuge, H. Garcia-Molina, and J. Hammer. She was a Guggenheim Fellow in 2000.

Dr. Widom teaches a free Introduction to Databases course to the public. This course was most recently offered beginning in January, 2013.

How did your passion for computer science develop?

That's an unusual story. I actually went to a music conservatory as an undergraduate. I took a course in music that was about using computer programs to analyze music. I then started taking more computer science courses. I actually got a minor in computer science before going on to get my M.S. and Ph.D. in computer science. I was a junior in college before I got interested, which is late (but not too late, obviously).

What got you interested in nontraditional data management? Can you talk about Deco and how it optimizes query processing?

It was a little different from the research that I did for my dissertation. I went to an IBM research lab after I got my Ph.D. and before I went to Stanford and they were strong in research in data management.

Deco is a system that accesses humans to help answer questions about data, specifically to help gather and process data.

What inspired you to offer your free introductory database course? What would you say was your favorite or the most rewarding aspect of teaching this course?

I was inspired because I had already created the videos for use inside Stanford. I had lots of online quizzes and exercises. When Stanford decided to offer courses publicly, I decided to be one of them.

The most rewarding thing about it was the sheer number of students who took the course and how grateful they were. I got lots of chocolates in the mail.

What is the most exciting project on which you and your students are currently working?

I'm not going to favor any one project. I think all of them are exciting. Deco is exciting, and I have students working on large scale graph processing, which is also great. I always enjoy all of these areas of research, and I change topics frequently.

What advice would you offer girls and women interested in a career in computer programming? How do you think we can encourage more women to get involved in STEM fields, generally, and change the perception of these fields as being inappropriate for women?

I think there are two things that go on, maybe three. One is intimidation from males. We certainly see that at Stanford. We have males who have been programming since they were 6 years old and women who did not decide to start so young. At the college level, it's important not to allow that to discourage women. Just because they didn't have a head start doesn't mean they are not as capable.

My advice is don't get intimidated by boys acting like they know everything. Also, it's not as geeky a career overall as it might seem; there are all different kinds of jobs in computing and technology in general.

I think the problem starts early in middle school and high school. I don't have a good answer; I hope that people at that level can find answers and keep girls involved. I don't understand it; my daughter is in high school and her advanced math class has mostly boys, so it's happened already by that time.

Nicole Zeckner

Ms. Nicole Zeckner runs a popular blog called "Pure Geekery" (puregeekery.net) where she discusses topics related to technology and other geeky areas of interest. She is the Quality Assurance Engineer/Automation Engineer at Zotec Partners.

How did your love of technology begin? What made you decide to pursue a career in technology?

My love of technology began when I was around five years old and my parents bought me a toy laptop for Christmas. I took that thing everywhere and played with it non-stop. When I was a little older we started getting hand-me-down computers from my cousins who were in high school. I'd game on those as well. When we were finally hooked up to the internet, I was blown away by everything that was suddenly available to me. I started writing web sites with easy generators, moved on to WYSIWYG, and finally HTML. I'd write HTML markup in my notebooks during my classes when I was supposed to take notes, to get ideas of what I wanted to do when I got home. I also started playing around with the Windows registry to see what I could change, and what would break.

When it came time to pick a career, computers seemed like a natural choice. I studied Informatics at Indiana University-Indianapolis. When I graduated I had a job as a Quality Assurance Analyst, which fit my desire to figure out how things work and how to find weak points in our programs.

What inspired you create your blog "Pure Geekery"? What inspires the topics about which you post?

I had a tendency to "over share" on Facebook and Twitter. I kept thinking about putting my thoughts into blog form, but thought that no one would be interested in yet another geek culture blog. However, I kept seeing my Aunt's blog (birdchick.com) take off and heard about her experiences so I decided to give it a shot.

My inspiration comes from whatever I'm reading or thinking about at the moment. For a while I would ask on Twitter if people would be interested in a certain topic. My uncle (the husband to my Aunt mentioned above) replied and said "You're missing the point. It's if you find it important that matters." When I started doing that, I enjoyed myself much more and saw my page views go up.

What insight (if any) have you gained from your blog – maybe from comments readers have left – into the extent of modern-day acceptance of women in the geek world?

I haven't had much yet. My blog is still fairly new. However, being on Twitter has opened my eyes to the sexism still prevalent in the community. Since I have been fortunate enough to not run into sexism, I thought it was on the way out. Speaking with other women about their experiences has made me realize how far we have yet to go.

Have you experienced any sexism while pursuing your career? If so, how have you overcome it?

I have been lucky enough to avoid some of the awful scenarios I see posted about on various forums. I have tended to work for woman owned companies or on teams that are mostly women, so I feel that has had a big impact on my experiences.

Please tell us about your current projects. What excites you the most?

Right now I'm working on sharpening my programming skills to move from Automation Engineering into Software Engineering. What excites me the most though is the progress I'm making on Pure Geekery. A good friend of mine is going to start writing with me, and I love that people are reading and enjoying what I'm writing. I'm hoping to meet more people in the community and learn from them.

What advice would you offer girls and women thinking about pursuing a career in technology? What do you think is the greatest impediment to women's success in technology/computing today and how can they overcome it?

When I was in school, I was teased and picked on a lot for being into computers. I can see how that might make some girls choose another path. I'd say follow your passion; even if your peers aren't supportive now, you will have new peers that are.

Right now, I feel the biggest impediment is that girls just don't know their options and what is out there. It is assumed they won't like STEM fields, so they are never encouraged to pursue them. The way to overcome this is to speak out about what you like and are interested in. Make sure you are educated in your options. And ask for what you want.

Do you think that there are things that we can do, maybe as a society or in schools, to encourage women in STEM fields or make them feel more belonging in those fields?

In my school system, we didn't have career day, which is something that should be in every middle and high school. If we were to showcase women who are successful in their field alongside men who are successful in their field it would make it just seem normal.

I also feel like we need more women teaching in the STEM fields. Teachers make excellent mentors and role models, and women teachers would make girls more comfortable in the classroom or asking for help.

Lixia Zhang

Dr. Lixia Zhang is a computer scientist, Professor at the UCLA Henry Samueli School of Engineering and Applied Science, Association for Computing Machinery (ACM) Fellow, and board member at the Asia Future Internet Forum. She played a major and central role in developing the architecture of the internet as we know it today, and continues to work in developing the internet of the future. She won the 2009 IEEE Internet Award and was named the holder of UCLA's Jonathan B. Postel Chair in Computer Science, which is given to a "faculty member of significant stature in computer science who will continue the great strides Postel made in Internet-related research"[23]. Dr. Zhang is currently leading a major project funded by the NSF and spanning twelve campuses to develop new internet architecture.

Your pursuit of science despite the obstacles you faced as a young girl is inspirational. What were the forces that motivated you to study independently and keep learning?

When I was very young I liked to read and was curious about the whole world. In particular I liked math. In elementary school I borrowed books – there were very few books in China, so I got my hands on any books I could. During the cultural revolution we lost the opportunity to study, but I always wanted to learn, so I read whatever I could.

---

[23] Wong Kromhout, Wileen. "Lixia Zhang named to UCLA's Jonathan B. Postel Chair in Computer Science." *Featured News Archive*. UCLA, 2012. Web. Accessed 28 March 2013. <http://www.engineer.ucla.edu/newsroom/featured-news/archive/2012/lixia-zhang-named-to-uclas-jonathan-b.-postel-chair-in-computer-science>

How did you decide to focus on engineering and computer science?

I came to the United States in 1979. Because I liked to read, I had the habit of going to the bookstore every week. When I was young, the bookstore was one block away from my house, so I always went there. I had the same habit when I started at California State University; I went to the bookstore every weekend. When I was there, I saw "Computer Networks" by Andrew S. Tanenbaum, who is a well-known author in networking. I had a look and I figured that this is really interesting, that this is what I'm going do. I just decided then and there. Those days I was tight financially, but I spent 30 dollars to buy that book, which was a big purchase for me. It was just an instinct, a hunch.

Since that time I knew I would do computer networking. When I looked for the next school to attend, Cal State only offered a Master's, and I wanted a PhD. Those days very few universities were involved in computer networking; MIT was one of the few that was. I applied there and was so lucky that I got in.

Many people asked me over the years how I got into MIT given where I came from. I say that I don't know; God was nice to me. I think one reason was that I got very good recommendation letters. I came to Cal State with little background and I spoke little English, but I tried really hard. I studied as much as I could. I think that impressed some professors, who wrote good letters that got me into MIT.

When I look back, there were great people who helped me. Overseas, Chinese Professor Fleur Yano, who was acting Dean at Cal State, had gone to visit China. I had passed the entrance exam to become a graduate student there. Professor Yano was asked to bring a few students back with her. I didn't have much education at the time, but in 1979 she selected me (one of four students) to come to Cal State. I attended a course on English as a second language; only after taking TOEFL and the GRE could I take courses. Without Dr. Yano, I wouldn't have come to the U.S. in the first place.

When we started, she told us that we needed to apply to the next school because Cal State only offers a Master's. She took me to the library to look at a catalog in order to apply to a different school. I was a girl who came from China; I didn't know about the U.S. education system.

At MIT, Dr. David Clark was my thesis advisor. I wanted to do networking – people who build networks, not just theoretical studies. When I went to MIT, I was admitted to EE (Electrical Engineering) – engineering and computer science were two programs in the same department. But when I met Dr. Clark, he took me on to do research. I started working with him, and he helped me to cross all the hurdles and helped me transfer to the computer science program. He supervised me for eight years. At the time I didn't know how lucky I was. David at that time was chairman of the Internet Activities Board (IAB), which was a coordination group overseeing the whole of internet research and development. He got me involved not just in research but also in the early days of internet development. Some years later, I served on IAB (now Internet Architecture Board) as a member. Without David I wouldn't have made the internet my career.

I can summarize all of this in one sentence: God helps those who help themselves.

What projects are you working on now? What excites you the most?

I'm leading an NSF-funded research project called "Named Data Networking". NSF started an effort to promote research and development for future internet architecture. I remember in 2005 they started a program called Future Internet Design. In 2009 they released a solicitation for future internet architecture. This was a solicitation for a team proposal, to see what they would develop further. A number of ideas stood out and they founded the program.

I teamed up with Van Jacobson. He is proposing a new direction for the future internet. I have known him for 30 years, since MIT. We put together a project team and submitted a proposal; I'm going to be the Principal Investigator. It was funded in the summer of 2010. It's the only project I'm working on now, and it's a big one. We are sketching out the architecture for the internet in the coming years. The research is into its 3rd year now, and we are starting to prepare our next proposal to continue this effort.

Have you encountered any sexism while pursuing your career?

I must have. But I'm such an ignorant person; it's probably just my personality to ignore it, and a cultural difference. I think I just ignored it and most I didn't notice.

When you have a goal, just push forward with it. Everything else, you don't care about. It's not just being female; being a foreign student, there were a number of jokes. Being Chinese from the mainland was kind of an issue in events in my research area. I remember there were times I went to meetings and had to be escorted because the building was a secure building. I appreciate my advisor's support. I learned later that someone had asked Dr. Clark how he got a Chinese student. His answer was always, I am doing research; I don't care where the student comes from.

What advice would you offer girls and women interested in a career in computer science or related fields? How do you think we can encourage more women to get involved in STEM fields, generally?

I teach an undergraduate course on Introduction to Networking. I saw very few, maybe 10%, who are female. I want to talk to them, ask them why their friends don't come here. I've asked that question for two years. They say that networking is conceived of as being difficult. The message I want to tell those people is that networking is exciting and not difficult at all. Once you get in, everything is easy. I really want to break this glass ceiling that gives people this wrong impression, keeps people away without seeing how simple it really is. Once you break it, it's not hard.

What I tell young students is that I think that one should think about what one wants to do for life and not just unconsciously follow what most other people do. I said that I am ignorant before; I don't really care what other people do; I do whatever I really want to work on. This is the same thing as saying to follow your dreams. It can be something very practical. Do what you want to do, and don't get influenced too much by the effect of other people.

Interviews: Math and Science

Anna Kay Behrensmeyer..................p. 63
Rita Colwell...................................p. 67
Beatrice Hahn.................................p. 70
Margaret Liu..................................p. 72
Amy Mainzer..................................p. 78
Adriana Ocampo.............................p. 82
Janet Rowley..................................p. 90
Alexandra Rutherford......................p. 94
Jill Tarter......................................p. 98

Anna Kay Behrensmeyer

Dr. Anna Katherine Behrensmeyer, who goes by Kay, is a researcher at the Smithsonian Institution. She is the Curator of Vertebrate Paleontology in the National Museum of Natural History's Department of Paleobiology and co-director of the Evolution of Terrestrial Ecosystems Program. Dr. Behrensmeyer is known for her pioneering research in taphonomy, the study of how organic remains become fossils and how that process informs our understanding of the past. Her work encompasses aspects of anthropology, geology, paleobiology, evolutionary biology, and ecology.

How did your passion for taphonomy develop?

It started with my first paleontological expedition in Wyoming, when I was a beginning graduate student. The team was working in Paleocene deposits, and three different kinds of fossils were found together – charcoal, shark teeth, and mammal bones. Clearly these organisms didn't all live in the same place, but they were buried together. It was a puzzle, and I learned from the expedition leader that this was a problem in taphonomy, which at that time was a fairly new sub-field of paleontology. That was exciting, to be on to something new that needed figuring out. I also liked the fact that solving the puzzle required expertise in several different disciplines – geology, paleontology, and ecology – which eventually led me to become more interdisciplinary.

Your research has revealed how the process of fossilization and what does and does not become fossilized has biased our understanding of the past. Can you discuss some of the highlights from your findings – some of the most crucial ways in which our understanding has been affected?

My understanding of the fossil record and how it represents the past keeps evolving. From studying specimens, reading scientific papers, answering questions from students and the public, and especially field work, I continue to find new questions and answers and more questions about fossils and information they contain. Recently I have been thinking a lot about recycling – fossils represent the body parts of organisms that, long ago, escaped being recycled by the natural processes of decomposition. A long-term study of recent bones in Amboseli Park, Kenya, has taught me the most about why so few animal remains end up as fossils. Hyenas and other scavengers destroy a large number, and most of the rest weather away on the ground surface. "Lucky" bones get buried by wind-blown sediment or by trampling in soft ground – rapid burial is the most important first step toward becoming a fossil.

Have you encountered any obstacles in your career because of your gender? If so, how did you overcome them?

When I started graduate school in a geosciences department, there were a few professors who were biased against women, especially women who wanted to do a thesis involving field work on a non-traditional topic (e.g., paleoecology and taphonomy). Fortunately there were other professors, including my major advisor, who were forward-thinking and supportive. Basically I didn't let biased people or comments bother me – I ignored them and just went ahead and did what I wanted to do. This also worked later on when I encountered subtle or not-so-subtle biases against women – it's rare now but still can occur. I think women scientists, even now, have to work harder than men to get their ideas across. You have to speak up, make yourself heard, and contribute to discussions in a positive and congenial way without going on the defensive unless it is absolutely necessary.

What are your current research projects? About what current/future project are you the most excited?

I'm lucky to have a number of colleagues who are women, and one of them has shared leadership with me on a project to discover the paleoecology of the earliest mammals. We run field expeditions together in Arizona, camping and exploring for fossils in the Painted Desert. We even used horses and a mule to get into a remote area. We have found lots of interesting fossils and geology, but no mammals yet. Another exciting project with two women colleagues at the Natural History Museum is comparing mammal communities in Kenya over the past 100 years. These aren't fossils, but understanding what kinds of species make up communities today gives us a model for what we should expect in the past, and also provides some clues about what is missing in our fossil assemblages. I really enjoy being able to jump around in time, from the present to the Triassic (210+ million years ago) and back to the Miocene (~15 million years ago) and compare the different kinds of animals and ecosystems from these different times. It's the closest thing scientists have to a time machine.

How do you think we can encourage more women to get involved in STEM fields and change the perception of these fields so that women feel that they belong within them? What advice would you offer women interested in entering these fields?

Women and men need to know that there are always frontiers in paleontology or any other science – important puzzles that can be solved by curious, creative people. Finding these requires young people to realize that they can make new discoveries; they must have the confidence and work ethic needed to find questions to solve and then convince others of their value. Women can bring unique perspectives to the natural sciences, and there are many successful women in fields that require a special kind of patience, power of observation, sensitivity to others (empathy), attention to detail, and ability to multi-task and synthesize. These include animal behaviorists, anthropologists, and geologists.

Stubbornness, determination, and a sense of humor help too.

Rita Colwell

Dr. Rita Colwell is Chairman of Canon U.S. Life Sciences, Inc. and Distinguished University Professor both at the University of Maryland at College Park and at the Johns Hopkins University Bloomberg School of Public Health. Her research is on infectious diseases and global health. She served as the Director of NSF from 1998 to 2004 and has held many other advisory positions within the U.S. government and nonprofit science policy institutes. Dr. Colwell has been awarded 40 honorary degrees from institutions of higher education. She is currently developing an international network to address emerging infectious diseases and water issues, including safe drinking water for both the developed and developing world.

How did you become interested in microbiology and infectious diseases? What inspired you to bridge the fields of biological research and computer technology in your research to understand, track, and prevent the spread of cholera?

I have always been interested in medicine and originally planned to attend medical school. However, I met my husband-to-be (now my husband) after I had been accepted to several medical schools but decided to go on to graduate school with my husband. So we did our Ph.D. degrees together, he in physics and I in microbiology. My interests in microbiology derive from having taken a course as a student at Purdue University from a wonderful professor named Dorothy Powelson. She was inspiring and that is how I took interest in microbiology and infectious diseases specifically. When I was in graduate school at the University of Washington, my professor was Dr. John Liston. He and I worked on marine microorganisms and for my Ph.D. thesis I wrote a computer program to identify bacteria based on their phenetic characteristics. The work was subsequently funded by NSF for my postdoctoral work at the National Research Council of Canada.

While Director of NSF, you spearheaded efforts to promote science and math education as well as the participation of women and minorities in science and engineering. Can you please discuss what this time in your life was like – what motivated you to take the helm at NSF, of which accomplishments you made while Director you are most proud, and what the best and most challenging aspects of this position were?

I was asked by President Clinton to serve as Director of the National Science Foundation and Vice President Gore swore me in at the White House in the Roosevelt Room. Very impressive. It was a wonderful six years (the term of the NSF Director is six years). It was an opportunity to serve my country and I was both very pleased and very proud to do so. The initiatives I founded included launching the cyberinfrastructure program that has been critical in expanding the computer sciences and information technology. Also, I launched the biocomplexity initiative that brought interdisciplinary science to solve problems of the environment and I was able to increase the NSF budget almost to the point of doubling it (about a 70% increase over the six years). And finally, but not least, I was able to initiate programs like Advance, Igert, and other programs to increase the participation of women and underserved groups in science and engineering.

It was a wonderful time in my life with the opportunity to see how the national agenda for science and engineering could be fostered and expanded. The challenge was to be on my toes constantly to communicate with Congress, fellow scientists, and the public. I enjoyed this and was lucky to have good mentors and advisors, including my superb deputy director, Dr. Joseph Bordogna, working with me.

In your many positions and endeavors, did you encounter any obstacles because of your gender? If so, how did you overcome them?

I constantly encountered obstacles then and even now being a woman in science I continue to meet gender-based obstacles. However, one learns to move on and overcome barriers by perseverance.

What are your current research projects? Please discuss as well your current efforts to build an international coalition against water-borne infectious diseases.

My current research is focused on climate and health, specifically infectious diseases, namely cholera, and the interaction (or drivers) with the environment. Genomics plays a major role in the research and our current studies include the cholera epidemic in Haiti. I am associated with the Safe Water Network, an organization the headquarters of which is in New York City. It is working to establish safe water kiosks in rural areas of India and Ghana.

How do you think we can encourage more women to get involved in STEM fields and change the perception of these fields so that women feel that they belong within them? What advice would you offer women interested in entering these fields?

Science and engineering (STEM fields) offer tremendously interesting and rewarding careers. Women can succeed in these fields and the barrier to overcome is ensuring mathematics education early (K-12 grades) in the education of girls.

Beatrice Hahn

Dr. Beatrice Hahn is Professor of Medicine at the Perelman School of Medicine. Her research has explored the origin and evolution of HIV by looking to primates and understanding how the disease transmitted from them to us. She has also studied the origin of a deadly malaria strain in similar populations. She was elected to the National Academy of Sciences in 2012.

How did you become interested in the origins and evolution of HIV?

I had an opportunity to work on the molecular cloning of HIV-1 when it was first discovered by Dr. Robert Gallo. Obviously we were intrigued by this new disease that had more or less emerged from the blue. That is why I was interested in this new disease that had suddenly popped up.

Your research has elucidated so much of what has caused the HIV epidemic. What was the most surprising result that your research uncovered?

It's hard to say! Perhaps at least one surprising finding was, although the precursor of HIV-1 infects chimpanzees throughout central Africa, only those infecting one subspecies, the Central subspecies (*Pan troglodytes troglodytes*), have been transmitted to people. There is a large reservoir of chimpanzees that are infected with the precursor of HIV-1 throughout Africa, but only one type is transmitted; the question is why that is.

Have you encountered any obstacles in your career because of your gender? If so, how did you overcome them?

I never did. My situation was a bit unusual. I started to work with my husband as a post-doc onward; we always came as a package deal. It's one thing to discriminate against a person; it's another to discriminate against a couple.

What are your current research projects? Do you think treatment for HIV will be developed soon?

I work on HIV-1 vaccine development. I think there is a path to a protective AIDS vaccine but there are still several significant hurdles. I hate to put a timeline on it, but I would be surprised if we had anything in hand to give to people within the next ten years. I think the vaccine can be developed but it will take a minimum of ten years.

We have also more recently developed an interest in malaria because we discovered the origin of *Plasmodium falciparum* (the cause of malignant malaria) in West End gorillas.

How do you think we can encourage more women to get involved in STEM fields? What advice would you offer women interested in entering these fields?

The current funding situation would discourage anyone, so I'm very careful encouraging anyone. If this continues this is not reasonable. Society has to decide how much they want to invest in biomedical research for their own benefit, and research requires money. It's not sustainable; we are losing young investigators who simply don't want to deal with this, and I can't blame them.

Margaret Liu

Dr. Margaret Liu is a pioneer in the development of DNA vaccines, demonstrating their effectiveness in a variety of pre-clinical models of various diseases such as influenza, herpes simplex, tuberculosis, and papilloma virus. More recently, her efforts have focused upon HIV and cancer. As Principal of ProTherImmune, Dr. Liu currently consults in the fields of vaccines and immunotherapy for companies and non-governmental entities. She is a Foreign Adjunct Professor at the Karolinska Institutet in Stockholm and has received many honorary lectureships.

How did you become interested in medicine and immunology?

Medicine and immunology have a number of aspects that attracted and fascinated me. Of course one big reason I went into medicine was in order to help people, and to do so from both the scientific perspective (prevention, diagnosis, and treatment) and the personal side of caring for patients as human beings. The specific fields of medicine (my specialty is internal medicine and subspecialty is endocrinology and metabolism) relate to my interest in immunology in many ways. Both immunology and endocrinology involve ligands interacting with receptors to trigger a pathway of events. These interactions, pathways, and subsequent physiologic and pathophysiologic events are beautiful in their logic, complexity, feedback loops, and outcomes.

What are the most important differences between DNA vaccines and standard vaccines created from viruses?

DNA vaccines are small circular pieces of DNA that have just enough material to enable the body to make the antigen (i.e., the part of the pathogen that you want the body to make an immune response against), whereas standard viral vaccines are either whole live, weakened viruses or bacteria, a whole or partially purified virus, a piece of the virus (or bacterium), or a piece of it either purified or made recombinantly. This makes the DNA vaccine different in a number of important ways:

Only the antigen you are interested in can be given as the vaccine without other parts of the pathogen that might potentially be deleterious to the individual or could cause the immune response to focus on a part of the pathogen that isn't important for protection.

A DNA vaccine can induce a number of key types of immune responses, including antibodies, T helper cells, and cytolytic T cells. Typically, inactivated viruses or bacteria or isolated proteins (for example, the different types of non-live influenza vaccines) do not induce the cytolytic T cells. This form of immunity plays an important role for protection against a number of pathogens as well as for combating tumors, and crucially can be directed against internal parts of pathogens that tend to be more highly conserved between different strains of a virus, for example. It is thought that a "universal" influenza or HIV vaccine would benefit from the ability of a vaccine to generate these cellular responses. While live virus vaccines can induce such cellular immunity, a DNA vaccine should be safer than, say, a live (attenuated) HIV virus vaccine, since such a virus would potentially cause life-long infection.

DNA vaccines represent a technology platform that could be used to make a number of different vaccines with the same manufacturing process. Currently, each vaccine needs to have a unique manufacturing process, which can obviously be cumbersome. An analogy is that DNA vaccine technology is like figuring out how to make ice cream, and each new vaccine is simply a different flavor, whereas with other vaccine technologies, it is a bit more like making different kinds of dessert.

DNA vaccines are being developed for a variety of diseases including as prophylactic vaccines against infectious diseases and cancer, immunotherapy for cancer, and therapy for allergies and autoimmune diseases, whereas classical vaccines have been more limited in their applications.

Research on DNA vaccines has recently appeared in the news due to their success in treating otherwise-incurable leukemia. Can you talk about the potential of these vaccines – the extent to which they could truly cure cancer and possibly other lethal diseases?

Rather than focusing on this latest news release (since many different diseases and different DNA vaccines get the spotlight over the course of time), I'd rather address the general potential of DNA vaccines for all applications: prophylaxis of infectious diseases and cancer, immunotherapy of cancer, and treatment of autoimmune diseases (such as diabetes) and allergic diseases (such as asthmas), as well as veterinary applications. There are currently a handful of licensed DNA vaccines for veterinary applications: equine encephalitis (horses – but used as well in other species), hematopoetic necrosis virus (fish), and melanoma (dogs); in other words, two prophylactic vaccines for viruses and a cancer therapeutic vaccine. In addition, a product delivering a hormone, growth hormone, is licensed in Australia. A human therapeutic product, which is a gene therapy product to treat peripheral artery disease, was recently licensed in Russia. This is the same entity as a DNA vaccine, but instead of coding for an antigen, it codes for a therapeutic protein, so it demonstrates that the technology works in humans as a gene delivery technology.

The question has been if and when DNA vaccines (or DNA plasmids encoding therapeutic proteins instead of vaccine antigens) will really be broadly shown to work in humans and become licensed products. In preclinical models, they worked so easily for a number of diseases and types of diseases. But the immune responses in humans were generally disappointing. People thought it was that humans are larger than many of the pre-clinical animal models. But DNA vaccines worked in cattle, and now there are licensed products for horses and pigs. I think that it is useful to look at the field of monoclonal antibodies, which raised a lot of excitement when they were first made, yet it took a couple of decades for these so-called 'magic bullets' to be developed into successful products. And they have been truly transformational in terms of their applications to a variety of diseases such as cancer and autoimmune diseases. DNA vaccines have undergone continuous improvements to make them more potent and also to determine what diseases they will work for. We are now at the 20th anniversary for my group's publication of the first demonstration of protection by a DNA vaccine in a preclinical model of influenza. The improvements in the technology and the identification of the right antigens and target diseases have improved to the point that we are hopeful that DNA vaccines and therapies will become clinical realities in the not-too-distant future.

What projects are you working on now?

My work is divided into projects that I'm directly involved with and those for which I act as an adviser. I advise on a number of different specific vaccines and vaccine technologies, from the development of HIV, malaria, influenza, and TB vaccines and ways to deliver vaccines more effectively and make them more potent, to cancer immunotherapy, as well as on broader issues related to the development of vaccines for developing countries. I also have been involved both as a faculty member for vaccine and immunology courses and in the evaluation of biomedical training programs.

Which ones excite you the most?

Technologies that increase the potency of DNA vaccines (see above) and that enable oral delivery. Most vaccines require an injection – and hence trained medical personnel and the cost and safety issues related to sharps. An oral vaccine would offer tremendous advantages for global delivery and, importantly, would generate mucosal immune responses – most pathogens enter via the mucosa, so such responses are sort of the holy grail for vaccinologists.

Have you encountered any sexism while pursuing your career? If so, how did you overcome it?

Yes, I have encountered sexism, but fortunately, not a lot, or I was oblivious to it, since in comparison to the generations before, my generation had an easier time of it. And my mother was a tremendous role model, raising three children on her own after my father's early death, while simultaneously adding on a doctorate to her previous 2 master's degrees and dealing with a fair amount of bias because she was a minority. Mom raised us to not look at obstacles, but rather to focus on doing our best, even if we needed to be better than others who had doors opened for them. On the other hand, as I became more senior, other opportunities arose because there were fewer women.

What advice would you offer girls and women interested in a career in medicine, biology, or related fields?

My advice is to be positive, focus on achieving your dreams, do not shy away from something because someone says you aren't capable of it, but also don't do something to prove that you can. When I did my surgical rotation as a medical student at Harvard Medical School, a male surgeon-in-training said to me, "It's too bad you are a female because you would have made a good surgeon." Obviously some of his surgeon bosses were female, but they were few. I loved surgery, and that comment tempted me to go into surgery to prove that my X chromosomes didn't limit me. But I realized that while I would enjoy it, I needed to define myself rather than let others define me either negatively or in reaction to their comments.

How do you think we can encourage more women to get involved in STEM fields, generally?

I despair of how women are still objectified and stereotyped in the 21st century, and how so many women still buy into so much of this themselves. So the first thing is that parents, girls, and women themselves need to make the choices that encourage females from a young age to see themselves as of value – alone, not as derivatives of males, nor for their bodies/clothes/looks, nor for being liked. Women/girls need to understand that in order to best contribute to the world, they need to know and develop their gifts and interests rather than seeing their worth mainly in relationship to others. And the females of today should never take for granted the opportunities they have that have been hard-earned by the pioneering women of earlier eras.

Amy Mainzer

Dr. Amy Mainzer is an astronomer and the WISE (Wide-field Infrared Survey Explorer) Deputy Project Scientist. She is also the Principal Investigator of NEOWISE, "an enhancement to the WISE data processing pipeline that will facilitate solar system science, including discovery of new asteroids with WISE"[24], and of Near Earth Object Camera (NEOCam). Her work focuses on topics such as asteroids, star formation, and the "design and construction of novel instrumentation for ground and space"[25].

Dr. Mainzer has received numerous awards, including the 2012 NASA Exceptional Scientific Achievement Medal, 2011 NASA Exceptional Achievement Medal, 2011 and 2008 JPL Ranger Awards, 2010 Lew Allen Award for Excellence, 2001-2003 NASA Graduate Student Research Program Fellowship, and the 1996-1999 National Science Foundation Graduate Research Fellowship. She has an asteroid named after her, the 234750 Amymainzer, and has made appearances on the History Channel series *The Universe*.

How did you fall in love with astronomy? Was there a defining moment when you knew this was the life for you?

I fell in love with astronomy when I was in first grade, so probably 6 or 7, and I can remember how it happened. I had kid books on Greek mythology that I loved reading. I can remember going to the library and looking up stuff in the encyclopedia about the different mythological figures like Andromeda and finding two different entries – one for the mythical character, and one that had a picture of a huge, beautiful galaxy.

---

[24] JPL Science Division. "Amy Mainzer, WISE Deputy Project Scientist." *Evolution of Galaxies: People*. NASA Jet Propulsion Laboratory, California Institute of Technology. Web. Accessed 28 March 2013.
<http://science.jpl.nasa.gov/people/Mainzer/>
[25] Ibid.

I was hooked! After that I couldn't get enough of it. But the real credit goes to my mom, who made learning such a joy. Throughout my life, she always shared the excitement of learning and was herself curious about nature. She's a graphic artist by profession and a naturalist by inclination. My mom knows more about transferring liquid helium into cryogenic storage containers than most grad students in astronomy!

How did you come to work in the Jet Propulsion Laboratory?

Working at JPL is such a strange thing. In one sense, it's perfectly ordinary because I've worked here for almost 10 years now. Yet at the same time, I still get an odd twinge every time I drive through the front gate and see the sign, because it's that sign that I remember seeing in a National Geographic book in the library when I was 10 (no Internet then, so information was precious and hard to come by). I came here originally because I was working with JPL on a project called the Spitzer Space Telescope, and because I went to Caltech for grad school. When I graduated with my Ph.D., there was a job opening on another NASA space telescope called the Wide-field Infrared Survey Explorer (or WISE for short). When I started, WISE was just getting going, and seeing it through launch and operations, then getting to do the science with the data, has been an amazing trip! I can't wait to do it again with another mission.

Did you encounter any obstacles to pursuing your dream because of your gender? If so, how did you overcome them?

The beauty of science is that it truly is for everyone. Each one of us does science whether we know it or not – every time you try something to see what happens, or wonder about what makes something work the way it does, that's the process of science. Science desperately needs the brains and talent of people from all walks of life to solve hard problems like climate change and heart disease. There are many people who don't think that girls and women should do science, but they are wrong. There are a lot of subtle and not-subtle ways that people have told me over the years that I didn't belong because of my gender. One of the most helpful ways I found to overcome this is to be a mentor to others coming through the pipeline.

Tell us about your current projects. What are you working on now? What excites you the most?

Right now I am working on studying asteroids with the WISE data. WISE is a terrific asteroid-hunting spacecraft, and we are using the images from the mission to better understand the asteroids and comets in our solar system. In particular, I'm focusing on figuring out how many asteroids there are that get close to the Earth, and what they are like. I'm leading a team of scientists who are studying many different aspects of the asteroid and comet data from our mission. Studying science is like watching a thrilling TV show or reading a book that you just can't put down – when I'm researching a science question, I can't wait to find out what happens next! The biggest excitement for me is learning new things about nature. It makes me love and appreciate life in the universe even more.

What advice would you offer girls and women thinking about pursuing astronomy as a career? What do you think is the greatest impediment to women's success in astronomy today?

Astronomy seeks to answer basic questions that people ask, like who we are, how did we get here, and where is "here" in the first place? Girls and women must be astronomers – we need the participation of lots of smart people if we're going to figure out the answers to these difficult questions. There is a long and proud tradition of women astronomers going back to ancient times. Plus, it's incredibly fun! It's also a career that allows you great independence and flexibility in how you manage your time and live your life.

There are many people who still don't believe that women and girls deserve equal treatment, let alone belong in technical fields like science and engineering. Yet there are a lot of forces for good out there who are helping to change that. Finding and seeking out those supporters of women in science (both men and women) can be a great source of strength when times are tough. That you are reading this book is a source of hope that we are progressing toward a more fair future. To girls and women out there I say welcome to astronomy – you belong here, studying the universe.

Adriana Ocampo

Ms. Adriana Ocampo is a planetary geologist and the Science Program Manager at NASA Headquarters' Science Mission Directorate. She studies the geology of planets throughout our solar system. She is one of the scientists responsible for discovering the 'Crater of Doom', the Chicxulub impact crater that was left by the asteroid that caused the extinction of the dinosaurs 65 million years ago. She mentors girls and women interested in her field through the Latina Women of NASA and many other venues.

How did you fall in love with space geology? Was there a defining moment when you knew this was the life for you?

I was one of those space cadet kids ever since I was a child. I was intrigued by the stars and space in general. Humans had just set foot on the moon and that had a great impact on me. It meant that the impossible was possible; I was a child of the Apollo missions. Even though I was really in an environment where space exploration was a faraway dream – living in a developing country. There was no space agency and no plans to build one, so I rarely got exposed to anything like that. However, I had a father and a mother that encouraged me to learn and study.

As a child I would go to the roof of my house with my dog and look at the stars. I was always questioning, what are those points of light, are there people like us out there. It was my passion; the calling came early to me. I was fortunate to be raised in a family where parents said that there was no limit, that you can achieve anything, that if you are persistent and study hard your dream would come true. I was raised with that belief.

When my parents came to the United States, the first thing I asked was where is NASA? We were in Los Angeles near the Jet Propulsion Laboratory (JPL) and I started volunteering there. I volunteered as a technical aid even before I graduated from high school and eventually as I started college JPL offered me a paying position, and that helped me pay for my schooling. I've been working for NASA since then.

On July 20, 1976, when Viking landed on Mars, the first images of another planet started coming down. I was able to witness that; I was fascinated; I couldn't believe it. Here was something millions of miles away but it looked like Earth. This is how my interest in planetary geology began. I combined geology, astronomy, and engineering courses to tailor a degree to my interest.

Can you discuss the process by which you discovered the Crater of Doom? What was it like to solve such a longstanding mystery?

It was amazing; I was very fortunate. I actually got to know Eugene Shoemaker; he was the first to do his Ph.D. at Cal Tech on impact craters. Before his thesis, people thought that the cause of the dinosaurs' extinction could even be volcanic, that it was an anomaly. He is the one who showed how impact craters helped shape our solar system and the universe. There was a paper that he wrote in the 70s on impact craters on how these craters could have impacted how life got to this planet.

Since 1980 when Walter Alvarez wrote a paper proposing that the dinosaurs went extinct due to the impact of a large asteroid on Earth causing a mass extinction 65Ma (million years ago), everybody was looking for the crater, and trying to find out what is this potential link that could have caused this massive demise. The challenge was who could find that crater. I went to a conference in Mexico where a geo-archeologist presented a paper on determining what had happened to the Mayan civilization through agricultural development, by trying to see if they could determine the agricultural patterns that they had using satellite images. Through that effort, they found this semicircle in the Yucatan Peninsula. They did not know the origin of the semicircle. I was in the audience and was intrigued. When I heard it and saw the images I immediately thought about a possible impact crater. You may say that I had impact craters on the brain. I talked to the speaker after the conference and asked him if he had thought of the possibility of an impact crater. He had not, however that led to a collaboration that resulted in the publication of a joint paper proposing the Yucatan Peninsula as the site of the "Crater of Doom".

We submitted the paper to Science, which took 8-9 months to review. It was so controversial. They rejected it. We then submitted to Nature. They said that we could do it only as a scientific correspondence, so we had to put a question mark at the end of the title. Shortly after, another group was researching this issue including Alan Hildebrand, who was doing his Ph.D. on it (I always say that we collaborated on it; I did it through remote sensing technique; he did it through direct sampling). Actually, a newspaper reporter in 1981 proposed the Yucatan Peninsula as the site of the crater, since he came across work done by Camargo and Penfield while doing exploration for petroleum, and they found a geophysical anomaly that pointed to the crater. So, I always say that we just rediscovered something that had lain dormant for almost 10 years, since it was proprietary geophysical data and had not been reported to the science community at large, and the link of the crater in Yucatan to the mass extinction was not made by them.

I was very fortunate to meet Dr. Walter Alvarez since I organized a Planetary Science workshop in Mexico and invited him to be the keynote speaker. And the day before the workshop we went to the field, to look for evidence of the crater, however it rained so hard that we had to turn around. We were very close from an actual outcrop that would have pointed us to the crater. If it wasn't for the weather we would have found it years ago. It took almost 11 years to find the crater. There is a little fishing town near the center of the impact, called Chicxulub, and it is customary to name a crater by the geographical feature that is closer to its center, hence the name of the crater. In today's topography the crater is buried underneath 1km of rock and half is on the surface and the other half is under water.

The community was so passionate; I remember going to science conferences where the science community had heated debates and felt very strongly that dinosaurs could not have disappeared by an impact from an asteroid. There were really lively discussions; scientists had very strong opinions. Even to this day it is controversial, but we have a wealth of evidence that the Chicxulub impact, if anything, precipitated the demise of the dinosaurs. The dinosaurs were the predominant species for over 250 million years on Earth. They [the dinosaurs] couldn't adapt to the instantaneous and catastrophic changes to the biosphere produced by the asteroid impact. It was 10km or 6 miles in diameter and made an enormous hole in the ground; you truly need a satellite perspective to see such a large impact crater. It is one of the few that have been preserved on Earth because it was buried under 1 km of sediment. The signature that is left is this sinkhole of rings; water finds the easiest way to go around, and the easiest way was the perimeter of the crater where the sediments are the thinnest. This is why you have that beautiful circle to this day; even the Mayans used it as an important site.

When it was found at first they were looking for petroleum; they didn't know that they were drilling into a crater, but then the cores got lost and it was hard to get a hold of samples to study them. The amount of material that got ejected was enormous; it had to be preserved in the surroundings. We found an extraordinary site in Belize where you can see the ejected sediments from the first days and months after the impact. I led six science expeditions sponsored by The Planetary Society that yielded an enormous amount of information and geological evidence on why this crater was so devastating and how it affected the biosphere of the planet. And the key answer is that the rock that the asteroid impacted was very rich in sulfur. Tons of sulfur was injected into the atmosphere to produce sulfuric acid clouds that covered the entire planet for almost 12 years. If the target rock had been made of basalt instead of sulfur-rich, the effects on the biosphere would have been less damaging. The sulfur-rich rock led to the highest amount of damage to all the living species at the time.

Did you encounter any obstacles to pursuing your dream because of gender prejudice?

One of the things I was taught by my parents is that 'no' doesn't exist, that there are just different ways of going around and finding a solution. Certainly, I was born in a country where I wanted to study something that was nearly impossible for a young girl, first because I was a girl, and then when I came to this country I had a completely different cultural tradition and spoke a different language. I was different from other students; there were a lot of challenges. Professors told me to my face that women were not made for geology because geology requires extraneous endurance; you have to climb mountains, be exposed to high and very low temperatures and extreme conditions. It's part of the test you have to go through to become a geologist. But I love that; that type of challenge made it even more interesting to me. When the first human mission to Mars will be chartered my prediction is that you will have a diverse set of astronauts and among them there will be geologists. The first people to go to other planets are geologists. Take the example of Apollo 17; the first scientist-astronaut to be sent to the Moon was a geologist. I think the same thing is going to happen when humans are sent to Mars; you will have geologists.

Even rovers like Curiosity are doing what a geologist would be doing when you go to explore: do recognizance, search, map, hammer, sample, take a core, bring it to the lab. Curiosity has an amazing built-in laboratory so it can sample and start to get results. It's a geological rover looking for the potential niches of past or present life. I am fascinated by that.

There are challenges as a woman in a scientific field; I was out of the norm, and there weren't that many female faces that I could relate to when I first started in this field. Today it is really comforting to see a lot more diversity in planetary science and science overall. I think it's definitely improving but we still have a long way to go. I like to tell young women that science is a fantastic field, and a fantastic profession. It provides the ability to answer core questions for humanity, to really see that science is not something foreign; it's part of our life; we are all scientists in one form or another. We look, explore, taste, exercise our senses. The innate curiosity that drives humans is the key element that makes humans scientists and explorers; in our hearts we are all scientists. I see that as a key element for a civilization that produces the best of what humans can be.

Tell us about your current projects. What are you working on now? What excites you the most?

I'm very fortunate to be working on New Frontiers; I'm the program director acting currently. New Frontiers has three main missions:

First is the New Horizons mission to Pluto. It will arrive in 2015 to this incredible dwarf planet and its fascinating system of moons. We will learn the secrets that Pluto has been hiding from us. As we focus more powerfully on that region of space we are finding more moons; now Pluto has five moons, but when the mission was launched we only knew of one, Charon. It is becoming more and more exciting as we go.

Second is the Juno spacecraft, launched in 2011. It is the first time we have had a mission to Jupiter launched with solar energy as the sole energy source. 450 Watts can power a full spacecraft with solar energy at that distance from the sun; this is amazing to me when we think that a hairdryer can use about three times that amount of energy. The suite of instruments on board is designed to understand the largest planet in the solar system with the most complex climate. The Jupiter system is like a mini solar system within our Solar System. There are about 66 moons around Jupiter; like a star it is composed of hydrogen and helium, and it emits more energy than it receives, so that's why it's called a proto-star. If it had acquired more mass during its formation, our Solar System would be binary and would have two suns. We are learning more and more how important Jupiter-like planets are to having Earth-like planets. Juno will arrive in July, 2016. On October 9, 2013, the spacecraft will do an Earth fly-by at 563 km altitude. It will use the Earth's gravity field to slow down and direct its trajectory toward the giant planet. On board both spacecraft [Juno and the New Horizons mission] are student experiments. On Juno we have a camera to engage students and the public at large.

Third is the OSIRIS-ReX, which will bring a sample return of asteroid RQ36. There was a competition that just closed where all kids under 18 could submit names to name the asteroid RQ36. We will announce the new name of the asteroid shortly. Potentially this asteroid could have a trajectory where it could intersect the Earth's orbit in the faraway future, so it is one of those asteroids we need to watch. We are sending a spacecraft to extract a sample to determine the chemical composition to learn about asteroids so that if we had to do a deterrent maneuver, we would be able to do it. It's an issue of the preservation of humanity in the future. Asteroids are the building blocks of planets and key to the understanding of how the Solar System formed.

All of these projects have budgets of over one million dollars, which includes the building of the spacecraft, instruments, launch, operations, and science return and analysis. I also am the lead scientist on the exploration of Venus with a group of scientists who are specialists on Venus, involving international collaboration.

What do you think is the greatest impediment to women's success in your field today?

Not believing enough in themselves, that they are capable of making their dreams come true, of being true to themselves. It's very important that any woman or human being who is interested in a scientific career be persistent that they can do it and they can make their dreams come true. I think if they truly believe in themselves that they will make it happen.

When I give talks, I start off with my philosophy of **STARS**:

Smile, life is a great adventure
Transcend to triumph over the negative
Aspire to be the best
Resolve to be true to your heart
Success comes to those that never give up on their dreams

That summarizes my philosophy to dream and never give up.

Janet Rowley

Dr. Janet Rowley studies human genetics and discovered chromosomal translocation – an abnormality that occurs when a part of one chromosome breaks off and attaches to a different one – as the cause of leukemia and other cancers, with different translocations being responsible for different cancers. Her work has enabled scientists to more precisely target their research for cancer treatment.

In 1984, Dr. Rowley was appointed the Blum-Riese Distinguished Service Professor at the University of Chicago. In 1998, she received the Lasker Award – one of three scientists – for her work on translocation. In 1998, she received the National Medal of Science, followed by the Benjamin Franklin Medal for Distinguished Achievement in the Sciences of the American Philosophical Society in 2003. Finally, in 2009, she was awarded the Gruber Prize in Genetics and the prestigious Presidential Medal of Freedom, the highest award that may be given to a civilian.

What inspired you to study medicine? How did you make the transition after getting your M.D. from being a physician to conducting research in genetics?

This journey has been a process of gradual evolution. In high school and as a freshman at the University of Chicago I liked the biological sciences. Many of my lab partners at the University of Chicago were pre-med students. We were taking the same classes, so I decided I would be pre-med too.

After graduating from med school, I got married after my internship and my husband and I started our family. I wanted to practice but only part-time, so I worked in the well-baby clinic several half days a week. I then learned about a full day job in a clinic for retarded children. This was challenging, but I did not have adequate training in neurology to understand the basis for the retardation in most patients. At this time, it was discovered that Down Syndrome was due to a chromosome abnormality. My husband was soon to take a sabbatical in Oxford, England. I could not practice, but I could study chromosomes (cytogenetics). I applied for, and got, an NIH (VSPHS) special fellowship to study in England. I started a research project that was not completed when we returned to Chicago, so I approached one of my professors about continuing my research project at the U of C. He agreed and so I began my career as an independent scientist, studying cytogenetics.

Your research on chromosomal translocation has had profound influence on our understanding of cancer development. Yet at the time of your initial publication of your findings, there was resistance in the field to your ideas. Can you talk about what this time was like for you – knowing that you had discovered something tremendously important and working to make other scientists and doctors see its importance?

Recurring chromosome translocations were not known to occur in malignant diseases before I discovered the first one in the summer of 1973. At this time, the general view was that because of their apparent randomness, these changes were a consequence, not a cause, of the cancer. The second translocation, the one that that caused the Philadelphia Chromosome (PH) in chronic myeloid leukemia (CML), seemed to be an exception. The PH chromosome had been discovered in 1960 by David Hungerford, collaborating with Peter Nowell; at the time it was thought to be a deletion of a small chromosome and the loss of part of the chromosome led to loss of genes important in myeloid cell maturation.

It was not clear that translocations were important in the middle 1970s. By 1977, I had discovered another translocation that seemed specifically associated with a rare form of leukemia and, by that time, I became a believer and a missionary. I felt that I was right and that they would be convinced at some point.

What is the most exciting project on which you are currently working?

The laboratory is currently directed by Dr. Jianjun Chen, who began as a post-doc in my lab about 12 years ago. We are studying changes in gene expression and in the levels of expression of small RNAs in acute leukemia cells that are carrying different translocations. The hope is that some of these molecules may be so important in leukemia transformation that they may be effective targets for therapy.

Have you encountered any sexism while pursuing your career? If so, how did you overcome it? Have you noticed any changes in the acceptance and encouragement of women in medicine over the course of your career?

I never expected discrimination, so I expect that I mainly overlooked it when it occurred. Although I was surprised to find out in 1944 that when I applied to medical school that there was a quota of 3 women in a class of 65. I had to wait 9 months to apply for the next class. But I was only 19 when I first applied and I had a full scholarship and lived at home, so I was not particularly bothered. In medicine and the biological sciences, there have been progressively more women, so I think that, by and large, the problems at the junior level and, to a lesser extent, at the senior level have lessened. Unquestionably, many women have a harder time proving their competence and capacity to manage laboratories and large programs than do men.

What advice would you offer girls and women interested in a career in medicine or related fields? How do you think we can encourage more women to get involved in STEM fields, generally?

I think that medicine and biology offer very rewarding careers for both men and women. There are a wide variety of choices once one gets a degree. I think that there are serious flaws in STEM education at present with an emphasis on facts, not on mechanism or principles of function that would be much more interesting to most students. Having young people do experiments even in early elementary school would be the best way to get them involved.

Alexandra Rutherford

Dr. Alexandra Rutherford is an Associate Professor at York University, affiliated with the History and Theory of Psychology Graduate Program. Her work examines the relationship between psychology and feminism from a historical standpoint. She is the project director for Psychology's Feminist Voices and coordinates the CENT (Constructing Empowering Narratives and Theories) research collective, a group of senior undergraduate and graduate students who meet on a regular basis to discuss their work and contribute to collaborative projects. Dr. Rutherford received the 2011 Award of Distinction from the Section on Women and Psychology of the Canadian Psychological Association and co-edits a feature in their newsletter called "Making Herstory".

How did your passion for psychology and behavioral science develop?

As an undergraduate at the University of Toronto in the early 1990s, I really had no clue what I wanted to do. I was fortunate enough to have the freedom to explore during my college years – I took music, French language and literature, biology, English, calculus, and psychology, among other things!! It soon became clear to me that psychology was my passion – I had a great introductory psych class that revealed the incredible breadth of the field. My first love was social psychology – the idea that you might be able to uncover things about people's social behavior and motivation that was not obvious to them was intriguing to me. The classic experiments seemed so clever, and I really liked research design. When I graduated from college, I wanted to pursue psychology as a career but I did not really know how to do that, other than to study clinical psychology (I did not really have any mentors to advise me at the time, so my knowledge of what to do next was somewhat limited!). I didn't realize how competitive it was to get into PhD programs in clinical, but luckily I did get accepted into one program and that set me on the path to what I do now. I found that I did love clinical psychology, but was also yearning to move beyond the controlled laboratory experiment as a research method. I was getting more and more interested in taking a historical approach, and that is what I do now. I am a licensed clinical psychologist and practiced for many years, but as an academic I study psychology historically. This includes questions like "How has psychology, in terms of both its research practices and knowledge products, been gendered?" and "How has feminism, from the late 19th century to today, shaped psychology and how has psychology shaped feminism?"

Your research has explored gender issues and attitudes toward women. What have been the most profound findings that you have uncovered so far? The most surprising?

My research is historical and examines the relationship between feminism and psychology over the 20th century as well as the ways psychologists' own genders and the gender norms of their times and places have influenced their work. The general finding that recurs in my own and many others' work is that gender operates in science on so many levels. Another way to say that is that science is gendered all the way up and all the way down – from the way questions are asked, to who is deemed qualified to ask them (and answer them), to what can actually be seen (and what is not seen) by scientists, all the way to how data are interpreted and findings are reported. This does not invalidate science – it just means that we need to examine science like we examine all human/social practices – critically, carefully, and contextually.

Have you encountered any obstacles in your career because of gender prejudice? If so, how did you overcome them?

I think there are many subtle ways in which gender prejudice still operates in academe, and of course in science. Although it is hard to know for sure whether these kinds of attitudes have affected me personally, I continue to run into the attitude that clinical and child psychology, which are predominantly female, are less rigorous than "harder" fields where the ratio of women to men is more even or favors men. Although you have to be really smart to get into clinical programs, I have encountered the attitude that the smart women who get into these programs are just there because they want to help people and this is somehow said in a demeaning way – as if helping people were an anti-intellectual endeavor!! I know there is still gender discrimination in terms of salaries at my university – published tables prove that. The response that this is because women don't negotiate as well as men infuriates me, as it blames and then places the burden on individual women to conform to some sort of masculine norm in order to get fair treatment (rather than acknowledging a structural inequity). Personally, I have only encountered one or two colleagues in my career who appear to me to be overtly sexist (although they would not see it that way). I deal with this by keeping my distance!! Luckily, I can easily avoid them and surround myself with supportive and feminist colleagues. This would not have been possible just a few short decades ago. In my interviews with feminist psychologists who were training before the second wave, stories of amazing sex discrimination and harassment abound. At that time there was not yet a community or collective consciousness around such unfair treatment.

What are your current research projects? About which current/future project are you the most excited?

I have a number of projects on the go at all times. One that is coming to fruition with a group of wonderful undergraduate and graduate student colleagues is a collective portrait of the first generation of women psychologists in Canada, many of whom will be quite unknown to the majority of psychologists. Another ongoing project is the Psychology's Feminist Voices Multimedia Digital Archive, which includes an oral history project that I have been leading since 2004. I and my research team conduct interviews with self-identified feminist psychologists to help unpack the relationship between feminism and psychology and establish an archival record for the field. I am also working on a paper that explores how discourses of masculinity affected early to mid 20th-century psychology in terms of who was deemed an appropriate kind of psychological scientist. You could be a woman and be a scientist, but you had to be a certain kind of woman!!

You are the project director for Psychology's Feminist Voices, exploring the narratives of feminist psychologists worldwide. What are the greatest challenges still facing female scientists? How do you think we can encourage more women to get involved in STEM fields? What advice would you offer women interested in entering these fields?

Greatest challenge facing female scientists: finding a way to combine work and family. This seems to be one of the last frontiers for women in many fields, but in science especially given the timing of one's training and the career expectations. This is a challenge that must be met with structural, societal, and culture-wide changes. No one person can solve this problem.

How to encourage more women to get involved in STEM fields: As a society, we need to start very early portraying science positively to girls and we need to combat gendered cultural stereotypes about women and science at every turn. We need to make the structural changes required to support both women and men who want to have lives and be successful scientists. There are some wonderful initiatives out there to get more women and more racial/ethnic diversity into STEM. Diversity is key to creative and relevant science of all kinds.

Advice to women entering these fields: a) find and use your mentors, b) work collaboratively with other women and supportive men (nobody can do everything alone), and c) make sure you love what you do! When things get rough, this may be the last thing that sustains you!

Jill Tarter

Dr. Jill Tarter is an astronomer whose work has focused on the exploration of space for habitable planets. She was director of the SETI (Search for Extraterrestrial Intelligence) Institute and has worked with NASA as a project scientist. She has advocated for the need for proper scientific education. She received the 1989 Lifetime Achievement Award by Women in Aerospace, the 2001 Telluride Tech Festival Award of Technology, the 2003 Adler Planetarium Women in Space Science Award, Wonderfest's 2005 Carl Sagan Prize for Science Popularization, a 2009 TED prize, and two public service medals from NASA. Dr. Tarter's work was illustrated in the film Contact, with Jodie Foster consulting with her for her character of Ellie Arroway.

How did you fall in love with astronomy and the search for extraterrestrial life? Was there a defining moment when you knew this was the life for you?

I started life as an engineer, earning my Bachelor of Engineering Physics from Cornell. At the end of those 5 years as the only woman in my class, I decided that if engineers were as boring as my professors, I'd find more interesting problems to solve with my considerable and hard-won problem solving skills. I stayed at Cornell and took graduate courses in multiple departments, finally finding a course on star formation taught by Prof. Edwin Salpeter – I was hooked. I went to grad school at UC Berkeley's astronomy department doing a thesis on Brown Dwarfs (a name I coined). I was raising a young daughter so grad school took a lonnnnnnnnng time. Between my first year when I was supposed to learn to program a PDP-8/S computer (the first ever desktop – with no language, it had to be programmed in octal) and my last year, the computer had grown obsolete and was given as a piece of surplus equipment to Prof. Stuart Bowyer, who was trying to start a SETI project with the UC Berkeley Hat Creek Radio Observatory 85 foot telescope. Stu recruited me to SETI to program that old PDP-8/S. I read the Cyclops

Report written by Barney Oliver and John Billingham and was hugely impressed by the fact that I lived in the first generation of humans who could try to do experiments to answer the old human question "Are we alone?", rather than just ask the priests and philosophers what we should believe. I was around at just the right time with just the right talents to begin this scientific exploration and I got hooked – and have stayed hooked, on SETI.

Of your many research projects, which provided the most promising evidence of sentient life on other planets? Where in our universe have you found the strongest evidence for life?

To date there is NO EVIDENCE for life beyond the planet Earth – there is evidence of the conditions that might once have supported life, or perhaps might do so today – that is, there is evidence for potential HABITABILITY elsewhere, but as yet no evidence of INHABITANTS. Mars, Europa, Callisto, Ganymede, Titan, or even Enceladus might be inhabitable within our solar system, but there's a lot of technology development and observational exploration before we can answer the question of whether they ARE or WERE inhabited. Beyond our solar system, SETI is really the only game in town right now. We are excited that after decades of selecting stars that we thought might host planetary systems, the Kepler spacecraft and ground-based observatories are showing us where planets actually exist – that's now where we are pointing our telescopes. There are no guarantees; we may be looking for the wrong thing, but at least we're looking where there is likely to be habitable real estate.

Did you encounter any obstacles to pursuing your dream because of your gender? If so, how did you overcome them?

In high school I had to just plain ignore all the gender-biased advice against taking shop rather than home economics (I took both) and against taking physics (I loved physics, but couldn't take advantage of an opportunity to attend Saturday classes at Columbia University because I was also a Drum Majorette marching and twirling a baton at Saturday football games). Later as the only girl in my engineering class, I made a conscious decision to date architects and never engineers (who in those days showed up for dates with slide rules on their belts). I was also locked into the female dorms each night, unable to work with my male colleagues on sharing the solutions to problem sets – so I did all of them myself and got a better education as a result. Although I was on the Dean's List every semester, at graduation I was told that because I was a woman, I only qualified to be an HONORARY member of the engineering honor society Tau Beta Pi. Years later I was told that I would be eligible for FULL membership status for a fee… no thank you. Also, when I decided to marry at the end of my junior year, my 5-year tuition and fees scholarship was summarily withdrawn (like my high school counselors, the corporate sponsors of the scholarship simply assumed that marriage would mean children and an end to my scholastic/professional activities). I was crushed – my fiancee and I had carefully planned out our finances for the completion of undergraduate school and then graduate school and the scholarship was integral to those plans. Fortunately Dale Corson, then Dean of the Engineering School, went to bat for me and cemented my understanding that there can be wise as well as stupid people of both sexes. Decades later, when Dale Corson was the President of Cornell University, I served on a special scientific advisory committee he had for Arecibo Observatory and I was able to thank him again, personally as a working scientist. So you just do what you have to. I remember discussing this with Professor Margaret Burbidge – a woman who is a great hero of mine – and she said that when you get denied an honor or an opportunity because you are a woman, it feels like you've been kicked in the stomach, but you just figure out how to do an end run around the obstacle and get what you want anyway – good advice!

Tell us about your/SETI's current projects. What are you working on now? What excites you the most?

Dr. Gerry Harp is now the Director of the Center for SETI Research at the SETI Institute (I retired in June). He and his team are using the Allen Telescope Array that we built over this past decade to search for radio signals that would be indicative of another technological civilization. Gerry has lots of new ideas about how to use the exponentially improving signal processing capabilities to begin looking for additional types of 'engineered' signals. My job now is fundraising to find the money to support Gerry and his team, not just this year, but next year and the year after that – as long as it may take. It isn't easy, and I'd be pleased if you could help me tell the story about the need to support this fundamental scientific exploration.

What advice would you offer girls and women thinking about pursuing astronomy as a career? What do you think is the greatest impediment to women's success in astronomy today?

I always suggest that they listen to themselves. Don't listen to what 'they' say, whoever 'they' are. Figure out what you like and don't like and make realistic judgments about what you are good at. That last part is probably the hardest – girls and young women often do not give themselves enough credit when they attempt to do self-evaluation.

Interviews: Gaming

Celeste Anderson..............................p. 103
Tara J. Brannigan..............................p. 108
Shanna Germain................................p. 114
Sheri Graner Ray...............................p. 118
Stephanie Harvey..............................p. 122
Jane Jensen......................................p. 125
Kate Killick.......................................p. 128
Lindsay Morgan Lockhart................p. 132
Rhianna Pratchett............................p. 135
Siobhan Reddy.................................p. 138
Alana Smith-Brown..........................p. 140
Caryn Vainio....................................p. 145
Nia Wearn..p. 150
Margaret Weis..................................p. 154

Celeste Anderson

Ms. Celeste Anderson is a professional gamer. She has gamed her entire life, first casually and later competitively, is an expert at first-person shooters, and has competed in numerous Halo competitions nationally. In addition, she is a speedcuber, able to solve the Rubik's cube in less than 25 seconds. She is sponsored by PowerA. She was recently a contestant on TBS' King of the Nerds reality series and was crowned King of the Nerds.

How did you fall in love with gaming? Was there a defining moment when you knew that professional gaming, specifically first-person shooter competitions, was for you?

When I was very young, I spent a lot of time with my cousins and it seemed that casual gaming was a big part of all our lives. It was something we did together and it felt very natural. I didn't really think much of it until I moved cities and a lot of people were noticing that I constantly wanted to play video games on my spare time. Being extremely shy and introverted, I kept to my studies and played a lot of games when I had the chance to because it was nice to escape into a story and into a world that was full of thrill and curiosity. I knew I had fallen in love with gaming when I just stopped caring what people thought and submerged myself into games.

There wasn't a defining moment when I knew I wanted to pursue professional gaming. I believe it was the consistent exposure to the competitive gaming world that encouraged me to see what it was like. After my first tournament at the Fan Expo in 2006 where I placed 2nd in a Halo 2 tournament, I had this sudden fire in me come out of nowhere. It had been a very long time since I felt passionate about something and I knew from then on that competitive gaming was going to be a big part of my life.

What got you interested in professional speedcubing? What do you enjoy most about it?

I always wanted to solve a Rubik's cube and one day when I was working on a National Video Game Tour across Canada, a boy was sitting at a table solving a cube. He was solving it in less than 13 seconds and I was floored. One thing that can always attract my attention is people who have astonishing talents and show a lot of ambition. I spoke with him briefly about it and later down the road we somehow got reconnected via internet. We became best friends and he taught me how to solve it. I also found out he was one of the top speedcubers in North America and that's when I got really excited to learn about his life. We started dating and just as much as competitive gaming was a part of my life, I wanted to be a part of his and explore speedcubing. I definitely wanted to support and be included with his hobbies; it just so happened that I ended up loving the hobby a little too much! After a year of practice, I managed to go from 3 minutes to 25 seconds. It no longer felt like a struggle to do the algorithms since it became muscle memory and quick computing. I enjoyed the new competitive atmosphere, but what I do enjoy the most about speedcubing is the goal to always do better. It was never so much about competing against other people as it was always just trying to challenge and outdo yourself. A side bonus is that people are always pleased to see someone actually solve a cube, so that's always a great feeling to enjoy.

What was it like to be on TBS's King of the Nerds show? What were your favorite experiences competing with and against your nerd/geek opponents?

It was amazing and hands down my favorite experience that I have ever been a part of. It was stressful but a lot of fun because I was out of my comfort zone and usually if I am, I have no ability to fight my anxiety and worry!

It was always one of my dreams to compete in a Reality TV Competition show when I was little because I watched a lot of Survivor, Amazing Race, and Big Brother. Not only did I want to see how well I could do, it was also important for me to challenge myself and get out of my shell. I learned a lot about myself and I had a blast living in Nerdvana. The competitions were so intense; I must have lost so much sleep while I was there because I was always on edge!

What I loved most was getting to be around other people who had things they were passionate about. Being around other nerds/geeks always feels like you're with family and even if we were in competition mode a lot of the time, we got to hang out and enjoy each other's companies. It was the perfect environment for me – hanging out with other nerds, living in a nerd heaven, and competition, which is in my blood.

Tell us about your current projects and upcoming competitions. What are you working on now? What excites you the most?

After the show, I decided to go back to school and get on the path so that one day I can create my own video games. Unfortunately, the competition scene for me is a little slow because Halo 4 is no longer on the MLG Circuit – the main competitive event that I attend. As of now, I'm concentrating on school and casually gaming; it's been extremely exciting to be a part of TBS' Competition Reality TV Series: King of the Nerds because it has opened a lot of opportunities! I am looking to attend the World Championship Rubik's Cube Tournament this year (2013) in Las Vegas and hopefully, if Halo 4 has a great competition event coming up, I'll definitely go to that!

Have you encountered any obstacles to pursuing your dream because of your gender? If so, how did you overcome them? What advice would you offer girls and women thinking about pursuing professional gaming as a career? What do you think is the greatest impediment to women's success in gaming – whether playing generally or competing specifically – today?

The obstacles that I have encountered being a female have been extremely difficult and, sometimes, very disheartening. There were a lot of times when I didn't believe I could continue to pursue professional gaming because, as much as people were excited to see females in the gaming world, there were a lot more people looking at your every move and continuously discouraging you. I was constantly judged and looked down upon and it really hurt sometimes. Females aren't common in the competitive gaming world and once you submerge into that world, there are a lot of things that are thrown at you. Good and bad. They always say that a lot of people concentrate on the bad things that happen in their life and forget the good and, being a shy and quiet person, it was a real tough battle with my insecurities. It took a while to overcome the obstacles and the negativity that are attached to a female gamer, but I think it is the genuine friendships I formed within that community and remembering who you are as a person that really hit home. I learned to disregard the negative comments and remember that I love what I love – nothing can change that. If you're a female and you're looking to go into professional gaming, you need to make sure your heart is in it. It takes a lot of dedication and time. The most important thing is to get into the right mindset and stay on track with it. Do not let others get you down and always be humble. Always work hard and believe that you can accomplish anything if you put your mind to it! I cannot express the importance of always staying true to yourself. If you love gaming and competing, then I recommend pursuing professional gaming as a career. It's made me who I am today and I've grown so much through my experiences in it. The greatest impediment for a women's success in gaming is that you'll always feel like you have to prove yourself; a woman's mindset can get overloaded with too many goals that stray off of just enjoying the experience of gaming. Success in gaming is gained through hard work and keeping a good head on your shoulders, which you can apply to most things in your life! There are a lot of women out there that have no idea how to succeed with continuous discouragement! Remember that you have people who will always support you and that's all that matters!

Tara J. Brannigan

Ms. Tara J. Brannigan is the Community Marketing Manager at PopCap Games, the creators of free online games including some on Facebook. She provides a line of communication between game developers and the players themselves. In addition to creating games, she also creates jewelry, masks, and other crafts. Ms. Brannigan has publicly denounced sexual harassment at game conferences and other types of prejudice against female gamers.

How did your love of gaming begin? Tell us about the path that led you to your work at PopCap Games.

To be perfectly honest, I'm not sure I can really pinpoint when it began. The first game I really remember playing regularly was Super Mario Bros with my aunt Mary. She's only 7 years older than I am, so we were more like sisters at that age and often spent time playing games together on her NES. We found our first bug when we discovered that accumulating too many free lives would eventually switch the life counter over to a negative value. If you die at that point, the game ends. We were angry and frustrated for a few days after we discovered that, but it didn't take long until we were back at it.

Later on it was Sonic the Hedgehog and a variety of other console games. However, I don't know that I really considered myself a gamer until I played Doom. That was really the first game that I not only enjoyed, but also spent hours mastering and replaying. That was the turning point at which I really actively started paying attention to which games were coming out and wanted to learn more about how games were made. I remember agonizing over a letter to John Romero to ask him if he had any advice for someone looking to get into the industry. I don't think that I actually expected a response, but was beyond excited when he wrote back with some personal advice and encouragement. It was a small thing, but it really made a difference in making me feel like it was something I could pursue. I'll always be thankful for that response.

For the first few years out of high school I pursued 3D modeling & animation as my route into the industry. And while I like to think I was decent at it, I eventually realized it wasn't for me. Instead, I took a part-time gig testing games and found my entry into the wild world of the game industry. I loved testing games, and while I took a brief break from the industry to build my skills as a QA [Quality Assurance] outside of games, I eventually returned to the industry that I love. What started as a contract QA job at Microsoft for the Hired Gun team ended as a full time position as a Program Manager for what would be the Primetime & 1 vs 100 for Xbox LIVE project. It was on the 1 vs 100 team that I got my taste of and fell in love with community management. Eventually a really exciting opportunity arose at PopCap that would allow me to expand those skills and it was time to make another jump!

You've tweeted that there are a good number of women at PopCap – what about the company and/or environment has allowed that to happen?

PopCap as a company is a lot like its games in some respects: open, inviting, and just a heck of a lot of fun for everyone. That alone can be a big draw for people looking to find a home in the game industry. By presenting an open, fun environment, you're bound to attract people of all demographics. I think PopCap has done a really great job of that, and it shows in the diversity and strength of the company as a whole. We make games that appeal to everyone. Having the input and creative force from a wide variety of people is seen as a big benefit.

In addition, when I joined the company I was completely blown away by the inclusion of the 'Workforce Culture' team, a fantastic group of women who were dedicated to the mission of building an awesome, fun place to work. Right out of the gate, new hires to the company were introduced to this team that was there to help you get started and generally support you in your new role. It might not seem like a lot, but setting that initial tone as a company that values its employees on a personal, individual level made a very strong impression on me. Our industry can have its issues with being a bit of a ruthless machine, and knowing that PopCap had made a commitment to ensuring employee happiness really set a great tone for my new role.

Please tell us about your current projects. What are you working on now?

I'm currently the Community Marketing Manager for one of our social titles on Facebook. It's a fun little hidden object game with some really unique characters and a fantastic sense of humor. I love the community surrounding the hidden object game genre and the diverse group of people that enjoy our game. In addition, I've been working on a few various side-projects that are meant to help better support and unify the larger overall brand. It might not sound extremely exciting, but I love working on projects that work across franchises to help create a better sense of community across games and within the company itself.

Outside of my professional job, I dabble in random metalsmithing and jewelry projects. As an extension of that, I participate in various jewelry-related communities and attempt to share some of my experience as a community marketing manager with artists and makers who are learning how to market their work. I love when my passions collide and I'm able to help provide guidance or support in some fashion.

Please tell us about the sexism you have experienced in your career. How have you overcome it/dealt with it?

As a bit of a preface: Most of the people that I've met in the industry are not sexist and don't actively promote sexist attitudes. The vast majority of people I've worked with through the years are great people, some of whom I count among my best friends. Any time this topic comes up I like to stress that the bulk of the people I know in the industry are great people. However, there is definitely room for improvement, and in comparison to some of the other industries I've worked in the game industry still has some room to grow.

The most hurtful experience I had was when I was promoted at one of my first testing jobs. I worked extremely hard at the job and was regularly given great feedback from my managers on the quality of my work. One day I came in to find that I'd been promoted to a lead position. I was really surprised and excited. Upon hearing the news, one of my coworkers coldly said something to the effect of 'Yeah, well it's pretty obvious why'. I was confused and when I asked for clarification I was told that it was because I 'have nice tits'. It wasn't long before I'd heard rumors that I'd slept with a manager and that I didn't deserve the position. It was utterly infuriating. I understand now that it was driven by jealousy and resentment, but had it been a male coworker that had been promoted to the same position, I have serious doubts that it would have been ascribed to his physical appearance or inferred that he'd slept with the boss. I'd like to say that I made some big stand or something to that effect, but in reality I just continued to do my job well and eventually left the company for a better paying role outside of the game industry.

Inappropriate touching thankfully seems to have receded a bit in the past few years thanks to the efforts of venues such as PAX, but nearly every woman I know in the industry has been inappropriately touched at industry events by complete strangers. If this happens to you, speak up; tell the person it's unacceptable and get the event's enforcement staff involved if necessary. No one has the right to touch you without your consent, and the more this sort of behavior is seen as unacceptable, the less likely it is to occur in the future.

Outside of that, one thing I see fairly often is men in the game industry making decisions around what goes into the game without considering their potential female audience and/or making decisions based around stereotypes. In most cases I don't think this is intentional or ill-willed.

The best way to help combat this is just to be present and to offer calm, reasoned opinions from your own perspective. Encourage your team members to seek out your opinion when designing and making decisions throughout the process. A team that seeks out and listens to a wider range of perspectives around what they're making has a much better chance of creating something that not only doesn't offend, but also actively appeals to a larger audience.

One of the teams at Microsoft did a fantastic job of this when trying to design the clothing for their female character. They were an almost entirely male team, and while they were perfectly capable of designing outfits for their character that they thought were neat, they sought out opinions from their female coworkers. The result was a great dialog about what worked and what didn't (high heels on hiking boots!) that led to an overall better design. It didn't compromise their vision, but instead made it more appealing to a larger audience overall. A win-win situation all around!

What advice would you offer girls and women thinking about pursuing a career in gaming? What do you think is the greatest impediment to women's success in this field today and how can they overcome it?

I think one of the biggest impediments to a woman's success in this field is really that first step: getting into the industry and sticking with it. It can be difficult to not be intimidated when you're new to the industry and you're not seeing many examples of other women in that same role. I am fortunate to have my mom as a great role model to look up to. While she's not in the game industry, she's an engineer in a very heavily male-dominated field and has never let it stop her from pursuing her career goals. She's a great role model and has always been there to encourage me and challenge me in a positive manner when I felt like giving up.

Thankfully these days finding a role model in the industry is easier than ever. There are more of us every year and many of us are willing to lend a helping hand, answer questions, and generally provide support. It's all a matter of finding the right people and connecting! Learning how to network (and maintain that network) is single-handedly one of the greatest skills you can develop for yourself in this industry. Join the conversation, make connections, find a mentor, and you'll not just have an easier time in the long run; you'll likely develop some fantastic, lasting friendships in the process.

In addition, learning how to advocate for yourself can go a long way towards growing your career. Make sure to take note of your successes, so when you go into the review process you're not fumbling for things to discuss and leverage in your career discussion and development. This can be as simple as filing away any 'thanks for the great job with _x_ task' e-mails into a special review folder for reference, in addition to keeping track of your accomplished objectives throughout the year. It's not always easy to talk about your accomplishments and successes, but it's critical to your long-term success in the industry. No one is going to manage your career for you. Just doing a good job and hoping that your efforts will be noticed seldom works out, so make sure you take the initiative and put your best foot forward!

And finally: Don't give up! If you eventually decide that the industry is not for you, that's okay and nothing to be ashamed of. However, if you love the industry and want to be a part of the joy that is making games, keep at it and don't get discouraged. You'll find your way in, meet a lot of great people, and hopefully make something fantastic that many people will enjoy and cherish!

Shanna Germain

Ms. Shanna Germain is a game and erotic novel writer and editor. She has done work in each of these areas separately – creating a new game called Numenera as well as writing erotic novels – and has also merged the two genres with her book Geek Love about geek-themed erotic encounters. In 2010, Ms. Germain was nominated for Best of the Net and a finalist for the John Preston Short Fiction Award. In 2009 she won first place in Anthology Builder's Match-That-Cover Contest, and in 2008 she was a Pushcart Prize nominee and recipient of the 2008 Rauxa Prize for Erotic Poetry.

How did your love of gaming begin? Please tell us about your path from playing tabletop RPGs to creating your very own game, Numenera, and what you have enjoyed most about creating Numenera.

I've been a gamer for as long as I can remember, from the early days of Pong, Frogger, and Bunnies & Burrows.

I started playing D&D as a happy accident. When I was in high school, I played on the boys' soccer team (because we didn't have a girls' team). So I had a lot of guy friends who were sporty in a very geeky way, if that makes sense. We spent a lot of time listening to Led Zeppelin and the Cure, talking about Lord of the Rings and Fahrenheit 451, and running through the woods pretending we were orcs.

One weekend, one of my friends said to me, "Hey, we're going to canoe across the lake, go camping, and play D&D. You should come with us." I had no idea what kind of game "Deendee" was, but I liked canoeing and camping so I said yes. My first game took place out in the woods near Cayuga Lake, while sitting on my backpack and borrowing a friend's dice. I ended up as a dwarf cleric. That was the last time I let someone else build my character.

Now, the second answer is this: I was recently asked this question in another interview and I gave an answer similar to the one above. Right after it was published, a long-time friend of mine who read that interview e-mailed me and said, "You are wrong. D&D wasn't your first tabletop RPG. How could you forget Bunnies & Burrows?"

Numenera is actually the brain child of Monte Cook, a long-time game designer who's worked on D&D 3rd Edition and a number of other games. So it's much more his game than mine. I'm doing some of the writing for the game, and I'm the lead editor, both of which I'm loving. Getting to play a part in creating this wholly new science fantasy game and world makes all of the creative parts of me very happy.

What inspired you to create Geek Love? Can you give us some teasers about what will be included in the collection?

As an erotic writer and a huge geek, I love the intersection where the sex and geek worlds collide. There's so much sexuality and sensuality in all things geek. Cosplay, dungeons, leather and subversive culture – it all intertwines in very cool ways.

Geek Love was created to celebrate that. I wanted to work with geeky writers and artists to make a book full of sexy librarians, gamers, superheroes, and computer programmers. We have some fantastic stories and art in the collection. There are drawings and photos of mermaids, hot gamer dudes, superheroes making out, tentacles, and library sex. We have stories of binary love, comic book collectors, gamers getting it on, and every other form of geek imaginable.

Can you also give us some teasers about your upcoming book, Leather Bound? What are your thoughts on the way women are portrayed in erotica today?

Sure! Leather Bound is a tale of a very sexual woman who runs a bookstore with her best friend. It's a tale of love and lust, full of bondage and books and beautiful men and women.

There are some fantastic depictions of women in the erotic world – realistic, self-aware women who are willing to claim their sexuality make me happy. Of course, sometimes (as in any genre), there are some female characters who make me feel a little crazy. I struggle with characters in the modern world who know nothing about sex or themselves. With the internet today, there is no excuse for a character to not be able to learn at least a little something about sex.

Have you experienced any sexism while pursuing your career? If so, how have you overcome it?

I'm not sure I would call it sexism. More like discrimination. The reason I make the distinction is because I find that both genders can be equally discriminatory to women in both the writing and the gaming industries. I've never felt like I got turned down for a job because of my gender, but I've had people suggest that the only reason I'm successful is because I "have a good smile" or that the only reason that people buy my books is because they think I'm hot.

I mostly ignore those kinds of comments when they're aimed at me. You can't be in this business long without developing seriously thick skin, and if someone's going to be that close-minded, I'm not interested in interacting or working with them anyway. I do try to provide education to people when I can, to help them understand why their words or misconceptions are harmful and destructive.

What advice would you offer girls and women thinking about pursuing game development or novel writing as a career? What do you think is the greatest impediment to women's success in these fields today and how can they overcome it?

I would say go for it, never give up, and always listen to constructive criticism and positive feedback, but never to assholes. Writing is a craft, and as with all craft, it requires a lot of work and time to hone your skills. Also, always be polite, kind, and professional. Good writing and a great attitude will take you far.

I think that the biggest impediment in the gaming industry might be that there are still so few female role models. I would encourage women to find people in the industry that they can look up to (male or female doesn't matter, as long as they're supportive) and learn as much as they can about both the craft and the business.

Sheri Graner Ray

Ms. Sheri Graner Ray is a creator of computer games who has worked with companies including Electronic Arts, Origin Systems, Sony Online Entertainment, and Cartoon Network. Her work includes Star Wars Galaxies, Ultima, and Nancy Drew. She wrote a book on gender in gaming called "Gender Inclusive Game Design – Expanding the Market" and is considered a leading expert on the topic. Indeed, in 2004 she was named one of gaming's Most Influential Women by the Hollywood Reporter. In 2005 she received the International Game Developers' Association's Game Developer's Choice Award. She co-founded Women in Games International and is its Executive Chair.

When were you introduced to computer games and gaming? When did you know that game development was your dream job?

I got into computer games by way of table top gaming, meaning table top role playing games like Dungeons and Dragons. In 1989 I had a weekly Dungeons and Dragons game going with five other people. We had a new player join us who was working for Origin Systems, a game company in Austin. About six months after he started playing with us, he told me they had an opening for a writer and he thought I'd be a natural. So I gave him my resume and a couple of writing samples. Two weeks later I had an interview with Warren Specter and two weeks after that I started as a "writer" at Origin Systems.

Honestly, I never thought it would last more than a year or two. But there was no question that I knew it was exactly what I wanted to do. I work with some of the most brilliantly creative people making things that bring people fun and happiness. I wouldn't trade it for the world.

Did you encounter any discrimination while pursuing your dream because of your gender? If so, how did you overcome it?

You know, I don't like to talk about the incidents I've run into. I've found it really does no good. Instead I'd rather focus on the positive things that have gone on in my career. Focusing on the bad things people have done to me because I'm a girl gives those actions power over me and I won't let that happen! ☺

Can you talk about what you think are the most important gender-related issues in the world of computer games today? Do you think that things have improved for female gamers? Has the way women are portrayed in games improved? To the extent that things have not improved, what do you think are the biggest obstacles?

There are several important issues in computer games today. Probably the first is getting women into the industry. The good news is that is improving. When I started we were probably less than 3% of the industry. Today we are 11% and growing. I think the biggest jump has occurred because of the growth in game educational programs. Because there are more girls in the classes, we are seeing more girls wanting into the industry.

A second large issue is getting women who are already in the industry to understand how important it is for them to step forward and be mentors for the young women just breaking in. We have a wonderful group called Mentornet.com that Women in Games International is working with to bring mentors to all women who want in.

As for the way women are portrayed, I do not feel it has made as big strides as it could have. We still have games such as Bayonetta coming out where apparently the less armor she is wearing, the tougher she gets... which is completely ridiculous. Can you imagine if they portrayed male characters the same way!

At this point the biggest obstacles are still getting in to the industry. It's a tough industry to break into regardless, but for women there's that extra hurdle of gender. I think in order to break down this barrier, we have to continue to shine a light on it... bring it to the attention of the industry... for it to finally go away.

What practices can we employ to create/promote gender-inclusive game design?

The thing we have to do if we want to make games more gender inclusive has nothing to do with putting the game in a pink box or making it about shopping. It's about understanding the different ways men and women approach entertainment technologies. You have to understand things like punishment and reward cycles and how the different genders approach that. You need to understand learning styles so you can make sure your tutorial is accessible for everyone. Things like what the avatars look like and emotional vs. visual stimulus... in other words, there's more to making games that appeal to everyone than just adding ponies and lipstick!

What projects are you working on now? What excites you the most?

What I can tell you is that I'm about to realize my ultimate dream. I am in the process of opening my own game studio here in Austin! We will be working on small tablet games to begin with, then working our way into some PC RPGs. It's going to be a lot of hard work, but I couldn't be more excited! So watch for Zombie Cat Studios, coming soon!

What advice would you offer girls and women thinking about pursuing game development as a career? What do you think is the greatest impediment to women's success in game development today?

Network.

The game industry is a glamour industry. We have more people who want in than we have jobs. So the way you get in is get to know people. Volunteer to help at conferences. Join the IGDA (International Game Developers Association). Go to a Women in Games International mixer. With today's social media, networking is as close as your Facebook page and Twitter. But you MUST do it. No job is going to fall into your lap. It is only by working at it yourself that you can make this dream come true. And make no mistake... it is a dream job! :)

Stephanie Harvey

Ms. Stephanie Harvey is a professional gamer known to the gaming world as missharvey. She is a 4-time World Champion and professional Counter-Strike player. She has played on several female-only teams including CheckSix Divas, SK-Ladies, emuLate!, and UBINITED. She works at Ubisoft Montreal as a game designer and has worked on Prince of Persia: The Forgotten Sands (XBOX 360, PS3, PC) and James Noir's Hollywood Crimes (3DS). She is also an M.NET Game Reviewer at Musique Plus TV Channel.

When were you introduced to video games and gaming? When and how did you decide to go professional and enter tournaments?

I've played video games for as long as I can remember. My parents are really open-minded people and even though they were not playing games themselves, they introduced me to technology at a very young age. Afterwards, it was in my hands and it just stayed as a passion for years until I started attending local tournaments for fun, just to watch my friends play. Eventually, I started getting more serious and had the desire to compete nationally and then internationally. It required money to do so, and by proving myself a few times I eventually got sponsored and became pro.

How do you think your background in architecture has helped/influenced you as a game developer?

My background in architecture helped me much more than what people think. Designing a building is very similar to designing a game. The thought process is almost identical and my vision of design was naturally transferred towards gaming. I believe in "function before form" and I feel it is one of the most important guidelines I had to keep in mind in both fields. What is the purpose of what I am creating and what is it supposed to do? Then when you nail that, you can think about what it looks like.

The way Nintendo designed Mario Galaxy is a great example of that theory. Also, the major difference between architecture and gaming is the interactivity you can have with the players. Buildings are not there yet, but I know some companies like Microsoft or Google are already working towards having interactive homes so maybe one day both worlds will unite.

What insights has your experience on several hugely successful female-only gaming teams given you into the sexism in the industry and what it takes to overcome it?

It has its up and downs but mostly it made me grow rapidly as a person on really sensitive issues because I was a female in a dominantly male world. The biggest learning experience for me is that no matter the sex, you can succeed and reach your dreams if you work very hard and put everything you can into it. As a female, no matter of which community you are a part, sex is a part of our daily lives. You are a nurse? Even if it's a female-dominated job, I am sure lots of them have comments about sexy nurse outfits from their friends all the time. The same applies to me in gaming. You need to learn to let it go and be strong. If you can back yourself with hard work, skill, or anything that isn't related to you being in a position because of your vagina, then you will succeed and be respected, but it will be hard. Just keep believing in yourself.

What are your current projects? What excites you the most?

I am actually very excited about every project I work on. I currently have two official jobs (game designer and gaming TV reviewer) as well as my gaming team, which for me is 24/7. The girls are my best friends and we practice for over 30 hours a week. We also run our own organization by dealing with sponsors, interviews, leagues, etc. Everything else that I do is a bonus. I would love to be more involved in videos (I've been working on and off on an online show but since I drive the project by myself it is not easy to always find the motivation) and I really want to write something, either a book, a blog, a presentation, a comic strip, or a web series... I am just not sure what to do yet as I always want to touch everything. I'm taking my time to figure out which one would be best for me at the moment.

What advice would you offer girls and women thinking about pursuing game development or professional game playing as a career? What do you think is the greatest impediment to women's success in gaming today?

My advice is DO IT! Do it for yourself and don't listen to anyone else telling you otherwise. I love to work with my female coworkers and it is still refreshing to play with my female team even after 10 years of knowing them. Be laid back about the comments you can get from others and don't forget that anonymity on the internet is a big issue and most likely you will be another victim of it. It shouldn't stop you from pursuing your passions and if you want to work in the industry, you should. We need more women in gaming and the more there are, the fewer prejudices there will be.

Jane Jensen

Ms. Jane Jensen began her career with a bachelor's degree in computer science and a job doing system programming for Hewlett-Packard. Her love of gaming eventually merged with her love of computers to lead her to Sierra Online, designing several computer games including the Gabriel Knight adventure series, the second of which was Computer Gaming World's Game of the Year. Ms. Jensen has also published novels, some of which were adaptations of her games and others of which were original stories. One of them, Dante's Equation, was nominated for the Philip K. Dick Award.

Since then, Ms. Jensen founded Oberon Media and worked at Zynga. Most recently, she and her husband formed Pinkerton Road, a game development studio based out of their home. The studio will provide subscribers access to the games they produce through a "Community Supported Gaming" model.

When were you introduced to games and gaming? When did you know that game development was your dream job?

I got a BA in computer science and began working for Hewlett-Packard doing low level code like Network drivers. But I really wanted to be a writer. When I discovered Sierra adventure games, I feel in love with them and knew I wanted to write games as a career, so I applied to work there and got lucky.

What would you say has been your favorite project so far – the one that excited you the most, or has the most lasting power for you?

Probably working on the first Gabriel Knight game – mainly because it was my first and it was so thrilling to be living my dream.

Have you encountered any discrimination while pursuing your career because of your gender? If so, how have you overcome it?

I haven't encountered much discrimination. I think gaming is a pretty high-tech field, so the women that are in it are smart and seem to be accepted at face value.

Can you tell us a little about what your plans are for Pinkerton Road? What inspired you to create this studio?

I wanted to get back to doing adventure games again and to have more control over the final result. Kickstarter made it possible to get funding, otherwise we probably would not have been able to do it.

What new games are you currently working on (either through Pinkerton Road or otherwise)?

An adventure game called Moebius and another one that is yet-to-be-announced.

What advice would you offer girls and women thinking about pursuing game development as a career? What do you think is the greatest impediment to women's success in game development today?

First, I think you need to have a real passion for it. If you have the passion, and you're prepared to work hard, there is no inherent barrier for a woman. But I think that's true of any profession. People are most successful when they are really focused in their passion and their inner drive and they have a strong vision of where they want to end up. As for the logistics, for game design I recommend that people either look for a specific game design program or do a joint computer science/English degree. Even though I don't program anymore as a designer, learning to think logically like a programmer – if this then that – is really helpful as a game designer, because it's basically writing fiction as a logic diagram. And it's a competitive field you so have to be prepared to work in QA or as a programmer or doc writer until you get a chance to show what you can do.

Kate Killick

Ms. Kate Killick is the founder and lead artist of Angry Mango, a small group of game designers that created Mush, which won the 2011 British Academy of Film and Television Arts New Media award. She holds a degree in Computer Games Design, receiving first-class honors from the University of Wales. She is particularly interested in experimental, independent games and games for social change.

When were you introduced to games and gaming? When did you know that game development was your dream job?

I've been into games for as long as I can remember. My earliest memories are of sitting on my Dad's knee playing a DOS version of Galaxians, which probably makes me sound older than I am! Gaming was always a social activity for me: teaming up with my sister to defeat Zelda bosses, inviting my friends over for Pokémon battles, Minecraft sessions with my friends at uni. It's always been one of my favourite hobbies.

When I started thinking about going to university, I had been doing bits and pieces of digital art, coding, and Flash games for a few years, but I didn't really know that much about indie games or what a career in the industry entailed. I had no idea you could study games at university; I had a vague idea of taking CG animation and possibly going into film. Luckily, when I was doing my art foundation year, a lecturer from the Computer Games Design degree came round to give a talk about the course. It blended my passion for art, my obsession with computers, and my love of gaming so perfectly – I knew instantly it was the obvious thing for me to do. I remember going away from the presentation trying to work out why I hadn't figured it out sooner!

What inspired you to create the award-winning Mush? What were the best and most challenging aspects of creating it with the small team at Angry Mango?

Mush started as an entry for the competition Dare to be Digital and when we came up with the idea we actually only had about two weeks before the entry deadline! We knew we needed something that would stand out to the judges, so we aimed to come up with a unique mechanic that also made creative use of the mobile phone's input methods. The mechanic of changing your character's emotions evolved from a prototype that some of the other team members had previously worked on, called Giant Ego, which features a character whose head grows and shrinks as compliments and insults are hurled at the player. We also wanted to create a really distinct aesthetic, so we looked at a lot of contemporary illustration for ideas of how to visually set the game apart from other vector art-style games.

Working in a small team definitely comes with a lot of ups and downs, particularly when you're trying to complete your studies at the same time! You have quite limited resources and have to take on a lot of different roles – I would have loved to have a project manager, but it's just not feasible for such a small team. The plus side is that you learn to work with each other and develop a great team dynamic – everyone has a big stake in the project and can see their ideas in the final product. It's never just a job.

Have you encountered any discrimination while pursuing your career because of your gender? If so, how have you overcome it?

I wouldn't say I've encountered any discrimination in terms of the opportunities I've had, but there are certainly times when the male dominance of the industry is apparent. Going to big games expos and seeing that the majority of women working there are being used as decoration is painful, but even more depressing is going to industry conferences or awards and seeing so few women on stage. It doesn't seem that women in the industry receive recognition or the opportunities to have their voices heard that men do. There isn't always a huge amount you can do about it as an individual – I think the most important thing is not to be too shy to express a controversial opinion and to point out sexism for what it is.

What projects are you working on now? What excites you the most?

I'm in between projects at the moment, but I'm working towards setting myself up with a sustainable game development business. I really enjoyed working on a mobile platform for Mush, and I'd love to expand to tablet games as I think there's a lot of unexplored potential there. I always get excited seeing what other indie developers are making, and recently there's been a lot of cool stuff coming out for tablets that I need to get my hands on!

What advice would you offer girls and women thinking about pursuing game development as a career? What do you think is the greatest impediment to women's success in game development today?

My advice to girls and women considering a career in games would be this: game development has become a very, very broad industry in recent years. There was a time when I wasn't sure I was doing the right degree because I didn't seem to be into the same AAA games as a lot of my coursemates, and I didn't feel like a "proper" gamer despite having loved games all my life. When I started to get involved with indie and mobile games, though, I realised how varied the games spectrum actually is.

I think it is important to be realistic about what you're getting into; the fact is, you will find yourself in the minority in a lot of situations and it will be frustrating at times. I've read some horror stories about the discrimination women in technology have faced, particularly when it comes to user comments on the internet, although I think that's part of several much wider issues. Perhaps I've been lucky, but I haven't encountered anything like that myself.

Overall, standing out because of your gender can work to your advantage, but at the same time it can direct attention away from your work as a designer or programmer. I suppose you have to find a bit of a balance. I'm always happy to talk about gender in games, because it's important to be vocal, and it's an important issue, but I don't ever want to be hired because of gender rather than merit.

I certainly don't think women should feel discouraged from going into a games career. If you're passionate about technology, or design, or games, then it is a vibrant and exciting industry to be a part of, with a great deal of opportunities to offer.

Lindsay Morgan Lockhart

Ms. Lindsay Morgan Lockhart (alias: missdoomcookie) is a game designer and writer at Microsoft Game Studios. Her work includes fantasy MMOs such as Rift: Planes of Telara and Vanguard: Saga of Heroes. Ms. Lockhart is also a writer and avid traveler.

When were you introduced to video games and gaming? When did you know that game writing and design was your dream job?

I've been gaming for as long as I can remember. My mother is a computer programmer, and has been since before I was born, so we always had computers in the house. I liked to say I learned reading and math from games, which might not actually have been true, but the Reader Rabbit series from the Learning Company definitely helped. We got our first Nintendo when I was five, and that only cemented my love of games.

I wasn't actually one of those people who knew they wanted to be in the industry and labored to get into it, which always makes it hard for me to advise people on how to get in. I'm a storyteller, and have been telling them in some form or the other since I was a little kid. My degree is in creative writing, and I'm always telling stories in different forms. I never even thought of doing it in games until an opportunity was presented to me to be a game designer/writer on the MMO Vanguard. I took the opportunity and have been doing it ever since.

Can you tell us about what inspired your work on Rift as the Defiant Lore Lead? What was your favorite part of developing that game?

I had been working on many high fantasy MMOs prior to joining Rift, and so in Rift, I saw the opportunity to shift the fantasy genre a little, which is what inspired the spellpunk approach to the Defiants. We were not making a science fiction game, so it would have been inappropriate to push them too far into actual technology, but fantastical technology helped differentiate them from the Guardians as well as previous fantasy games. The dynamic approach of the game's systems also informed our approach to the lore, which is to say that we were always striving to set up a world in flux. Incorporating story beats that would enable a dramatically shifting world informed the decision to have our game focus on planar invasions. They create a gripping visual language for our game story. The challenge of dynamic content and dynamic storytelling was definitely the most fun part of working on Rift and differentiated it the most from my previous projects.

Did you encounter any obstacles to pursuing your dream because of your gender? If so, how did you overcome them?

No, as I mentioned, I sort of fell into this work, so there wasn't a "pursuit" period. :) And since I started in the industry, I've never had trouble finding new opportunities or moving up within my teams, so I can only assume it hasn't been.

What are your current projects? What excites you the most?

I'm currently working on an unannounced project, so I should probably avoid this question. :)

What advice would you offer girls and women thinking about pursuing game development as a career? What do you think is the greatest impediment to women's success in game development today?

Make games. It's absolutely true of this industry before you are in it or even after you are in it that you are going to be doing the job before you have the job. Every promotion I've ever received has come after I was doing the job duties of that position, and it was made official. So, to back up a bit, you have to show to prospective employers you know what it means to make good game experiences. A lot of companies offer their toolsets for free, so download them and build mods and show you've got the stuff.

I think that one of the biggest impediments is the fact that there are so few women in it now. If that sounds like a cyclical problem, it absolutely is. Connections are essential in the industry. It opens up doors both to get into the industry and to continue getting jobs later on. I've only ever once gotten a job at a company where I did not know anyone, and that was only contract work. Who do men tend to know? Other men. It goes beyond that, though. If women don't see other women in the industry, they are less likely to think of it as a possibility. So, we need more female role models who are also reaching out to their female connections.

Rhianna Pratchett

Ms. Rhianna Pratchett's work spans the genres of video and computer gaming, comic books, and journalism. She is known for her work on the games Overlord, Viking: Battle for Asgard, Heavenly Sword, and Mirror's Edge, as well as a comic series with DC Comics based on the Mirror's Edge world. She has contributed to books on games narrative writing and works with the IGDA Writers' Special Interest Group and the Writers' Guild of Great Britain to improve games narrative writing. Recently, Ms. Pratchett began the use of hashtag #1reasontobe, highlighting reasons why women should work in gaming. In addition, her father, Terry Pratchett, revealed that his daughter will take over his popular Discworld series.

How did you come to love the worlds of gaming and comic books?

I've been a gamer since I was six years old. I'm an only child and my father was very into electronics and computing, so naturally I became interested in what he was up to. We used to play games together (I would draw the maps) and he would pass on his old machines to me. I also dived into his comics collection as well (including things like 2000AD and Watchmen) although games were my first love.

What is special about each of these different media for telling stories? What would you say has been your favorite project so far – the one that excited you the most, or has the most lasting power for you?

With comics you have a wonderful fusion of imagery and narrative, and the way you use the space on the page can bring so much to the pace and flow of a story. The tie-in comics for Tomb Raider and Mirror's Edge allowed me to explore the background and relationships of the characters in a way that there just wasn't time and space to do in the games. It was a very satisfying way of building out the narrative worlds.

I think my favourite game projects have been Overlord and Overlord II. They were really as fun to make as they are to play. I had a great relationship with the developers, Triumph Studios in the Netherlands. Working with a smaller team meant that alongside writing duties, I also got to cast and voice direct on the games, which really allowed me to shape how the narrative evolved from page to screen. We also had a fantastic team of voice actors, as well, who were a real hoot to work with, especially Marc Silk who voiced Gnarl and many of the minions.

Have you encountered any sexism in your career pursuits? If so, how did you overcome it?

Not sexism in regards to me being female, which has never been a problem because it's always been about my skill set, not my gender. However, I have encountered a degree of sexism when it comes to the use and depiction of female characters. Although I think that is getting better, in general. Basically you have to deal with it by offering alternative ideas and solutions, and pointing out that originality is more appealing to a broader audience than the same old tired clichés. By and large people aren't trying to deliberately be sexist when it comes to character depiction and creation, but they can often fall into familiar grooves and tried-and-tested ideas.

Please tell us about your current projects. What are you working on now? What excites you the most?

I'm working on another game for Square Enix/Eidos that I'm not allowed to talk about yet, unfortunately. However, I'm most excited about the work I'm doing outside of games at the moment. Particularly the screenplay I'm writing, which is an adaptation of the novel Warrior Daughter, by Janet Paisley. I'm doing the project with script development support and funding from the BFI and Creative Scotland and it's been a great experience writing a long-form story. My background in writing female characters that exist in violent times has come in very handy!

What advice would you offer girls and women thinking about pursuing comic book or game writing as a career? What do you think is the greatest impediment to women's success in these fields today and how can they overcome it?

Just go for it. Make sure you have a strong, broad knowledge of your field and what editors and developers are looking for. Go to lots of conferences and talks to learn about the industry you want to enter into from those currently working in the trenches. Be prepared to work hard to hone your skills and develop your talent. You can bet that the guys are doing exactly the same thing.

The opportunities are out there, but you have to kick the doors down yourself; they won't just open for you. And kicking doors down is all part of the fun!

Siobhan Reddy

Ms. Siobhan Reddy is Executive Producer at Media Molecule, an indie game development company that produced LittleBigPlanet, a puzzle platformer video game series. These games focus on user-generated content and gameplay. Ms. Reddy has produced other games including Airblade, Burnout 3, and Burnout 4, traveling across the world to pursue her gaming dreams.

When were you introduced to video games and gaming? When did you know that game development was your dream job?

We always had played board games as children and my brother was the one who was more into games. I used to play them but to be honest for the longest time I was more into music, film, theatre, fanzines, & technology all as separate things. It was a bit of a "eureka" moment when I realised that these could all be combined when making games.

Can you discuss the process that led to the development of the hugely innovative LittleBigPlanet? What inspired you in creating this game?

I had known Mark, Alex, and Kareem socially for about 8 years or so. They invited me to join Media Molecule just before setting it up to handle production. I was ready for a change from Criterion and so jumped at the chance. They showed me their early thoughts before I joined and it was clear that they had some really awesome, solid ideas that they wanted to pursue. When I actually started working with them it was really a matter of trying to knit these together, to make sure each of them got to pursue the thing that they were into.

Did you encounter any discrimination while pursuing your dream because of your gender? If so, how did you overcome it?

I haven't ever been stopped from doing what I love doing. Having a production mind means that you do all sorts of work covering a range from the menial like ordering pizza through to actually leading the team and making the decisions that this requires. I definitely have experienced people assuming that I am administrative rather than the role that I am. This can be very frustrating, but it's easily remedied.

What projects are you working on now? What excites you the most?

We are working on two projects. I'm inspired by people and our limitless imaginations. I get excited by all stages of the process. I'm inspired by the idea of making projects that bring people a little closer to some collective moment inside the shared mind of the molecule.

What advice would you offer girls and women thinking about pursuing game development as a career? What do you think is the greatest impediment to women's success in game development today?

Do it!! This is industry is the most vibrant and interesting industry that you could find yourself a part of. We can create worlds, stories, experiences from the ground up. It's so exciting. So exciting ☺. I am part of a couple of groups at the moment investigating why young women don't see it as an interesting place to work and I hope that we can change that. Change has to happen from within and so I really want to see more women join so that we can.

Alana Smith-Brown

Ms. Alana Smith-Brown is a tabletop and live-action roleplayer, Batman fan, and chess fan who also enjoys math, science, and problem-solving video games. Most recently, Ms. Smith-Brown was a contestant on TBS' Kings of the Nerds reality show. She is starting a gaming blog and writing a book based on one of her games.

How were you introduced to the world of comic books? What made you fall in love with them, and why is Batman your favorite?

My Grandparents owned a lake house; there were no TV or video games. One rainy day I found a bunch of my older brother's comic books and started reading them. They were rather tattered and worn from my brother but they still had a full story in them. It was a collection of a few Batman comics as well as a couple X-Men. By this time both of these sets of characters were on TV, animated for kids. It wasn't until I was older that I started collecting comic books, first with my allowance and then they were the reason I got a job while in high school. Batman is my favorite because in the animated series from the 90s he was the first male figure that said women are equal to men. Women can do anything men can. Catwoman, Red Claw, Harley Quinn, and Poison Ivy are all strong female characters. They helped shape me into what I am today, a go-getter and do-it-myself kind of person. Yes they are all villains, but Batgirl didn't come until later in the series. I also love Batman because he would solve problems with his brain. He doesn't need to kick the crap out of someone to get things done.

How did you get introduced to live-action roleplaying? I read on your Twitter page that you are running a LARP – can you tell us about it? What are your favorite RPGs?

I used to be a huge Anime fan. My first Con I ever went to was an Anime Con in Vermont. They had an evening of LARPing. I had never heard of it before but it sounded like so much fun! Dressing up in costume and pretending to be someone else for the evening? Yes please! That was the Con that introduced me to Vampire: The Masquerade. Once I went home I had to search the internet over to find a copy of Laws of the Night so I could start one myself. None of my friends were interested in regular play of the game so I ran a couple of One-shots on my 19th and 20th birthdays. I had never had so many people show up for one of my birthdays. All growing up only 1 to 4 people would show up, but now running my own LARP I had 22 people come to celebrate my birthday with me. It wasn't until last year that a few of my friends finally had the time for a monthly LARP. So I am again helping run Vampire: The Masquerade, this time with help. It's rather difficult to run a LARP with just you as the Storyteller (ST). So now there are 5 STs with a regular player base of 35 to 40 players. We are growing every month because we give out bring a friend experience points so they can continue to make their characters more awesome. In fact the villain I used in my one-shot for my birthdays is now a villain they have to deal with in the monthly LARP. We are running it as a TV show with plots and season finales, with the exception that we don't know how our players will react to things when we send a plot hook out. For example, last game I brought in a character as a plot hook for a specific character. He pointed a gun to my non-player character's (NPC) head. I surprisingly was able to talk my way out of it and he bargained with me over not telling a rival that he was there. My NPC lived and now I can use her for future plot devices for this player character (PC).

I love systems that let the player control what things look like. One of my favorites is Silvervine Games. I love them so much one of the characters I made for their game is now a tattoo on my arm. They call their system a shared narrative. So both the player and the GM can create the world together. For example one of the powers you can buy is flight, but you have the power to choose if you are flying with wings, or maybe you have a jet pack to get where you are going, or maybe you have a magic ring that takes you into the air. It's those kinds of things that made me fall in love with this game.

Another system I love is Golden Hour by Windmill Games Co. In their set of games you get to be a character set on a TV show from the anime multiverse. Each show has a TV rating so you know who can play what game. All the way from TV-Y7 with ADGNEPSEF 555 to TV-MA with Wuxia. They really give the player a lot of freedom to do what they want. These games are best played with those who have huge imaginations. People can really surprise you with their creativity in this game.

I started seriously roleplaying with Dungeons & Dragons between 2nd edition and 3.5. I really enjoyed 3.5 as a system. I tried 4th edition when it came out but it felt too much like a power gamers game and less of an adventure. Which is why I switched to Pathfinder! I love Pathfinder. It's a smooth transition to Pathfinder from D&D 3.5. In fact my next tattoo I'll be getting is of my Monk character from my friend Brian's campaign. I love the art in these books and the easiness to read the sections when you are looking for something. Everything Pathfinder does is amazing. Their booth at the big Cons is really inviting and I love the fact that you get to talk to the writers and artist. I even bought a few of the novels based in the Pathfinder world.

What was it like to be on TBS's King of the Nerds show? What were your favorite experiences competing with and against your nerd/geek opponents?

It was really awesome being on King of the Nerds. My favorite moments while being on the show were when we all got to sit around the table and just talk, either at meal time or while playing games. I met some of the most interesting people on the show. Life-long friendships were made.

Tell us about your current projects/activities. What are you working on now? What excites you the most?

Some of my girl gamer friends and I will be starting our own blog mid-February. We will be talking about everything from finding Lovecraftian themes in video games to GM tips and how to have fun at your first Con. I love tabletop gaming. It's great getting together with your friends sitting around a table and telling a story together all night. I am eventually going to turn one of my gaming stories into a book. I'll be participating in NaNoWriMo (National Novel Writing Month) again this year. I didn't get very far last year but I was able to get most of the storyline out of my head and on to paper. So I'm preparing myself for that much writing by starting this blog.

Have you encountered any obstacles to pursuing your geeky interests because of your gender? If so, how did you overcome them? What advice would you offer girls and women thinking about pursuing a career in the comic book or gaming industry? What do you think is the greatest impediment to women's success in comics and gaming today?

Some of the obstacles have been finding a gaming group. Since my area has a rather small population of gamers it's hard to find a group to game with regularly. Many groups are used to the "Gamer Girlfriend" AKA the girl who sits there and doesn't know what she is doing. While in my relationship it's different because I know about the games and my husband is there just to spend time with me. That's why I started going to Cons. I started local with Running GAGG in Geneseo and SimCon in Rochester and UBcon in Buffalo. Then I moved on to the bigger Cons Origins in Ohio and GenCon in Indianapolis. I met friends who want to play games with me. We have get-togethers just for that, Gaming Sleepovers. We play to all hours of the night and then get up in the morning and game over breakfast. It's so much fun! So I overcame my obstacles by finding new people to share my love with. It's never too late to make new friends when you can find them with similar interests.

To the women and girls pursuing a career in comics and gaming: you can do it. You have great ideas and you can make them happen. Yes there will be bumps in the road and yes there will be nay-sayers. But you can do it. I believe in you.

Probably the hardest part is getting past all of the negativity on the internet. I have yet to actually meet someone who will say mean things like that to my face. Other than "Go away. We don't play with girls." Don't worry, you can start your own group of just girls. There are enough of us out there. It's not just a boy's club anymore. There are a ton of women going to Cons now and even more so couples bringing their families. There is no such thing as "Fake Geek Girls", just girls who want to learn more about comics and video games. They can even kick your ass doing it.

Caryn Vainio

Ms. Caryn Vainio is a UX/UI (user experience and interface) designer at Z2Live. She received her degree in astrophysics but found her career in gaming – she is known as Hellchick by Quake players. Ms. Vainio has been outspoken, including on her blog, about gender issues and prejudice in gaming.

How did your love of gaming begin? How did you transition from getting your bachelor's in astrophysics to pursuing a career in developing games?

When I was a kid, my dad used to take me to the arcade on Sunday nights. I LOVED it. I looked forward to that every week.

At the same time, my stepfather had bought some of the new Atari computers, like the Atari 800 (yes, I'm that old), and we had a Colecovision as well. So I was playing games on those systems as well. I got immersed in text adventures like Zork and wanted to know how to make my own, so my parents bought me books on BASIC programming and I would make little text adventures and distribute them to my friends.

I fell away from gaming for a little bit in my teenage years, but I came back to it right around the time that Wolfenstein 3D came out. I loved that game. Not long after that I played Quake, and then played it online for the first time, and I was utterly hooked on this concept of multiplayer, super-fast competitive gameplay. I was addicted.

I had gotten my bachelor's degree in astrophysics and had planned to continue on at the same school for my Ph.D., but the university cancelled the Ph.D. program for astrophysics. So I had a year where I was stuck. The university hired me to teach freshman physics and I continued to work on my research with my professor while I waited to apply to other programs. But in the meantime, I was playing a LOT of Quake and writing about it on PlanetQuake. Eventually, GameSpy, who owned PlanetQuake, asked me if I wanted a full time job in California running the site. I hadn't really considered up to that point that I could get paid to do something that fun, so I went out there to see if I'd like the place. I loved the company and its culture, and so I took the job. I figured that if I ever wanted to go back into science I had plenty of time to do so. I haven't yet. I do miss science quite a bit, but I'm also doing something I really enjoy apart from that.

What's your favorite game/project that you've designed so far? What do you find to be the most exciting part of user interface/experience design?

There's probably a difference between the project I had the most fun working on and the project I'm the most proud of. And it's hard to even pick just one in those categories, so there's probably some overlap here and there.

The projects I had the most fun working on were Monday Night Combat at Uber Entertainment and Quake IV at Raven Software. For Quake IV, I couldn't believe that after years of being a Quake devotee, I was actually working on a Quake game. The team I worked with was hugely talented, and a lot of us are good friends to this day even as we've spread out across the country.

I had just as much fun working on Monday Night Combat, and I'm also particularly proud of that work. We were a small, really tight-knit team that grew out of Demigod, a game we worked on at Gas Powered Games. We had so much fun playtesting the game every day – probably the most fun playtesting I'd ever had since Quake IV.

My favorite part of UI/UX design is problem solving. On the one hand, you might have a fairly complex or deep system that the game designers have created; on the other, you have to convey all of that complexity and depth to the player in a way that's easy to understand and doesn't impede their enjoyment of the game itself. Sometimes that problem is REALLY hard to solve.

Please tell us about your current projects. What are you working on now?

Unfortunately I can't tell you much about the projects I'm working on now at Z2Live except to say that they're really fun mobile games. It's been really fun translating my skills over to mobile. People always assume that mobile games are always casual games by nature, but that's not true, and it's really fun seeing us take concepts from more hardcore games and put them into our mobile games, where we want to hit that sweet spot between games you can play when you have a few free moments on your cell phone and games that strive for more complex, deep gameplay.

Please tell us about the sexism you have experienced in your career. How have you overcome/dealt with it?

That's a pretty broad question for such a big topic!

I've seen sexism in various forms over my career, which is now spanning over ten years. When I first started out as a female gamer in a mostly male-dominated gaming genre, I saw a lot of sexism online – people that didn't think I was really a girl, people that told me girls can't actually play, and people that assume I must be fat or ugly or any number of unpleasant things, simply because I'm playing a game.

In my career, I've been accused of having gotten a job in gaming because of my gender, or because I must have slept with someone to get it. I was even sometimes prevented from talking to people I needed to talk to in order to do my job, because the person I needed to talk to had a history of working poorly with women, and people were afraid of what would happen.

And then there are the female game characters. I've worked on projects where the range of female characters, if they existed at all, were limited to the pretty ridiculously-proportioned or underdressed. And when I raised questions about it, I was often met with blank stares from male colleagues, or told that the sales data and demographics suggested that this was what their customers wanted, and that tied their hands and they weren't to blame.

It's been better these days professionally, but I still see sexism in the industry and many of my female friends have experienced far more of it than I have. How do I overcome it or deal with it? I try to point out that it still exists in this industry when I can, and hope that some of my male colleagues will begin to notice what's happening and help to stop it (and I'm definitely seeing more and more men in the industry speaking up against sexism in games). And I try to be really, really good at what I do, so that there are no questions about whether or not I deserve my job and can do it.

What advice would you offer girls and women thinking about pursuing a career in game development? What do you think is the greatest impediment to women's success in this field today and how can they overcome it?

My first piece of advice would be to never let someone else dictate to you what you're "allowed" to do. If you're drawn to games and you want to make games, then go out and make them. People told me as a kid that women weren't meant to be in science, and I told them they were wrong, and I went and got my degree in science anyway. No one can stop you from doing what you love except yourself and your own self-doubts.

Secondly, make games. Don't just say you WANT to make games... actually make them. There are tons of kits out there that let you make games, and they're free. Download them and start making them. You don't need a degree or to go to a special school to study game design; you just need to start making games. And you don't even need a fancy software kit to do it – grab a pen and some paper and start drawing out some game boards and pieces and cards and just make a game.

I think the greatest impediment to the success of women in this field is the vicious cycle of low gender representation and the lack of mentors. If women don't see women in a field they're interested in, then their interest in that field lessens. That means even fewer go into the field, which causes an endless cycle of never having enough women to interest other women in participating. And how we overcome that is a multi-faceted process – we need to show the men in the industry that sexism does exist even if they themselves either don't see it or think they don't contribute to it, and that more diversity in female characters in games will lead to more women seeing that games aren't just male fantasy engines.

Nia Wearn

Ms. Nia Wearn is a senior lecturer in Games Design at Staffordshire University, where she lectures about Game and Level design, Narrative, Production, Business issues, and Marketing. She is currently pursuing her Ph.D. studying online collaborative games design and is active in the #1reasonwhy movement.

When were you introduced to computer games and gaming? What made you decide to focus on conducting research into and teaching game design as a career?

I have an older brother – 5 years older – and we had a techie journalist father that brought computers into our house from about as early as you could easily get them – so I grew up around computers. Either with great foresight, or as a method of babysitting, my mother would make my brother play games with me – so I watched him play, and then as I got older we played a lot of games together, usually cooperatively where we could. I'd make my own cooperative roles – so I'd be navigation or map making if he played a text adventure. I think I still know where all the secret rooms are in Wolfenstine 3D. He also introduced me to paper-based roleplaying games – a hobby I continued for years; it's his dice I play with now.

As I got older I got into Web Design, and more to do with graphics design – although I'm not artsy and I'd already fallen out with the art teacher about classifying comic books as art, so I took Computing along with Archaeology, English Literature, and Sociology at A-Levels (at the same time I was studying Science Fiction in classes at the local university) and was running and designing websites and playing games. When I had to choose a university course I went through the list of anything relevant, crossed out everything that involved an art portfolio or anything with programming and that left a handful of courses around the UK, which I duly applied for.

The course I ended up on, my first choice, BSc Hons Interactive Entertainment Technology at Staffordshire University, was a complete mish-mash of things, so I forged out a path through it, taking in marketing & e-marketing as well as basic 3D Modelling and Animation and towards the end of it found myself much more interested in what the player might think of assets I was making and how that would fit into the bigger picture of gameplaying – but we didn't have any formal games design classes. I followed on my undergraduate degree with a Masters in Digital Games at Liverpool John Moores University – where, amongst producing games, we also looked at the context of games in society and the effects they might have on players.

In that year I went down to a Games Symposium where I realised it was possible for me to be a 'games academic' – which I'd never really thought about before – and pursued that angle as opposed to going into 'The Industry'. I was lucky to get a job back at Staffordshire University after a year of working in a college to help teach what was the successor to my old course – BSc Hons Computer Games Design.

As I found my feet I started doing a bit of research and developing first modules and then whole degree programs looking at the wider aspects of games in society, or more from the player point of view. My students are amazing and it's been great to see how they react and develop to thinking about the games that they make – not just how they make them.

What has been your most exciting research project or finding so far?

It wasn't a research project to start with – but it's fast becoming my main area of research – but working out the best ways to get students to make games has been fascinating. I've long been in charge of our core, cornerstone, 2nd year group games project and I've tweaked it every year, building on experiences from the previous year and the changing student body. At the same time as working on large scale group projects I've been involved in Global Game Jams – growing the annual event into one of the largest in the world (well, we were in the top 20 this year I think) – and we've brought some of those rapid prototyping elements into academic modules too. I can honestly say the first time we ran it I was so sure our students would be unable to make anything that I was almost in tears when they demoed their games at the end of the 48hrs. It does also mean I cut them no slack in lessons now – I know how good they can be...

Have you encountered any obstacles to pursuing your dream because of your gender? If so, how did you overcome them?

Yes and no, nothing has ever been direct – but for a long time I was the only person who taught the production side of things, and my awards or modules were often seen as 'easier'. It's much less of a problem now than it was, but I think the students we get have matured a lot, and also diversified slightly. I used to be able to name every female student we had on a games course and there's too many to do that now. I have been very lucky – I haven't suffered the same kind of abuse and disregard other women I know have spoken about on-line – I'm pretty vocal on Twitter etc. and I don't think anyone has ever made reference to my gender.

What are your current projects? What excites you the most?

It took me a long time to realise I'm passionate about how people make games, how people play games, why they buy them etc. – just not the actual process of making them. To that end I'm involved in some projects to do with modifying behaviour with games and the wider scope of behavioural economics. I'm starting to base my Ph.D. research on Ludoliteracy, and if what we teach and how we teach are reflected in how students work in time-pressured events like game jams – and applying production methodologies and people management techniques like SCRUM into games education on a wide scale. We've got a massive rejig to our group projects coming up, and I'm in charge of the organisational aspects of that – which is head scratchy enough at the moment. I'm also doing a few other things, co-running a monthly board game club, mentoring as part of the #1reasonwhy movement, and working on speaking about careers in games and games education in schools.

What advice would you offer girls and women thinking about pursuing game design and related fields as a career? What do you think is the greatest impediment to women's success in game development today?

I fully understand why some girls don't want to work in the games industry as it stands at the moment. However I also know how much groups change, and usually work far better when they are a little more mixed up. I'm also aware it's not at our level – college and universities – but something happens much earlier than that – I'm just not sure what it is. I do know it can be an excellent, diverse, and rewarding field to go into, where you can craft your career however you want pretty much. I was very lucky to have supportive parents and family, and now a supportive husband and circle of friends – none of whom are very games-y which is nice, but I'm also known as the one with 'the coolest job in the world' and I'm frequently introduced as such, which can be a little bit embarrassing even if it's true. What is nice to see in the 6 years I've been in charge of open days for our courses is that the girls coming to us are much more confident and self-assured.

I think anyone who wants to make it in the games industry can, and I think a lot of the old issues are falling away anyway. I hope that any girl or woman knows herself well enough to have a good idea of what she wants to do, and how she gets there – and if not who she can ask for help. The other thing to remember is that no one knows what they're doing, really, deep down when it comes to making games. It's such a young industry that changes so quickly; there's always a new angle to look at or a new avenue to exploit so there really are plenty of exciting and perfect opportunities for everyone.

Margaret Weis

Ms. Margaret Weis is the famed writer and editor of many gaming universes and stories including the Dragonlance novels and game modules with Tracy Hickman. In addition to many more novels and games, Ms. Weis has formed her own gaming company, Margaret Weis Productions, Ltd. Her company has produced many RPG lines including Serenity and Battlestar Galactica. Most recently, it has released the Marvel Heroic RPG for which it has already won three ENnies: a gold for Best Rules and two silvers for Best Game and Product of the Year.

Ms. Weis was named one of the Millennium's Most Influential Persons in adventure gaming from Pyramid magazine, stating that she and Hickman were "basically responsible for the entire gaming fiction genre" (Haring, S. D., 1999). In 2002, she was also inducted into the Origins Hall of Fame for her work with Dragonlance.

You have said that you enjoyed Tolkien's books and never really read any other fantasy. What was it about his books and world that grabbed you and (if his books were in fact your inspiration) made you want to write your own fantasy?

I read Tolkien in 1966 when I was a college student and the books were sweeping across college campuses. I was caught up in the beauty of the language, the imagination, the story-telling. My friends read them and we spent hours in the student commons talking about them. The fact that the books became part of the 60s counter culture added to the mystique. These books were OUR books. Books for the young. Our parents and teachers had never heard of them. I read them over and over and they still hold a very special place in my heart.

When were you introduced to the world of gaming and shared universes? What made you decide to pursue work as an editor (and ultimately a writer) with TSR?

I read about TSR and Dungeons and Dragons in an article in Publisher's Weekly. I thought the game sounded like it would be a lot of fun for my children and me to play together. A game that stimulated the imagination. A friend of mine ran a game for my family and we all loved it. I was fascinated by the company and continued to follow the amazing success. When I saw an ad in PW looking for game editors, I applied.

I was working for a small publishing company as a novel editor at the time. TSR sent me an editor "test". Unfortunately I didn't know anything about the D&D game, so I flunked the test rather badly. However, serendipity or fate intervened. TSR's book editor, Jean Blashfield Black, was looking for a novel editor who was also a writer. She ran into my agent, Ray Peekner, who said he knew someone who would fit that criteria and that I had already submitted an application.

Jean went to the game department, found my "test", and called me on the phone. I went for an interview and she hired me on the spot.

What would you say has been your favorite writing project so far (and why)?

I'm loving working on the Dragon Brigade series I'm writing now. It's so very different, not traditional fantasy, with muskets and magic, saints and demons, dragon-riders and airships and floating continents. Probably the best times were the years working with the DL team to create Dragonlance. We had so much fun together. Those were good times, good memories.

What made you decide to form Margaret Weis Productions? If you can tell us, what is the project on which you are currently working that excites you the most?

MWP grew out of my love for gaming. Our first big success was the Serenity RPG. Our new project, the Marvel Heroic RPG is doing really well. We were honored by winning two ENnie awards. The Marvel game is receiving rave reviews from the fans. Nothing beats sitting down at a table and playing your own game!

Did you encounter any obstacles to pursuing your career because of your gender? If so, how did you overcome them? What advice would you offer girls and women thinking about writing fantasy and/or developing games as a career?

Actually the only time I ever really encountered any gender discrimination was when I wanted to play softball with the boys in grade school and the teachers wouldn't let me. I played anyway and they finally gave up. Of course, I had to wear a dress because girls weren't allowed to wear jeans. So I ran the bases in my frilly petticoats!

There were only a few women in the game industry when I began work at TSR in 1983, but that was not because of discrimination. The huge majority (one survey at the time found 90%) of D&D players at the time were male. It was difficult to find women who knew anything about the game. Those who did and who wanted to be a part of it were encouraged. Women worked as book editors and game editors. Jean Black was head of the book department at TSR. Jean Wells and Laura Hickman (with husband, Tracy Hickman) were best-selling game designers. Rose Estes's Endless Quest books based on the D&D game were hugely popular.

I don't know about the experience of others, but for myself, no one in the RPG industry ever told me I couldn't do anything because I was a woman. Usually it was because I had missed my dice roll...

As for advice, I would say that you should do your homework, learn everything you can about the field you want to enter (unlike me flunking that the D&D editor test!). Show that you are interested. Take time to get to know the people. Do freelance work, even if it doesn't pay much. Volunteer to work for the company in chat rooms, etc. If they tell you that you can't play softball with the boys, just go ahead and keep playing, frilly petticoats and all!

Interviews: Science Fiction and Fantasy

Danielle Ackley-McPhail..................p. 159
Marta Acosta.......................................p. 165
Linda Addison....................................p. 170
Beth Bernobich..................................p. 176
Patricia Briggs...................................p. 180
Jacqueline Carey...............................p. 183
Rose Estes..p. 187
Esther Friesner..................................p. 193
Sara King..p. 200
Genevieve Pearson..........................p. 204
Anne Rice...p. 211
Pamela Sargent.................................p. 218
Lucy Taylor..p. 226
Lisa Tuttle..p. 230
Carrie Vaughn...................................p. 234
Chelsea Quinn Yarbro......................p. 237

Danielle Ackley-McPhail

Ms. Danielle Ackley-McPhail is a fantasy writer and the author of the Eternal Cycle series. She is the editor of the Bad-Ass Faeries anthologies, containing unique depictions of fae from myriad authors including Trisha Wooldridge, Elaine Corvidae, and Ms. Ackley-McPhail herself. She has contributed writing to many other anthologies as well, including Through a Glass Darkly by Lite Circle Publications. She has won several awards including the 2009 EPPIE Award for Best Anthology Complete (for Bad-Ass Faeries 2) and the 2007 Dream Realm Award for Best Anthology (for Breach the Hull).

How were you introduced to the world of fantasy writing? When did you know that writing and editing in this genre was the career for you?

You know, growing up I read pretty much anything and everything, so it is hard to say what anchored me to speculative fiction as a writer. I guess you would have to say I started gravitating in that direction in my freshman year of high school for two reasons: 1) the summer before, I lived with my sister and my only reading options were law books, nursing books, or Piers Anthony (any guess which I picked?), and 2) my freshman English teacher had a thing for mythology. In doing a report on Chiron I discovered a love of deconstructing myths, which gave me an understanding of how the fantastic could develop in a "real" world. See, there's enough true-to-life out there. There's enough every-day and grim reality. I wanted to explore the potential of magic and wonder and possibilities and speculative fiction gave me so much more room to play.

What inspired you to create the Eternal Cycle series and its main character, Kara O'Keefe? What are your thoughts on the way women are represented in fantasy today?

Well, the idea of the Eternal Cycle series came out of a volunteer group I used to belong to online. For a number of years I worked for a writing site on AOL called the Amazing Instant Novelist. Many of the volunteers would create a private chat room and we would just talk shop, basically. My supervisor was also a speculative writer and one day he was sharing tales of his various careers, including a brief stint as a pawnbroker. His story didn't have anything quirky about it, but something about the combination of him and a pawnshop made me think "Hmmm… now what could I do with that?" It was a diversion. I never consciously set out to write a novel. I was addicted to the story and the feedback I got on the message boards when I posted an excerpt. When I finally clued in to the fact that I was actually writing a book I got serious. Due the clips of what I had already written (young girl, heirloom violin, magic) it was natural to link my storyline to Irish mythology. With this in mind, I named my villain Olcas, which in Irish means Evil, and I started to read up on Irish myth and legend. What is one of the first things I run across? A notation about Carman and her three sons: Calma, Dubh, and Olcas. They terrorized Ireland until they were destroyed by the Sidhe. There was so much to work with there, just in that little notation. I had to run with it. When I was researching that, too many other things fell into place not to pursue them and my story-turned-novel was all of a sudden a trilogy. There was so much to play with in the mythology and the depth and richness I was able to weave into the story frankly ran away with me. So, I guess you could say I was inspired by a wealth of possibilities. As for Kara, she just walked up and insisted on her place in the tale. Not much deliberate thought went into her. Don't take that the wrong way. I didn't have to develop Kara because she was real to me from the very first, even when all I had was that one fragment of a story. I did a lot of learning of who she was as a person, but her identity was always secure. I did struggle at first, though, because a lot of the situations she found herself in made her come across as whiny and wishy-washy. She and I sat down, had a talk, and Kara grew, found her strength, and stared down the dark. Sadly I think that women in fiction overall, not just in fantasy, fall into about three primary categories: weak women who need to be rescued, damaged women who have to overcome the past, and babes with balls, where for the most part they are euphemistically guys in a dress. This isn't across the board or all the time, but a high percentage. We need to find a balance as writers. Strive for the complex potential we all possess, men or women. If we can set aside society's preconceptions our characters will have the depth of real personality.

What has it been like to edit the Bad-Ass Faeries series, including writing by so many great authors?

The Bad-Ass Faeries series has been a labor of love... stress on the labor part. We had a phenomenal idea, recognized the potential, and ran with it. For me it tied in heavily with my own love of mythology and finding the twist that allows me to make something my own. No matter what I'm writing I love to take the reader's expectation and turn it on its ear. This series is tailor made for that. Just the title alone gets a reaction... a huge grin, mostly, though there have been the occasional deep frowns. Some people see what they think of as profanity and can't get past that. But you know, bad-ass is not necessarily bad. We like to tell people to think Bruce Willis with wings. For the most part, though, this series makes people think and see things differently. We have fun with it. Sometimes there is a message, sometimes we're just shaking people up and making them pay attention. It is a lot of work, but the joy when we see the readers' excitement... more than worth it. This is a series that has a life beyond the editors and authors that have participated in it and that is something every author dreams of. It was even referenced in a New York Times article a few years back as a good sampling of the urban faerie genre. And heck, let's admit it... it's also a hell of a lot of fun! We've been fortunate enough to receive submissions from some great authors just from that fact alone. People that normally might not have the time to consider small-press projects. I am regularly getting approached at conventions by people who want in.

What projects are you working on currently? What excites you the most?

I don't know if you might have noticed or not... but I am a consummate overachiever. I could write a book just on the projects I have lined up right now. Probably about seven novels at this point, and definitely three anthologies. Not to mention graphic and web design and audio work. I take on too much, but I can't seem to help myself. Of most immediate concern is The Redcaps' Queen, the novel I'm supposed to release (at the time of this interview) in six months. I really should get that written. It is the sequel to my biker faerie novel, The Halfling's Court, and continues some secondary storylines from that novel. I'm also in the midst of reading submissions for Bad-Ass Faeries 4: It's Elemental and Eternal Flame (book 2 in the Legends of a New Age series). What I'm most excited about, though, is my next steampunk anthology: Gaslight and Grimm: Steampunk Faerie Tales... and talk about big names! If I can pull off what was promised, this is going to be my best collection yet, with some truly amazing talent involved in the project.

Have you experienced any sexism in your career? If so, how did you overcome it? What advice would you offer girls and women thinking about pursuing fantasy writing or editing as a career? What do you think is the greatest impediment to women's success in this genre today and how can they overcome it?

You know, I can't say that I have. Discrimination, yes, but not anything I could specifically point to as sexism. See, I'm small press. There are always prejudices against that because some people see that as second-rate... a bare step above self-publishing. In fact, many people assume... or did at the beginning... that I self-published. Because of that I had trouble getting on serious literary panels at some conventions and at times was pushed off on assistants in some author appearances because I apparently didn't rate the attention of the person in charge. Once I even had a Community Relations Manager at a Barnes and Noble back out of an arranged author event when they realized I was small press. I have never had anyone complain because I was a woman. I think in part this is because I never give them the chance. I remain focused and pointed in the direction I want to go. Of course, I have had a few shocked and perhaps skeptical reactions when people find out I write military science fiction. In the early days of the Defending the Future anthology series, when I was still the only woman among the ranks, I jokingly dubbed myself "Bob" (in fine Black Adder tradition) when I was dealing with the business end of the books for the editor. Military fiction of any time is definitely a field where women are not well represented. We did combat that... book four in the DTF series is called No Man's Land and every story in the collection is written by a woman author. Ironically enough, there are more military veterans in that book than the entire series combined.

My advice: decide what you want to do, what you need to know to accomplish that, and pursue it single-mindedly. Don't buy into the assumption that something can't be done. Try it first because if you don't you've already failed. If you don't succeed, try again because that is how we grow and improve. Come at it from another direction, try different things, make an effort. You would be amazed at what you can accomplish just by trying. You might not always succeed, but the possibilities that open up when you embrace opportunity are amazing.

If you want to be a writer, associate with other writers. Talk about the craft and the business and learn what you can before you drop yourself into the middle of it. If you want to be an editor, learn what it takes and be prepared to work hard.

I think anyone's greatest impediment today is accepting the preconception that something can't be done because it hasn't been.

Discover for yourself because you will be amazed what you can accomplish when you take impossible out of your vocabulary. Things are tough enough in this business without letting false roadblocks stand in your way.

Marta Acosta

Ms. Marta Acosta is a speculative fiction author best known for the humorous Casa Dracula series featuring Latina heroine Milagro de Los Santos. She has also written about a socialite named Nancy under the name Grace Coopersmith.

Ms. Acosta's book "Dark Companion" has been nominated for the Best Fiction for Young Adults award by the American Library Association's Young Adult Library Services Association (YALSA). She has a blog at vampirewire.blogspot.com where she blogs about her writing, interviews, other news, and some geeky pop-culture.

How were you introduced to the worlds of science fiction and fantasy? When did you know that writing in these genres was the career for you?

I always read fantasy as a child and, of course, so much of children's literature is fantasy: talking animals, fairies, wizards, ghosts, time travel, magic spells... I especially loved the magical world of C.S. Lewis's *The Chronicles of Narnia*. I read a wide range of fiction and non-fiction, and fantasy and science fiction are genres I very much enjoy.

In high school, I was introduced to classic science fiction by an older girl who had inherited hundreds of sci-fi novels from her sisters. I believe we met when I was 15. She was reading a book on back campus, Robert Heinlein's *Stranger in a Strange Land*, and when I asked her about it, she told me that I wasn't "mature" enough to read it – which made the story irresistible. We became best friends and she loaned me her books. We read sci-fi voraciously. We took physics together and talked about what the future would bring. We were fascinated by the world – and worlds – beyond.

She went on to UC Berkeley, majoring in computer science, and then to IBM and Apple. I think this was one of the benefits of an all-girls school:

we were comfortable pursuing math and science courses. I celebrate that sort of girl geekiness in my contemporary gothic novel, *Dark Companion*.

When I went to college, I learned quite quickly that science fiction wasn't considered literature. I wanted to be taken seriously as a writer so I wrote those grim, spare, too earnest, third-person, present tense short stories that creative writing majors always write. Although it would be lovely to be taken seriously as a writer now, I've given in to my humorist's instinct and frequently use first-person, past tense, which is a more natural conversational voice. The supernatural and fantasy elements in my novels are metaphors for issues of gender, race, and class. Or sometimes I include a paranormal element just for fun. I think the wonder of speculative fiction is the "what if?" of it all; humor adds a "why not?" spin to the "what if?"

What inspired you to write the Casa Dracula series? What did you draw on in creating its protagonist, Milagro de Los Santos?

My inspiration to write the novel came directly from my annoyance at a science fiction movie I was watching. The movie was set on Earth in the near future. Everyone was running around in Lycra bodysuits. There was no racial or ethnic diversity in the population and the usual guy hero and pretty love interest who must be saved. I was ranting about clichés in speculative fiction and saying, "Why aren't there any Latino vampires? Why are they all rich, sophisticated European guys? Maybe vampires are snobs."

As a humorist, I took that notion and ran with it. Milagro de Los Santos is a bright, sardonic, aimless young woman who becomes entangled with upper-class, Type-A vampires. They consider her a gold-digging, tacky party girl. She is only a little kinder in her assessment of them. I gave Milagro a bit of Elizabeth Bennet's cleverness, Bertie Wooster's blithe self-delusion, and Jane Eyre's essential loneliness.

Milagro is not a media stereotype. She's not the girlfriend of a gangbanger, or a pregnant immigrant, or a naïve and submissive daughter. She's like a lot of real Latinas: smart, affectionate, funny, and warm-hearted. She wants love, and she also wants to pursue her passions: gardening and writing crazy political horror stories.

Your writing, including the recent novel "Dark Companion", includes intelligent and resourceful female characters. What are your thoughts on the way women are represented in science fiction and fantasy today?

Now that we're post-Buffy, there's been quite a change, especially with novels. Women readers and women writers dominate the paranormal and urban fantasy book market, as well as speculative television series. Female characters aren't merely decorative communications officers, but leading characters frequently charged with saving the world. On American television, the characters, which may have originated in novels written by women, are predominantly directed by men, and the scripts are primarily written by men. So the female characters are defined disproportionately by men. Most men in Hollywood lack Joss Whedon's feminist sensibilities.

I loved Buffy Summers, the reluctant vampire slayer, but I've noticed an infestation of kick-ass chicks in both fiction and onscreen. While I enjoy a good chick brawler, and my heart was always with Kara Thrace of *Battlestar Galactica*, why must a female's prowess be physical? Yes, a few girls can beat up men. But a grizzly's going to beat up everyone. I want female characters who use ingenuity, collaboration, and consideration to achieve goals. I want speculative fiction to actually *speculate*, rather than merely slap a dystopian setting sans political/social context on a standard romance plot.

What current projects are you working on? What excites you the most?

My next novel will be released in July 2013, and I'm delighted to be the first woman writer to create a story about an iconic female character. I'm also working on a young adult Gothic mystery series and a humorous contemporary adult novel. I'm most excited about whatever I'm working on at the moment.

Have you experienced any sexism in your career? If so, how did you overcome it? What advice would you offer girls and women thinking about pursuing science fiction or fantasy writing as a career? What do you think is the greatest impediment to women's success in these genres today and how can they overcome it?

When I sold my first novel, I was startled that my publisher labeled me a writer of "women's fiction." Previously, I had been a writer. My situation was complicated by my ethnicity. Publishers were looking for a "Latina Terry McMillan," and I suppose my publisher hoped I would be writing about upwardly mobile Latina professionals hanging out with similarly hued girlfriends, and talking about men and the next career move.

I was asked to include more parties, more romance, and more descriptions of luxurious settings and clothes in my novel. Political and social commentaries were edited out. The book was given a cover with a brown-skinned woman with a red-ruffled dress, stiletto heels, hoop earrings, and a crucifix necklace. I was nudged toward a nicer, gentler type of humor. Niche marketing is critical for good book sales; however, incorrect labeling helps neither the author nor the reader. I can't exactly blame my publisher for asking for so many changes since I'm always the one who colors outside the lines.

Men writers are judged more kindly than women writers of equal skill and talent. Women are mocked even as they repeatedly revive the publishing industry. I might have a problem with that attitude if women didn't dominate book sales. Women have to stop apologizing for writing and reading about things that we think are important.

In terms of science fiction and fantasy, readers have uneasily relegated my books to paranormal romance and urban fantasy subgenres. "Uneasily" because the *Casa Dracula* books are primarily comedies. Those subgenres are largely written and read by women. I haven't faced any gender bias from other authors or readers of speculative fiction, which is not to say that it doesn't exist; I know that many men won't pick up a book written by a woman, but who's to say if it's because they're actually biased or because the publishing industry pushes women to write a particular type of fiction that many men simply don't find interesting.

As for impediments to women's success, please check with J. K. Rowling, Stephanie Meyer, Charlaine Harris, and Susanna Clarke. Women can and do achieve great success in fantasy and science fiction. Rowling's publisher asked her to use her initials so readers wouldn't identify her as a woman, but her identity was known after the first book and didn't harm her subsequent sales. Young women should write whatever they want to write and not worry about the reaction from guys. The rise of self-publishing also changes the landscape. If a young writer doesn't want to concede to a publisher's demands, or if she is really writing outside the box, she can self-publish and control her story.

When my next novel is published, I'll be dealing with devoted fanboys who may not appreciate my interpretation of a beloved character. But at least I'll have finally and truly earned my geek cred and created a female character who feels honest to me.

Linda Addison

Ms. Linda Addison is the author of several collections including "How To Recognize A Demon Has Become Your Friend", containing short stories and poetry. She has published in several magazines including Asimov's Science Fiction magazine. She is the first African-American recipient of the world-renowned Bram Stoker Award, and has received a total of three: in 2001, the award for superior achievement in poetry for "Consumed, Reduced to Beautiful Grey Ashes"; another in 2007 for her poetry for "Being Full of Light, Insubstantial"; and her third in 2011 for "How To Recognize A Demon Has Become Your Friend". She has contributed her work to several award-winning anthologies.

How were you introduced to the world of speculative writing? When did you know that writing in this genre was the career for you?

My first memory of being attracted to speculative writing is reading fairy tales in elementary school. My imagination soared at the idea of talking animals and magic. When I started making up my own stories around fifth grade they were versions of Alice in Wonderland, full of portals that took me to magical lands.

Storytelling was very natural in my house. I was the oldest of nine children and my mother would often make up stories, involving magic, to keep us entertained before bedtime. I was surprised later to find out that storytelling didn't happen in everyone's home.

My recognition of wanting to be a writer came early. The first time I held a book in my hands was in school, one of those "See Dick Run" books. The teacher read it and I knew right then that I wanted to make up stories that would be in books that other people would read. I had no idea what the process of creating a book was but I was completely in love with making one.

I went from fables to science-fiction novels and short stories. My mother and I loved to watch scary movies together which also influenced my interest in horror.

Which of your many stories and poems stands out for you as the most memorable, the one that was the most enjoyable to write, or the one with the most lasting power?

It's impossible to pick a favorite child from my work. I usually think a lot of my latest pieces, mostly because I'm always working to improve my writing.

I was at Necon (an annual writer's conference in Rhode Island) and someone on a panel about zombies said no one could write a zombie story where the reader would feel compassion for the zombie. I love a challenge, and wrote a story called "Unrequited" that is in my latest fiction and poetry collection (which received a HWA Bram Stoker award) "How to Recognize a Demon Has Become Your Friend" (Necon EBooks). The story is about a zombie that falls in love.

The one story, at this point, that has the most lasting impact on my career is "Twice, At Once, Separated" from Sheree Thomas' Dark Matter collection, published by Warner Books in 2000. The collection received a lot of attention because it was the first collection of speculative stories from African-Americans.

There are two reasons my story in "Dark Matter" is important to me. I had been previously published in the speculative field, but it brought recognition to my being African-American (which isn't obvious when a story or poem is sent to an editor) and many other African-American authors writing science-fiction, fantasy, and horror outside the handful known to the world.

The other reason it's significant is that I'm in the process of writing a science-fiction novel based on the characters and world I created in that story.

You work during the day as a computer analyst. How do you balance a full-time job with writing?

Many writers have to do a day job to pay bills. The balance is not always easy. I don't do a lot of the things that others do to relax, like watching television, etc. I tape some shows to watch later, but most of my extra time after managing life, family, and bills is spent writing (or doing other things and wishing I was writing).

In general, I'm always journaling bits of ideas, conversation, character traits during the day and night. I've learned if I get a great idea, line, whatever, and don't write it down – it's gone. I go back through my journals when I'm working on a collection of poetry or fiction for seeds to build on.

When I start a new writing project I try to set an amount of time to write every day. Every book I've written was done by working on it every day, even if it's only for a few minutes. When I'm traveling back and forth to work I work on editing what I wrote the day before.

Now with light-weight computers that can be carried every day, I'm delighted when I have to wait somewhere or get delayed = an opportunity to write!

What current projects are you working on? What excites you the most?

As I mentioned I'm working on a science-fiction novel based on my story from Dark Matter. It takes place thousands of years in the future. Humans have left a poisoned Earth behind and are traveling through space in multi-generational space ships searching for a new Earth. Some humans live inside the ship in a forest environment; others have their bodies in stasis and live in a virtual world with an artificial intelligence that runs the intricate systems that maintain their environment. Things begin to go wrong (else why read on ;-) and twin sisters are an important part of saving the day.

I'm always excited about characters when I write. So these sisters have been living in my head for years and I'm happy to start telling their story. I should say telling it again. I wrote one version of the book, but I'm rewriting it from scratch (because a great deal of the first version was my figuring out the story).

Once a book comes out there is plenty of business to be done (getting reviews, doing readings, etc.) so while writing this I'm also doing promo for two collections that I wrote with other authors.

"Dark Duet" (Necon E-Books) is a poetry collection written in collaboration with Stephen M. Wilson somewhat influenced by musical themes. Stephen contacted me about doing the book with him. It was an amazing experience since Stephen lives in California and I'm in New York. The whole project was done through e-mails. Our styles are different in that Stephen's poetry can move over the page, making shapes, and my work is more standard. I was excited to do something different. Some poems we wrote together, others were written in a kind of call and response. I'm extremely proud of the final results.

"Four Elements" (Bad Moon Books) is a collection that I initiated. The idea was to have a four part book written by four women who had won HWA Bram Stokers, with each choosing an element. Mine is Air, poetry written as a journey through space and time. Rain Graves, Charlee Jacob, and Marge Simon created poetry and fiction for the other three sections: Fire, Earth, and Water.

Have you experienced any sexism or racism in your career? If so, how did you overcome it? What advice would you offer girls and women thinking about pursuing speculative writing as a career? What do you think is the greatest impediment to women's success in this genre today and how can they overcome it?

I haven't experienced any racism directed against me even though I had a strong sense when I started writing science-fiction in the 70s that the field was dominated by Caucasian men. I was deeply gratified to see Uhuru in the Star Trek television show. The show presented a future with a mix of races in the future and this was the future I saw.

The only way an editor knew your race was if they met you at a convention. I started attending conventions later in my career so I just presented my writing over the transom in hopes of getting published. Even though I was one of the few African-American authors at a convention, I wasn't aware of being treated less than others. In fact it was a plus because people would remember me and in the networking world of conventions that was a good thing.

Early in my career I considered writing under the name 'L. D. Addison' to mask the fact that I was a woman. I read many articles on the writing process and other women writers were saying that we shouldn't have to hide behind a different name so I decided to use my name and concentrate on writing well.

Writing well means that if my main character is male, it should be clear through the writing. I developed a stubborn approach; if an editor had a problem with my name being 'Linda' but my main character was 'Joe' and I believed I wrote it clear enough to be obvious of the sex of the character then that was the editor's problem.

I never got any feedback to know that this was a problem as I started sending work out. My first four published stories had two stories with female main characters and two with male main characters. I like to believe the stories sold because they were well-written. It's hard to know since writing and publishing is somewhat face-less. That is not so true now that many authors are in social networks, blogs, etc.

The best advice I can give any woman wanting to publish speculative work is to write as well as you can. It doesn't matter what race your character is, whether they are human or alien. Write a believable character that the reader will care about and become emotionally invested in. Create a story with a beginning, middle, and end that pulls the reader through so they can't put the book or e-reader down.

Writing well is the best revenge to feeling you are swimming against the pre-defined stream.

Write what matters to you, what you care about, what you're curious about.

If you're into science-fiction, read cutting edge science, then daydream about some new discovery.

The greatest impediment would be for the writer to believe or spend any time on the process that being a woman or a minority will hold back your success. Success in getting published is accomplished by writing well and spending time making sure work is being marketed/submitted to the correct publisher/publication. I spend a lot of time checking markets and informing people in my social networks of new work they can buy, readings that I'm doing, trying to get reviewed, etc.

Beth Bernobich

Ms. Beth Bernobich is an author of speculative fiction including the River of Souls series. Her first novel, Passion Play, was the winner of the 2010 Best Epic Fantasy award at the Romantic Times Reviewer's Choice Awards. She has also written the Lóng City series for young adults and the romantic mystery "Ars Memoriae". In 2011, she released a collection of short stories called "A Handful of Pearls & Other Stories", which was nominated for the Best Indie Fantasy/Paranormal award at the Romantic Times Reviewer's Choice Awards.

How were you introduced to the world of science fiction/fantasy writing? When did you know that writing in this genre was the career for you?

I've always been a reader. I read all kinds of books – SFF, literary, mysteries, romance, historical fiction. I also come from a family that likes to tell stories. Even so, I didn't even think about writing my stories down until I was almost thirty. But one day, I was reading a rather dreadful book – a book that I hoped would be light entertainment, but that turned out to be rather tedious – and I stood up, threw the book down, and said, "I can do better than that."

I couldn't at the time, but I'm stubborn, so I kept at it. As for why I ended up writing science fiction and fantasy? I can only say that whenever I come up with an idea for a book or story, it inevitably has an element of the strange or fantastical. (Okay, that's not entirely true. From time to time, I do get ideas set in the ordinary world, but I tend to lose enthusiasm before I finish them.)

What inspired you to create the River of Souls series and its main character, Ilse Zhalina?

The series evolved over time, with so many rewrites and revisions; I can't remember what initially inspired me. But about mid-way through, I realized I wanted to write a story about the balance between fate and free will, and what would happen if we were given another chance, or even several chances, to do the right thing. Mixed in with that is Ilse's personal story as she escapes her father's control, only to suffer through terrible abuse, and finally survives, and goes on to achieve the freedom and sense of self that she never had before. While I never ran away from home, I am a rape survivor, and I wanted to show a more complex portrayal of survival than one usually finds in SFF.

Have you experienced any sexism in your career? If so, how did you overcome it? What are your thoughts on the way women are represented in science fiction and fantasy today?

I haven't experienced what I would call direct and personal sexism, as in, someone telling me directly that my work is less important because of my gender. It's more of a pervasive attitude about women's writing, and about how women are depicted in SFF. There, yes, I come across sexism all the time. Women writers simply forgotten, overlooked, or dismissed. Women in binders, so to speak. Women objectified on book covers. Women objectified in the text through the male gaze. Women characters, when they are included, relegated to secondary roles, or as prizes to the main male character.

I haven't overcome it, and I won't, until we get rid of that mindset that says women's work is not as important as men's. But as part of working to change that mindset, I write. And I try to be as true to my subjects as I can.

What current projects are you working on? What excites you the most?

I'm currently in between book projects, so I'm writing a short story or two set in the River of Souls world. However, I've been looking through my list of possible projects, and the one that excites me the most is one I call "Not Mansfield Park." I'm a huge Austen fan, and while I think MP has flaws, it does a fabulous job of showing family dynamics. The flaws, however, inspired me to come up with a different take on the story, one that would make Fanny less of a drip. A couple pages into writing down my notes, the story took a hard turn into the strange, including old magic, polyandry, and an alternate Christianity. Once I finish my contracted novels, I want to write NMP. I also need to find a real title for it. *g*

What advice would you offer girls and women thinking about pursuing science fiction/fantasy writing as a career? What do you think is the greatest impediment to women's success in this genre today and how can they overcome it?

Write what excites you. Write what bothers you. Work on your craft first, then learn the business inside and out so you know what to expect from the choices you make. That's advice I'd give to any new writer.

The greatest impediment continues to be invisibility. That's true for any writer, but women writers continue to be ignored, forgotten, and dismissed simply because of their gender. Joanna Russ's How to Suppress Women's Writing is just as true today as it was in 1983. We've made progress, but we have a long, long way to go before women writers and their work are considered equal to male writers and theirs.

How to overcome that? Well, talking about women writers whenever the subject of writers comes up. If we see yet another top-ten list with only men, remind the list maker with names of women authors. If we see yet another all-male anthology, write to the editor and ask why. If an article about epic fantasy or hard science fiction is male-centric, post a comment to mention women writing in the field. It's a long slow slog, but silence is our enemy. And until we change the attitude that women's work has less value than a man's, SFF will continue to be a boys' club, with women included as second-class citizens.

Patricia Briggs

Ms. Patricia Briggs is a fantasy and urban fantasy author who is perhaps best known for the character of Mercy Thompson, the Native American who can shapeshift into a coyote, with a new book in the series coming out this year. She has also written the Alpha and Omega series set in the same world as her Mercy series. In addition to her novels, she writes short stories and has contributed to several anthologies. She won the 2009 RT Reviewers Choice Award for Best Urban Fantasy Novel for her book Bone Crossed.

How were you introduced to the world of fantasy? When did you know that writing in this genre was the career for you?

I come from a family of readers. My sister read primarily science fiction and fantasy and handed me Andre Norton's Year of the Unicorn when I ran out of horse books to read, which was my first fantasy novel – though I had been reading fairytales for as long as I remember. When I decided to write a book, fantasy seemed the right choice of the genres I read most often. I felt like I didn't have the background to write SF. And, although I enjoyed reading romance, I couldn't imagine staying interested in writing a romance for the entire time it takes to write a book.

What inspired you in creating Mercy Thompson – her character and the world in which she resides?

Writing is, partly, a process of making decisions. There were three decisions that I made that Mercy and her world were defined by. The first was the decision to set the stories in the Tri-Cities rather than a larger city like Seattle or Portland. The second was to make Mercy a shapeshifting coyote – which meant that she was terribly underpowered to be dealing with vampires and werewolves and that she had to be Native American. The third was that I wanted her to have a job that was grounded in reality, something she would have to get up every morning and go do or not make her mortgage. We had two Opel GTs we had sitting in our backyard while my husband was working to make one running car out of the pair when I started writing the first book – and he'd been keeping our ancient VWs running for years. Mechanicking is something I knew enough about to make it real – and, if she owned her own garage, it was something to use to apply tension to the stories.

What are your thoughts on the way women are represented in fantasy today?

In general, I think women are very well represented in fantasy, especially urban fantasy. Fantasy is a genre with a long tradition of strong female characters going all the way back to the 1930s with women like Red Sonja (Robert Howard) and Jirel of Joiry (CS Moore) that continued though the end of the twentieth century and the beginning of this one with writers like Andre Norton (Mary Alice Norton), CJ Cherryh, and David Weber. Urban fantasy, the subgenre I am currently writing in, is dominated, almost to the point of cliché, with strong female protagonists.

Tell us about your current projects. What are you working on now? What excites you the most?

Right now I'm finishing up a couple of short stories to fill out an anthology as well as one for another graphic novel project with Dynamite. I'm having a lot of fun playing with characters and storylines that wouldn't carry a whole book, but are perfect for a shorter length tale. Next up is the next Mercy book – and this one is going to be a humdinger. Hanging out with my imaginary friends is always exciting. :)

Have you ever encountered any obstacles in your career because of gender prejudice? What advice would you offer girls and women thinking about pursuing fantasy writing as a career? What do you think is the greatest impediment to women's success in this field today and how can they overcome it?

If my gender has ever been an obstacle, I haven't been aware of it. Most of the editors who are buying fantasy today are women – and most of the readers are also women. There is, I understand, still some resistance to women writing epic fantasy (a la Game of Thrones), which has more to do with the readers or the perception of the readers of the genre than anything originating from the editors. There are a lot of challenges in the world of publishing right now, but truthfully, I don't see much impediment to success that is dependent upon the gender of the writer. It might not have been true twenty years ago, but today, write good stories and no one much cares what gender you are.

Jacqueline Carey

Ms. Jacqueline Carey is a fantasy author best known for her bestselling Kushiel's Legacy series and her epic fantasy duo The Sundering. She has won many awards, including the 2001 Locus Award for Best First Novel, 2001 Romantic Times Reviewers' Choice Award for Best Fantasy Novel, Barnes & Noble's Top Ten Science Fiction & Fantasy of 2001 award, and Amazon.com Editors' Top Ten Fantasy of 2001 award for Kushiel's Dart, the Borders' Top Ten Fantasy of 2002 award for Kushiel's Chosen, and the Amazon.com Editors' Top Ten Fantasy of 2003 award for Kushiel's Avatar. Her recent book, Dark Currents, was named one of the Best Books of Fall 2012 by Publishers Weekly.

How were you introduced to the world of fantasy? When did you know that writing in this genre was the career for you?

My first venture into the world of fantasy was accompanying Lucy through the wardrobe into Narnia as a small girl, when my mother gave me a copy of C. S. Lewis's "The Lion, the Witch and the Wardrobe." That was the origin of my love affair with the genre. I began writing my first fantasy in high school, scribbling in the back of a notebook. Although I didn't take the hobby seriously, I persisted with it all the way through college. It wasn't until after I graduated, and spent six months working in a bookstore in London on a work exchange program, that I realized writing fantasy was my true vocation.

What inspired you to write the Kushiel's Legacy books? What did you draw on in creating the three trilogies' main characters (Phèdre, Imriel, and Moirin) and in creating the world itself?

A lot of disparate elements inspired Kushiel's Legacy; research into angelology, a trip to the south of France, a particularly vivid dream, a long-time love of historical fiction and novels that combine intrigue and high adventure. As for the characters, that's always been a part of writing fiction that's a mystery with a capital "M" for me, especially in the case of Phèdre, who's certainly my most provocative heroine. From the first inkling of conception, she was who she was – a highly sophisticated, divinely masochistic courtesan-spy. With Imriel, the process was more organic, since he began as a supporting character. Although he's still a child at the end of the first trilogy, he had so much baggage and angst; I knew he would be the logical heir to carry on the dramatic arc of the series. In Moirin's case, knowing that I was returning to a female protagonist, I wanted a heroine who could view what had become a very familiar world through fresh eyes, a heroine who was at the other end of the spectrum from Phèdre's sophistication.

Have you experienced any prejudice in your writing career because of your gender? If so, how did you overcome it? What are your thoughts on the way women are represented in fantasy today?

By and large, I've been fortunate. There's always a certain amount of casual prejudice – people often assume that as a woman, I write children's books, romance, or chick-lit, or that since it's fantasy, it must be YA. Not that those aren't all worthy genres in their own right, but I frequently have to explain, no, my books aren't appropriate for your Harry Potter-loving 12-year-old niece. I think women are represented very strongly in some subgenres of fantasy today, especially urban fantasy, paranormal romance, YA, and what they're calling "New Adult." Epic fantasy is probably the one area where women are underrepresented, and perhaps those in the field are underappreciated as it continues to be somewhat male-dominated.

What projects/stories are you working on currently? What future projects excite you the most?

As of this writing, I'm editing the second book in the Agent of Hel series, my take on urban fantasy. It's more light-hearted than the Kushiel's Legacy series, but a lot of fun, and it's invigorating to be writing in a contemporary setting, to be able to utilize pop culture references to comment on the subgenre itself. I'm excited about writing the third and final volume next. Beyond that, nothing I can talk about yet!

What advice would you give girls and women interested in fantasy writing? What do you think is the greatest impediment to women's success in this field today and how can they overcome it?

As most authors will tell you, the best way to learn is through doing. No two writers work the same way, and everyone has to find their own path. So... write. Write a lot. Build a world and explore it. Create characters and break their hearts. Take risks, and don't be afraid to make mistakes. Experiment. All the methodology – whether to outline in advance or wing it, write in a linear fashion or skip around, follow a rigid schedule or go with the flow of inspiration, edit as you write or worry about it later – emerges with experience. As you write, you'll discover what works for you.

With the industry in a state of flux, dealing with the rising influence of e-books and new avenues to publishing, I find it difficult to identify the greatest impediment to women's success in the field, at least in external terms. There are female writers who've found routes to success that didn't exist five or ten years ago; there are female writers who've found success via traditional routes. No doubt the industry will remain in flux for a long time. But one thing that will remain consistent is that it takes a tremendous degree of persistence to succeed in it, and persistence is the one thing you can control. No matter what impediments you face, keep trying. If you fail at first, try again. And again, and again. One day, success will be all the sweeter for it!

Rose Estes

Ms. Rose Estes is the author of many fantasy novels including the renowned Endless Quest series and Find Your Fate books, which were Choose-Your-Own-Adventure-type stories, the Greyhawk Adventures novels, and the Saga of the Lost Lands. Her work has included journalism, research, editing, young adult novels, and adult novels, including both fantasy/science fiction and books about dogs.

I was a sickly and frail child who spent a lot of time on my own. I was regarded as a child prodigy as I read from the age of two. I loved listening to a radio program called "Let's Pretend," where they enacted fairy tales and fantasy stories. I also read all of Jules Verne and Edgar Rice Burroughs (Tarzan and Jon Carter on Mars). I watched Saturday matinee serials of Buck Rogers and his arch enemy Ming the Merciless who lived on a planet somewhere in space. I also loved the fantasy and science fiction novels of Andre Norton.

My grandmother lived with us; she was crippled with multiple sclerosis and had no use of her hands. As a consequence, I read to her on a daily basis. She had many interests but was especially drawn to Jewish mysticism. I read the Kabala to her, and even though I understood little of what I was reading, I'm sure some of it stuck in my mind. These were probably the bases for my interest in these genres.

Quite honestly, I never thought of myself having a career as a writer even though the events of my early life gave me an appreciation and deep passion for the written word.

I had a superb English teacher in high school who demanded far more from me than the other students. I thought she was mean and finally worked up the courage to ask her why she treated me so badly; she replied, "Because you're capable of doing more." It became a challenge and I worked hard to not disappoint her. She taught me that if I were given a task that mattered, it was wise to take the task one step further than was requested. It was a valuable lesson that I have heeded all my life.

She also introduced me to Walter Cronkite who was a world famous journalist and radio newsman, even though I had no idea of his fame at the time. We spoke whenever he was in town and when I graduated he gave me a card with his phone number and told me to call him if I ever needed help.

I headed for Chicago and attended the University of Chicago on scholarship and worked a number of menial jobs before I gave in and called Mr. Cronkite. Immediately, I had a job at the Encyclopedia Britannica where I was taught how to do serious research. I also worked at the Chicago Tribune doing the same work. Eventually I worked at the Tribune alone for the grand sum of $40.00 a week.

Perhaps because I was young and extremely eager to learn everything, reporters began to allow me to tag along. In time I wrote many articles, all of which bore other people's bylines, which didn't matter to me; I loved it.

After two years battling pneumonia in the winters, I figured that if I were to starve to death, I'd prefer to do it where it was warm, so I returned to Texas.

This time I didn't need Mr. Cronkite's help, but answered an ad that said simply, "Wanted, someone who can spell." The job was being a copy reader for a major newspaper. I was at the end of a long line of adults. I won the job by being the only person who spelled all 100 words correctly, and, following my teacher's advice, gave a brief definition of the word. (The test was oral.) By now, I was earning $50.00 a week.

I was once again attending university on scholarship and worked every spare hour at the paper. One day I discovered stacks of new books on all topics sitting in the hall for anyone who wanted them. I took armloads every week and came to the attention of the book reviewer. We struck a deal; I could have first pick of the books and could even write reviews. I was to be paid $10.00 for every review.

He shared our secret with section heads of music, dance, theater, and best of all... restaurants! The deal was the same, $10.00 for every review. In return, I got to see and hear every performance and movie in town and could walk into the best restaurant and order anything on the menu for free! I couldn't have been happier or better fed. Once again, I had no issue with others' names being on the byline; I thought I was getting the better deal!

All this time, I had been majoring in biology, but for every science class, I took two of English, eventually graduating with a double major and a minor in history.

I had thought that biology and the sciences would be a practical career choice. It never even occurred to me that by the time I graduated and earned my Masters on the role of fate in the novels of Thomas Hardy, I had been a journalist for more than eight years. I had never thought of a career as something that could be fun, something that you would wake up eager to do every single morning. I thought careers were simply serious jobs that one did like a duty until at last you retired! It sounds silly now, but that is how I finally recognized that my path was to be a writer.

A failed marriage deposited me in rural Wisconsin with three children under the age of five. My choices were to head for a major city and earn decent pay as a journalist, with iffy issues of childcare, or stay in small town Wisconsin where my children were safe and find whatever employment I could. I chose Wisconsin and found a job with a small game company called TSR Hobbies that had invented an odd game called "Dungeons and Dragons." It had almost a cult-like following that few adults understood and most essentially regarded as something to do with dark matters and demonology. My job was trying to put it in words that would make it understandable and non-threatening to the general public.

On a trip to Iowa I found a second-hand book called "Choose Your Own Adventure," wherein the reader decided the course of the book. I immediately realized that this was the tool that D&D needed to introduce young readers to the genre/game and help adults understand as well.

However, TSR was not interested, no matter how I tried to convince them. I was told that if I believed it was such a good idea I should go home and write one myself.

The challenge had been issued and I was stubborn and determined enough that I did just that, even though I had never considered writing fiction. The book (handwritten on three legal pads) came to the attention of Random House, the publisher that was distributing "Dungeons and Dragons" all over the country. They recognized the importance of the books even if TSR did not. I was told to write three more books (in three months), which I did, and so began the "Endless Quest" series. The first four books were on the young adult best seller list for six months and the next two for an additional two months. They have sold more than 16 million copies and been translated into 28 languages. This was a record that held until the advent of "Harry Potter."

I eventually left TSR and signed with Random House. I was contracted by Bantam to write a young adult trilogy based on the prehistory "Clan of the Cave Bear" novels of Jean Auel.

Unfortunately, shortly after the first book of the "Saga of the Lost Lands" was finished, my editor quit. The new editor read the book and commented that "the vocabulary was a bit low and there wasn't enough sex or fantasy." I replied that it was a young adult book and there wasn't supposed to be any sex or fantasy. She wrote back and said, "Not anymore. Just go in, punch up the vocabulary and add some sex and fantasy!" And so I became a writer of adult fiction much to my surprise. These three books, "Blood of the Tiger," "Brother to the Lion," and "Spirit of the Hawk," remain three of my favorite books.

Gary Gygax, the creator of Dungeons & Dragons, lost control of TSR Hobbies after writing the first novel of what was to be a series called "Greyhawk." I was asked to continue the series and I wrote six of them, though I will be the first to admit that the first two books were terrible; I am embarrassed by them to this day. But while research could prepare me to write prehistory, not being a gamer put me at a disadvantage. The series was popular, however; sales were good and by book three the writing had greatly improved.

I was working on a series of contemporary fantasy novels set in Chicago when I was involved in a car accident and sustained an injury that killed the part of the brain that retrieves vocabulary. I had to learn my language all over again, starting with jumble word puzzles and children's vocabulary workbooks and then advancing to crossword puzzles. The first book, "Troll Taken," was finished and I was three-fourths of the way through the second book, "Troll Quest," when the accident occurred. It took me nine months to finish the last section and then only with the help of a friend. We would talk the next chapter out and he would outline it for me so that I could follow it like a road map.

It was one of the hardest things I've ever done, but stubbornness and a refusal to quit got me through it. I had seven contracts outstanding at the time of the accident and they were lost. I feared that I would never be able to write again and what had once been as easy as breathing would be gone forever. Being a writer was how I defined myself. If I wasn't Rose the Writer, who was I?

Many changes occurred over the next several years. I moved to the central Oregon coast, a place I'd always wanted to be, and married a man who was a brilliant artisan and owned a gallery. I was happy, but I wasn't writing.

For years I had collected vintage photos of dogs and their people dating from 1860 to 1930. I also had a large library of rare books about dogs. In 2006 I was contacted and asked to write the history of the Chow Chow in America for the breed club's centennial. I thought, being straight research, that I might be able to do it, so I agreed. It turned out to be one of the most difficult books I'd ever written, not because of the writing, but because the club had little saved material. Again, the ability to do solid research and my own library and photos produced a book that brought me more acclaim than any previous book I'd written. Best of all, it proved that I could still write.

This book and two others that followed were self-published and I have fallen in love with the freedom it gives to writers. No longer do I have to write what other people want, or deal with agents and small royalties. Self-publishing allows me to write whatever I want and, aside from the cost of the book itself, what's left is mine. I highly recommend self-publishing for any beginning writer.

My husband was diagnosed with cancer in 2006 and died in 2011. I now run the gallery and have filled it with exotic treasures from all the far off lands that I have never visited except through books and my imagination.

I still have two novels in me that I will write someday, but my next book will be on the history and development of the Labrador Retriever. Perhaps not as exciting as fantasy but I love dogs and it fulfills me.

The best advice I have to offer to anyone who wants to write is to first of all write what you are passionate about. Be stubborn and never take no for an answer if it is something you truly want to do. Always be willing to learn and, perhaps most important of all, hold yourself to higher standards than others expect of you.

Esther Friesner

Dr. Esther Friesner is a fantasy author and editor best known for her Chronicles of the Twelve Kingdoms, Princesses of Myth, Chicks in Chainmail, and Supernatural Suburbia series. She has won several awards including the 1986 Romantic Times award for Best New Fantasy Writer, the 1994 Skylark Award, the 1995 Nebula Award for Best Short Story for "Death and the Librarian", and the 1996 Nebula for Best Short Story for "A Birth Day".

How were you introduced to the world of fantasy writing and editing? When did you know that writing/editing in this genre was the career for you?

In grad school at Yale, a friend of mine came to the lunch table with a big yellow legal pad absolutely covered in writing. We all wanted to know what she was doing. "I'm building a world!" she replied. And I swear, my first thought was: "Oh, that sounds like fun. I can do *that*." So I did, beginning by (kids, do not read any farther as I am about to set a Bad Example for the youth of today) making world-building notes while in some of my, er, less-than-fascinating classes. The resulting world became the basis for four published fantasy novels, starting with my first-ever novel sale, Mustapha and His Wise Dog. That sounds good until you learn I intended to write a twelve volume fantasy series set in said world (The Chronicles of the Twelve Kingdoms) but it was not to be.

As for editing, it was another case of seeing someone else do it and thinking it would be fun and doable for me. My first endeavor was Alien Pregnant by Elvis (*that* will teach people better sense than to leave copies of National Enquirer-type newspapers in a science fiction convention green room!), but my most successful one was the Chicks in Chainmail series, with five anthologies and one omnibus published so far.

I always knew I wanted to be a writer. I loved stories from toddlerhood on, and my first recollection of creating an original tale was at age 3 when I dictated a downright bizarre poem-turned-story to my mother. (It involved a bunny rabbit, a barbershop, a haunted house, and a witch. Hey, I told you it was bizarre!) While I always knew I wanted to be a professional writer, I loved it enough to keep writing a part of my life whether or not I was ever published. Luckily and happily for me, I was able to have that dream come true.

What inspired you to write the Princesses of Myth series? What are your thoughts on the way women are represented in fantasy today?

Serendipity plays a big role in my answer to this question. The first two books in the Princesses of Myth series – Nobody's Princess and Nobody's Prize – are about young Helen of Troy. Before I came to write them, I was invited to contribute a story to the Random House YA anthology, Young Warriors, edited by Tamora Pierce and Josepha Sherman. At that time, I'd been thinking about Helen's character a lot, probably because of the movie, Troy. I thought there was more to her than being just another pretty face, even if it was a face pretty enough to start a ten year war. She was a Spartan. Even though she would have lived well before the Spartan culture of 300 (if she'd lived at all), that Greek state gave its girls the same athletic training as its boys (including the use of weapons) and its women enjoyed more freedom than Athenian women, for example. Also, in the myths she has two brothers, yet it is her husband, Menelaus, who becomes king of Sparta by right of having married her. It sounded as though in Helen's day the right to rule passed through the female line. Who knows?

So I decided to write a story about young Helen centered on the tale where Theseus of Athens (yes, the one who slew the minotaur) is so smitten with the beauty of teenaged Helen that he kidnaps her until her brothers rescue her. I thought that Helen ought to be able to rescue herself. It would have been too far-fetched for a girl, Spartan or not, to battle an experienced warrior for her freedom, but not all battles are fought with swords. I was very pleased with the results!

Apparently, so were the folks at Random House. I received an invitation to submit a proposal for a YA novel about Helen, which turned into two novels, which turned into the Princesses of Myth series. And there was much rejoicing. (I know; I was doing it.)

To the second part of this question: I haven't read widely enough in today's YA to give an encyclopedic reply, but from what I have read, I think a great deal of progress is being made. The Hunger Games trilogy leaps to mind, but so do many other books where girls are given a chance to fully realize their talents and potential. This is not to say that YA lacked this entirely in the past. As a girl, I loved the Edward Eager books like Half Magic, Knight's Castle, and Magic by the Lake. The girls in these had just as big a role to play as the boys including a scene where one of them unhorses Sir Lancelot.

The Supernatural Suburbia series put a twist on the witch, werewolf, and vampire mythos. How did you decide to edit (and contribute stories to) these very-different and humorous anthologies, and what was the experience like (including working with so many great authors)?

The idea for this series, unlike that for Chicks in Chainmail, was not my own. Full credit for the concept goes to the late Martin H. Greenberg. He was wonderful as both a professional and a person, and he is sorely missed. He approached me at a World Fantasy Convention to ask if I'd be willing to edit and contribute to this series; I leaped happily at the chance, and the rest – as they cliché – is history.

The editing experience for this project was unremarkable, i.e. !*Drama*!- free. Good. I hate !*Drama*! All the contributors involved were professionals, which is a term I apply to aspiring, unpublished writers as well as to those with long, respected track records. From my point of view, you count as a professional if you have a professional *attitude*. What's that? Simply put, it's the polar opposite of being a prima donna. When you get a rejection letter, you don't start snapping "How *dare* you?" and "Do you *know* who I *am*?" (Trust me, you don't want to ask this question. Ever. You're probably going to hate the reply.) The same goes for the attitude a writer shows when asked for revisions to a story. If you disagree with the editor's request, you discuss it in a civil manner. This is preferable to throwing yet another "Do you *know* who I *am*?" tantrum.

I know what they say about the squeaky wheel getting the grease, but my late father had a wise addendum to this: "Yes, and it's also the first one to be replaced."

Right you are, Dad!

What projects are you working on currently? What excites you the most?

I'm in the midst of the next set of Princesses of Myth books and I am very excited about it! Unfortunately, I can't share the titles because my editor has suggested re-titling them and we're working on that. What I can tell you is that the books are about the girlhood of one of ancient Ireland's most colorful women, Queen Maeve of Connacht. She's a wonderfully strong character and I'd like to use these books to present my notion of how she found that strength. I also want to address the serious subject of bullying and overcoming it. Maeve is a king's daughter, well-loved, beautiful, and… a target. This situation will arise in the second book, which I am in the process of writing, and I hope I do it justice.

Have you experienced any sexism in your career? If so, how did you overcome it? What advice would you offer girls and women thinking about pursuing fantasy writing or editing as a career? What do you think is the greatest impediment to women's success in this genre today and how can they overcome it?

I never experienced sexism but I know very well it does exist in the field of writing speculative fiction. It wasn't so long ago that women who wanted to write and publish "hard" science fiction had to assume male pseudonyms (James Tiptree Jr.) or conceal their female first names behind initials (C.J. Cherryh). Publishing is a business; no business stays afloat without sales, and if publishers bought into the Received Wisdom that "Readers don't believe women can write 'hard' science fiction, so they won't buy your books unless they think you're a man", there was little a woman could do if she wanted to see her books published.

The only instance of sexism I recall touching my work was when the Chicks in Chainmail series was in its larval stage. Or should I call it reverse sexism? No, that's not it, exactly. Sideways sexism? You be the judge: the title, Chicks in Chainmail, gave the publisher some moments of malaise, being concerned about how the capital-W *Women* might react to it unfavorably. He was eventually persuaded that *Women* have the smarts to tell the difference between a joke and a cheap shot. (I go on about this matter in the Introduction to the first book in the series.)

Coupled with this came the bemusing fact that very few male writers tried to contribute to the first book. When I remarked on this to one of my male colleagues he told me, "Well, we're scared to do it because we don't want the *Women* to take offense."

Wow. I didn't know we were so scary. Not scary enough to get equal pay for equal work quite *yet*, though.

For girls and women who want to have a career in fantasy writing or editing, it is Equal Opportunity Advice (i.e., it's the same as it would be for boys or men). I don't feel qualified to give a lot of advice as to getting a job in editing since I've only done it incidentally, but I presume some good, basic things you should do are: do your homework. Find out how one gets started (internships?). Find out what the opportunities for promotion will be. Find out how much you will be paid at each step along the route and then ask yourself honestly if you want to/are *able* to live on that pay.

If you're interested in concentrating on a particular genre, like fantasy, go to speculative fiction conventions where you might be able to engage working editors in conversation about any of the above.

As for writing fantasy, you must learn the art and the craft and the business of writing. Most of us know about the art of writing, but not much about the other two facets. The craft means learning the nuts-and-bolts of prose, basic things like good grammar and spelling, how to prepare a manuscript (including an e-manuscript) for submission, and above all, *how to finish what you start*. Complete your book before you try to submit it.

The business side is about money, both yours and the publisher's. Keep the day job, as they say. Do the math for how much yearly income it will take to keep yourself living comfortably and *safely*. That includes medical insurance. You can't write while you're sick. You can't write when you're stressed out about having a mountain of bills and no way to pay them. You can't write when you don't pay the rent and have no *place* to write.

Wanting to succeed can make an aspiring writer desperate. I remember saying, "I'll do *anything* to get a book published!" Fortunately, I didn't really mean that, but some folks do, and it can lead them into making some astoundingly bad decisions and choices. This includes falling prey to all manner of schemers who make their money by exploiting *your* dreams of getting published. Their methods are simple: they tell you what you want to hear. They tell you they're on *your* side. They tell you that superlatives fail them when asked to describe your work. They tell you that anyone who attempts to warn you away from them is just envious and wants to see you fail.

And they take your money. Gleefully. And probably find a way to make you pay for the "Kick Me" sign they've left taped to your back.

If you forget everything else, remember this marvelously simple rule, coined by writer James Macdonald, called Yog's Law: Money flows *toward* the writer.

(The webpage for the Science Fiction Writers of America has a useful section called Writer Beware. You do not need to be a SFWA member to access this resource. You should do so, ASAP. It's an education in the art of the scam.)

And after all that, I'm sorry to say that I have nothing useful to provide as an answer to the last question in this section. There's always The Economy to blame for writers getting lowballed on advances and payment for short stories, but that's not an impediment specific to women. Let me at least offer this: Don't undervalue yourself or your work. Know your personal limits. Remember that there's a difference between being easy to work with and being a doormat. Women are still being raised to be pleasers, to sacrifice our own dreams and ambitions so that others can achieve theirs, to remain quiet in the face of offense because we "don't want to make waves" or "just want everyone to *like* me."

Most important of all? Don't give up.

Sara King

Ms. Sara King is an author of science fiction and fantasy. She transitioned from fantasy to science fiction, and today writes in those genres as well as horror. She is noted for being a very fast writer, speed that improves her work.

Ms. King graduated from the Odyssey Writing Workshop in 2008. Her outdoorsy lifestyle is reflected in her vivid imagery in both her poetry and her novels. She is known for her After Earth series and has received Honorable Mentions for her work from the University of Alaska's 21st Annual Creative Writing Contest and the Writers of the Future contest.

How were you introduced to the world of science fiction? When did you know that writing in this genre was the career for you?

Orson Scott Card and Anne McCaffery were about the only two science fiction authors I read growing up. I actually never thought I'd write science fiction. Because, seriously, that was boring, right? I had this love of fantasy novels and that was my goal in life as a kid – become a fantasy writer. You know, tell stories about dragons and sorcerers and all that fun stuff. So I wrote a few fantasy novels (I think 4??) and then had this weird idea of a sci-fi/fantasy mix. (It was science fiction, but most of the book took place inside a fantasy game.) And, strangely, the moment I wrote that book, I've been writing sci-fi ever since. It was like this switch flipped in my head and suddenly there was no going back. Because honestly, science fiction is more fun to write than fantasy because it's more centered in reality, yet at the same time, literally anything can happen. I love that. I still write some fantasy because it currently makes more money in our market, but I would have to say that my true love is sci-fi.

You have advocated for increased readership of science fiction/fantasy magazines and short stories, concerned that modern technology is harming the field of speculative fiction (if I have mischaracterized your argument, please correct me). Can you comment on how this has happened – how speculative fiction stories and authors are being harmed – and how we can re-engage people with these magazines/publications? Do you think that there is something more magazines can do to utilize the internet to their benefit (e.g., online publishing and advertising, etc.)?

Okay, my statements were a bit misunderstood, here. I'm not saying that modern technology (the internet) is harming the field of speculative fiction. I'm saying that the increased cost of paper over the last forty years, combined with lackluster reader demand (who actually reads short stories anymore??) and everybody and their mother having Microsoft Word have made it very difficult for writers to make a living writing short stories. (Okay, it's basically impossible.) Whereas a writer used to be able to produce a 5000-word short story and earn a month's wages, now that same short story is enough to (maybe) pay the electric bill. If they make a pro sale. Which is like a 1/1000 chance. I think the biggest problem, though, is that so many sub-standard writers have Microsoft Word and decide that gee, it's so easy to write a story, why can't they just write one and make a million bucks? So they're inundating editors with crap, millions and millions of pieces of crap, which makes it increasingly difficult – and time consuming!! – for editors to slog through the mess and actually find gems. Which, in turn, brings the level of quality in the magazine down, which, in turn, makes less people interested in reading it. Vicious cycle. We're in one.

What are your thoughts on the way women are represented in science fiction and fantasy today? Do you think that things have improved for us?

Well, I've certainly been doing my best to better represent women. Though I haven't really read a lot of today's sci-fi. I think the current 'fad' (at least among editors) is hard science fiction, which focuses more on the technology than the characters involved. I STRONGLY disagree with that stance and thoroughly believe that a good story starts with the characters, not the events or the objects. That's part of what I'm currently trying to change in the publishing industry. I'd like to make science fiction about character again, not material stuff. Therefore, I've been starting a new genre, called 'character sci-fi', so that readers can immediately identify the type of stories that wrench their heart-strings and make their guts twist. I honestly can't say whether or not things have improved, aside from the fact that I know that a lot of sci-fi authors out there are now aware of women's feelings on the matter, and most of the dinosaurs who stereotyped, belittled, or ignored them are dying off.

Tell us about your current projects. What are you working on now? What excites you the most?

Ha! I have too many projects (44) to get excited about any one book. I think the next books I release will be the four ZERO books, a series that a lot of people compare to the Enderverse and Firefly, 'but in a good way'. Excitement-wise, I'd say I'm most excited to work on my first epic fantasy (Aulds of the Spyre), the next Outer Bounds novel (character sci-fi), and the next Guardians of the First Realm book (any of the 3 I'm currently working on).

Have you ever encountered any obstacles in your career because of gender prejudice? What advice would you offer girls and women thinking about pursuing science-fiction writing as a career? What do you think is the greatest impediment to women's success in this field today and how can they overcome it?

Actually, yes. Did you know that most women sci-fi writers use male pennames to publish their books because the common conception is that 'Girls can't write sci-fi'? Which is ludicrous. But it's definitely something

I'm working to overcome. My advice for other women interested in writing science fiction professionally is to definitely keep your own name. Do NOT fold to the pressure to use a male penname. That just exacerbates the problem. Eventually, if enough of us do it, we'll be able to change that public perception.

Genevieve Pearson

Ms. Genevieve Pearson is an author of action/adventure fantasy novels, including the Song of the Silvertongue series. In addition to her writing, she is a filmmaker and comic book fan. Despite facing a wealth of sexism in the film industry, she broke out on her own in independent publishing, and since then her books have been highly acclaimed. She was a contestant on TBS' King of the Nerds reality show and was the runner-up, having won the most nerd-offs of any contestant.

How did you discover and begin your love of fantasy books and writing? Was there a defining moment when you knew that writing fantasy was the life for you?

I've loved reading my entire life. My parents were both avid readers, and though we were poor growing up the one expense they never spared was books. We spent hours in used bookstores and in the library. That's when I began gravitating towards fantasy because of the rich and unique worlds created. I loved imagining places different than the one I lived in, where I could be strong and powerful. Because there weren't many stories starring girls like me, I began to come up with my own, and would share them with whomever would listen.

Around the time I was six, my mom started having me sit down and write for ten to fifteen minutes every day. She still has those notebooks, and the first note book is filled with "My name is Genevieve Pearson and my mom is making me write and I hate my mom for making me write." over and over again! But, at the very end of the book it says, "But I am bored and so this is the story of a little girl who wanted a kitten..."

That's when I really began to write. Once I got comfortable writing, I took a notepad and pen wherever I went and if I had a spare moment and I didn't feel like reading, I would work on one of my stories. They were all terrible. The biggest improvements came when I was twelve and we got a computer that I could use to write. After that, I could easily spend hours a day writing, and I often did. I would write my own stories, became involved in WRPG (where you write as a character in an RPG), and wrote fan fiction as well. I just wrote, wrote, wrote!

I was encouraged along the way. I met the fabulous Megan Lindholm (a.k.a., Robin Hobb) at a book signing. She generously agreed to come to my book group and talk when I was sixteen. She brought tons of books and gave us a lot of advice. I also read and found inspiration in other amazing writers like Lois McMaster Bujold and Octavia Butler.

There was no defining moment when I decided I wanted to be a writer. But I have always had a passion for storytelling, and my love of writing grew out of that. I have all of these amazing stories and worlds in my mind, and I want to share them, to pull others in the way I am. I want to set imaginations on fire. I want to help people escape their lives and maybe discover themselves along the way. By writing, I can do that.

What inspired your creation of Kyrie – her character and her world?

I was in West Texas for two months during tornado season. I'd never lived anyplace like it. I started joking with my husband that the weather there was like 'every day is judgment day.' Looking back, I can see how a lot of my feelings and emotions during that stay informed the story: We spent a lot of time at Wal-Mart buying supplies for our film, ate at all of these hole in the wall restaurants, visited family members who lived out in the country, hid in the bathroom during a tornado warning — all elements that found their way into the book. But the story was really born when one night I had a bizarre dream about Kyrie and Meriah and Nate (both were actually named in my dream). It was just like watching a movie. I woke up with part the story really clear in my mind. I wrote it down on my notepad and went back to sleep.

Kyrie's character grew out of her name. I heard the song Kyrie by Mr. Mister and the idea of a young pregnant woman feeling lost and alone and hearing that song on the radio came into my mind. And I thought, "Perfect!"

After I knew Kyrie's origin, I built her character from there. A girl a little different growing up in a small town might learn to adapt, but would always feel apart. She would be used to being the smartest in the class, so she'd be a little over-confident when it came to her decisions and judgments (a problem Kyrie runs into repeatedly early on). Feeling wronged as a child gives her an inner determination to always do what she sees as 'right,' even if, again, it winds up putting her in bad situations over and over again.

The story and the character kept rattling around in my head, and by the time we were driving home from Texas I pretty much had the whole story planned out.

That's how most of my stories come together: Impressions and ideas slowly coalescing into a sudden "woomph!" moment of inspiration, where it feels like the idea came out of thin air fully formed, though really it was brewing in the back of my mind for a while! Sometimes that moment of clarity comes in a dream, or sometimes while I'm wide awake.

What was it like to be on TBS's King of the Nerds show? What were your favorite experiences competing with and against your nerd/geek opponents?

Being on TBS's King of the Nerds was exciting and stressful. It was a really unique, once-in-a-lifetime experience. One of the best parts was meeting, for the first time really, other nerd girls like myself. I didn't have a lot of experience with women who had the same interests as I did, so that was great. I'm very competitive, so most of my favorite experiences were when my team and I won!

The hardest part was never having time alone. As a writer and an introvert, I'm used to being independent and I like to have time by myself to recharge. I really like people; I just need a little 'alone' time. On a reality show, you are never truly alone. There is always someone nearby, usually a camera person. I literally could not have five minutes by myself and that was very difficult. There also weren't very many books to read.

Tell us about your current projects. What are you working on now? What excites you the most?

My current project is the "Song of the Silvertongue" series, about Kyrie who is a half-Angel Nephilim and uses her songs to cast spells. I have four books planned, two of which are completed. I hope to get the next two finished over the next two years. I'm also working on the "Hidden Talents" series, about a young woman, Samantha, who discovers she has a very unique super power and goes on to form a team of superheroes — only to find it's not as easy as the comic books make it seem! There are several books in that series planned. Right now I'm hoping to complete at least two more of them.

Usually my most recent idea is the one that excites me the most. That's one of the hardest parts about being a writer; the newest idea is always the most interesting, but if you keep jumping from new idea to new idea, you'll never get anything done. As a result, whenever I have a new idea I write it down on what I call a "barf sheet" (basically, just a document with every detail about the idea I can think of) and store it in my "ideas" folder on my computer. This allows me to emotionally put the new idea aside so I can continue working on my current projects. But finishing a big project, looking at an 85k manuscript or a finished screenplay... oh, it's the best feeling in the world. You know you accomplished something in life, that you have something to show people that you did.

Please tell us about the obstacles you faced in your career because of gender prejudice. Where were you hindered in pursuing your dreams and where were you encouraged, and how did that impact your career path? What advice would you offer girls and women who run up against similar forms of sexism?

Initially I attended film school with the dream of becoming a writer and a director. Once in film school, I realized something 'was up' when, in a round-circle of introductions, the professor made a point to stop me immediately after I stated my intent to be a director and began to lecture me on the impossibility of being a director and having a family. He hadn't said anything to the boys. When I pointed out that Spielberg and Coppola had families, he scoffed and told me, "They also have wives who stay at home and take care of the kids."

I had a lot of great teachers at school, but it soon became apparent that the best opportunities always seemed to go to guys. The few opportunities that did go to women always went to those who operated within gender roles. The school's goal was to produce commercially successful filmmakers, and I guess they didn't see a girl who wanted to direct action/adventure as having the potential to be commercially successful.

After college, I continued to try and get representation as a screenwriter and a director, but again ran into roadblocks. Then, one day, I got a critique form in the mail that was curious to me; it said, "The hero in an action movie should not have a feminine voice." I began to wonder if my name was influencing the outcome of my submissions. I started submitting the same screenplay under an androgynous name.

Immediately, my results changed. I went from never placing in contests to placing regularly. I went from no-interest from agents to follow-ups. But ultimately, at one point or another, I'd have to reveal I was a girl and all of the interest would evaporate. Poof. I remember being interviewed and the guy on the phone just kept saying, incredulously, "But it didn't seem like it was written by a woman!"

I persisted and persisted and finally had a TV show I created picked up for development. Thus began another frustrating year until that eventually failed, as young shows often do.

After that, I was really depressed. I'd come so close to having my dream and lost it. I saw myself as a failure. Even though I worked really hard, I felt I must not have worked 'hard enough,' especially when I saw boys from my same program in college selling screenplays and TV shows and 'breaking in' in a way I couldn't.

But while I was in college, and in between film projects, I had taken to writing a book, "Chasing Power," just for fun and as a mental break from homework and stressful projects. "Chasing Power" emerged from my love of superheroes and my desire to create my own superhero universe that was a little more realistic than most but still had fun elements. Around that time self-publishing through eBooks was becoming more and more viable. I researched independent publishing and realized there was a lot of potential in it – the worst that could happen, after all, was that nothing would happen!

I also felt like after years of 'notes' from producers and agents telling me what to write, I wanted to create my own project and put it out in the world the way I'd originally envisioned it. I wanted to see if there was even an audience for the type of stories I wanted to produce or if I was barking up the wrong tree.

I published the book, and lo and behold, positive reviews started to come in. People liked it! For the first time in my life, I felt like I was reaching an audience that 'got' what I was trying to do. The funny thing is, all I've ever wanted to do was tell a wonderful story. It just so happens that my fantasy novels were what stuck.

I want young women to know, sometimes you have a dream, and you work your entire life to achieve that dream and then it doesn't work out the way you imagined. It's all right. Take a step back. Go back to the roots of what you love. Don't be afraid to try a different route. Maybe someday I'll still get to see one of my screenplays on the big screen, maybe not. Either way, I know in my heart I went out there and I fought the good fight for my dream. The important part is to always work hard, to always try and improve your craft, and to do work that you are proud of.

Anne Rice

Ms. Anne Rice is a world-renowned author of gothic fiction, best known for The Vampire Chronicles and The Lives of the Mayfair Witches, the former of which have been turned into movies, comic books, and Broadway plays. She has also written the series Christ the Lord and Songs of the Seraphim, the erotic Sleeping Beauty Trilogy under the pseudonym A. N. Roquelaure, and several other books. Her most recent book is the debut novel in The Wolf Gift Chronicles. She is one of few celebrities who keeps in personal touch with her fans, including an active Facebook page with over 700,000 followers. In 2003, she became the second woman ever to win the Bram Stoker Lifetime Achievement Award by the Horror Writers Association.

How were you introduced to the world of fantasy, horror, and supernatural literature? When did you know that writing in these genres was what you wanted to do?

As a little girl in the forties, at the neighborhood theater I saw the old classic films, Dracula's Daughter, Frankenstein, the various Mummy movies, etc., and I suppose this was my real intro to fantasy, horror, etc. As a reader I was slow, and it was not until I was about fourteen or fifteen that I read a lot of classic ghost stories by English authors and American authors like H.P. Lovecraft that I found in the library. I also read hard cover compilations from the library of science fiction short stories. This was long before I had ever set foot in a bookstore. But remember this was now the early fifties. Add to this that in Catholic school, I read the lives of the saints.

I also read comic books as a child, "Tales from the Crypt," that sort of thing that I found in the drugstore for ten to fifteen cents. But these were much frowned on as trash. I was quite impressed with some of the stories. I frankly loved fantasy and horror. Dracula's Daughter, the 1934 film with Gloria Holden, caused me to fall in love with vampires as doomed aristocratic beings of great sensitivity. Later on when I started to write, I retained my fascination with these themes. Why fantasy and horror resulted in "intensity" for me when I wrote, as opposed to the pedestrian realism favored by American literature at the time, I do not know. But that is what happened. When I wrote "Interview with the Vampire" in 1973, I was able for the first time really to touch my reality, to tell all that I knew. I had never been able to make pedestrian realism work for me.

You've mentioned that writing about supernatural creatures is, despite their varied powers, a reflection on humanity. What is it about writing about the supernatural that allows you to examine and discuss issues at the core of human existence, including themes of faith and good versus evil?

I feel a release when I am in the fantasy framework, to go to the very depth of the pain I feel, to seek the highest pleasure. Perhaps I need the "alternative reality" in which to be fully honest, fully myself. The metaphors of horror fiction work for me. The Vampire is a perfect metaphor for the monster in all of us, the lonely one, the predator, the outcast. And I feel alive when I'm writing from the point of view of a vampire. I do not think writers can ever completely understand why one frame works and another does not. We can talk about it and around it, but the truth is we cannot know. Why did the "Game of Thrones" theme and framework work for its author? Why is someone impelled to write musical comedy? We go where the intensity is; we return again and again to what works. My life has been strange, but isn't everyone's life strange? During the 1960s when I was in creative writing classes, the bias was in favor of realism entirely. "Great literature" was realism by Updike, Bellow, Roth, etc. But I simply couldn't be myself in that "genre." I could learn from great writers of all kinds, but when it came to pouring out my soul, I wanted Aristotle's list of ingredients for great tragedy: plot, characters, spectacle, pity, fear, catharsis – and I found the fullest expression of that in fantasy and horror. My teachers pondered "the death of plot" or "plot as faith" but I just wrote plots with vampires and other heavily imagined characters.

What are your thoughts on the way women are represented in fantasy literature today?

Actually, I don't think much about how women are represented in the genre. I don't read enough of contemporary fantasy literature to know the answer to that. But I can tell you what I've observed about how women are received in my fantasy fiction: they have a very hard time being accepted by readers. My male characters are much more easily accepted. When I write about a woman vampire as I did in the novel "Pandora," there are readers who will take offense at her "boasting," which would never happen with my male characters, Lestat, or Armand, or Louis, or Marius. And when heterosexual love scenes are included in my fantasies... as in "The Witching Hour" or "The Wolf Gift"... some readers are very quick to sneer and condemn the work as cheap romance in no uncertain terms. This simply never happens when I am dealing with all males, gay males, etc. "Interview with the Vampire" escaped all censure as a cheap romance because Lestat and Louis were men, even though Louis was really me in the novel. If "Louis" had been female and everything else the same, the novel would have been dismissed as "cheap romance," I have no doubt. I did not know this when I started out. It is something I've seen over time. If in the Wolf Gift, Reuben had fallen in love with a mortal boy instead of Laura, there would have no criticism probably of the relationship whatsoever. American audiences sneer at heterosexual relationships critically, though they actually want to read about them more than they want to read about gay relationships.

Now that The Wolf Gift has been released, what's next on your plate? What projects are you working on now?

The sequel to "The Wolf Gift," "The Wolves of Midwinter," will be out in October. This series is developing well for me with its own strange rules and ambience. It is very much about the "normal" life of Reuben and his "abnormal" life as a Man Wolf, about the interplay of the ordinary and extraordinary. I am also writing something else but it is too early to talk about it. And I want to write a third novel in my "Angel Time" series about Toby O'Dare, reformed contract killer, and his angelic mentors who send him back in "time" to answer prayers. I'm also trying to develop a TV series and will be working on that a lot in the coming months.

Your extremely popular Facebook page often is a place of discussion and debate among people with very varied opinions on everything. What has been most rewarding for you about this page?

I love hearing directly from my readers, asking them questions, reading their answers, seeing the articles they bring to the page, and starting discussions that often involve thousands. This is such a great pleasure that I can no longer imagine my life without "The People of the Page" as I call those who make this page with me. We are however having a devil of a time with the Facebook algorithm, which now censors the posts in that it only sends some to some people. I no longer reach the people I used to reach, and what I think is important is no longer relevant as to what people see from my page. FB is controlling it all in mysterious ways that are very frustrating. But frankly, I love being on the page, talking about writing, answering and asking questions, just chatting directly with people. I have always loved my readers. Seeing them at signings is a joy. FB makes it like a big party every day. The isolation I felt in the 80s and 90s is a thing of the past. This is just wonderful.

Have you ever encountered any obstacles in your career because of gender prejudice? If so, how did you overcome them?

Actually none. I think the world of writing, especially fiction writing, has always been good for women, and good to women from the beginning. Mary Shelley, the Bronte sisters, George Elliott, Amelia Edwards, and many others were so hugely successful as the novel developed and grew in popularity that the "bankability" of women has never been in question. Also I believe that writing is a field in which women can make gender prejudice work for them. A woman confined at home with small children cannot necessarily become a professional ballerina or violinist or movie director, but she can become a bestselling novelist. The outlay for equipment is minimal, and working in her spare time, in a bedroom or office garage, a woman can top the bestseller list. Her husband on the other hand might not be able to work in "time" to write if he is struggling to support the family as a full time doctor, lawyer, policeman, or clergyman. Of course all kinds of people become writers, no matter what the obstacles, but the field is tailor made for the stay at home woman. Also, if a young man comes home from Harvard Law school and tells his parents he wants to be a novelist, he might start a family crisis. But many a woman has simply "done it" without confronting anyone. No, I have never confronted prejudice.

Is there prejudice in how female authors are received by the public? I honestly don't know. Seems to me the Jean Auels and Danielle Steeles of the world sell millions of books, so I would say no. On the other hand, a young journalist did tell me in 1976 when she was interviewing me for "Interview with the Vampire" that she felt that the book was not being taken seriously because it was by a woman. She said that if a man had written the book, it would have been an event. Was she right? I don't know. I think the book was taken seriously and that it has become a success. But it was meeting with some resistance at that time. I honestly don't know if this had to do with my gender. I would say, all in all, I have not encountered gender bias. Sometimes things are said that are not nice or productive to a woman who succeeds, but it's not necessarily rooted in the writing profession. I do remember the head of a publishing house telling me once at a big book convention that "your job is go home now and take care of your husband's ego." I thought it was a ridiculous comment. I was standing in a huge house in New Orleans once (which I owned) and my contractor asked me if I ever cooked. He said, "I've never seen you cook." Of course no one would ask Stephen King or Saul Bellow such a question. But again, this has to do with being a woman in any profession, that kind of cheap denigrating treatment.

What advice would you offer girls and women thinking about pursuing fantasy/horror/supernatural writing as a career? What do you think is the greatest impediment to women's success in these fields today and how can they overcome it?

My advice would be the same as my advice to any and all writers: go for it. Reach for the fire from heaven. Be bold, be brave, and be stubborn. Write the novel of your dreams. Create the novel you can't find in any bookstore; write the novel in which you want to live. Protect your particular vision, your characters, your story, your voice. Don't try to sound like anybody else and never listen to criticism. Your originality is your greatest asset and will get you the most criticism in the beginning. Stick with what you want to write. Stubbornness is as important as talent.

All that being said, I can say that things are better now than they have ever been for fantasy, horror, and supernatural writers. The field is wide open. Vampire, horror, supernatural fiction has gone mainstream in the last decade or two decades. It is no longer "genre writing." TV and movies have supported this tremendous advance. Vampire novels, fantasy novels, horror novels top the best seller lists and are on the front counter of bookstores, and HBO series like Game of Thrones are making history with their high production values and popularity. We are in a new Golden Age of Television right now that fully embraces not only costume and historical drama, but all sorts of horror and fantasy drama as well. And the book business is as always wide open. This was not the way it was when I first published "Interview with the Vampire" in 1976. Vampires were looked on as a trash subject; horror was a genre; science fiction was a genre. I remember when Knopf, my publisher, published a hardcover novel called "The Mists of Avalon" by Marion Zimmer Bradley. They were perfectly astonished when this became a national bestseller. Up until then this author had been on the genre shelf and suddenly she was on the front counter. That might have been the very early beginnings of the shift towards fantasy and horror and science fiction going mainstream. The readers indicated to New York publishing and to the world that they wanted fantasy, horror, and supernatural fiction. I think they wanted old fashioned storytelling, plot, character, spectacle... all those elements Aristotle praised for tragedy. And they rewarded great fantasy and horror and supernatural fiction until New York publishing and the media took notice.

The main thing every writer needs is belief in self, to the point of stubbornness. The world is filled with people who will tell you you have no talent, or demand sarcastically "What makes you think you can be a writer?" Ignore such voices. Never invest in failure. Just keep writing, keep going, and today you can self-publish effectively if you do not get anywhere with conventional publishing. This is a great, great time to be a writer.

Pamela Sargent

Ms. Pamela Sargent is a prolific science and historical fiction author and editor. She is known for her Seed Trilogy (beginning with Earthseed), Venus Trilogy, Watchstar Trilogy, several alternate history novels, and numerous Star Trek novels with George Zebrowski. She edited the anthology "Women of Wonder: Science Fiction Stories by Women About Women" as well as several others celebrating women's contributions in science fiction. She won the 2012 Pilgrim Award for lifetime contributions to Science Fiction/Fantasy studies as well as a Nebula Award.

How were you introduced to the world of science fiction?

There wasn't any one introduction for me, but more like a series of exposures. The first science fiction novel I read was Man of Many Minds by E. Everett Evans. If you're wondering why it was that particular book – I was eleven at the time, and the school I went to had a program where students could purchase a group of paperbacks at a bargain price. This was back in ancient times, when a paperback cost about 35 cents and even less than that through this school program. I ended up with Man of Many Minds by mistake in one order, but was enthralled by the author's ideas. I actually thought he'd made up all the ideas, such as telepathy, by himself; I didn't know there was a whole body of work in which such ideas were commonplace.

This was also about the time that The Twilight Zone first appeared on television, so that was another gateway to the world of sf. I took to that program immediately and watched it regularly – same thing later on with The Outer Limits. By the time I was in my teens, I'd gone on to reading Arthur C. Clarke and H. G. Wells, but was still ignorant of most of the genre – the magazines of the time, Ace Doubles, the conventions where sf readers got together – all of that was unknown to me. It wasn't until I got to college and met George Zebrowski, then a freshman from New York City who actually knew a few of the writers and editors in the field and wanted to become a writer himself, that I was introduced to sf's subculture.

At the time, it seemed as though I found out about science fiction largely by chance, but looking back, it's clear something was drawing me to it both as entertainment and later on as a form I wanted to explore in my writing. What drew me to sf was my extreme dissatisfaction with the world as it was, a dissatisfaction shared by a number of people my age during the 1960s. I felt early on, even in childhood, that I wasn't suited for any kind of conventional life and that too many people were excluded from acceptance by the mainstream culture solely because of their gender, their ethnic background, or their weird interests.

By the time I graduated from college, I had sold two sf stories, mainly because George Zebrowski fished them out of a wastebasket and encouraged me to send them to editors. Another way of putting this is that before I knew what I was getting into and when I was still too young to know any better, I was a published writer, although writing and publishing did get a lot harder after that first bit of luck. And after all these years, I'm still living with George (who has also published a lot of sf of his own) and still writing.

When did you know that writing in this genre was the career for you?

Again, at the time it seemed more accidental than a choice. I became friends with people, in particular my college classmates George Zebrowski and Jack Dann, who were trying to become sf writers. I also gravitated toward a genre in which I could draw on my own experience to some degree (I was still at the "write about what you know" stage where I took that piece of advice much too literally) but use the devices of science fiction to distance myself from the story. In other words, I was able to avoid writing tedious, unoriginal, and clichéd autobiographical pieces that nobody, including myself, would have wanted to read. But to put it more positively, I saw a chance to ask questions about why things are as they are and how they might be different. Sf is a good place to ask such questions, which were probably at the root of my dissatisfaction with the world.

Of your many novels, what has been your favorite story or series? Which one excited/inspired you the most or has the most lasting power for you, and why?

I don't like to single out a favorite. Most writers don't from what I can tell. I often think that whatever I'm currently writing, or whatever is my most recent published work, should be my favorite because if it isn't, then I haven't improved or advanced as a writer. As far as readers go, though, I still get e-mails or other comments from readers who cite my 1986 novel The Shore of Women as a favorite. More readers are picking up on Earthseed since it was optioned by Paramount Pictures, and I also got a number of letters and comments about it from readers when it first came out in 1983.

Ruler of the Sky, my historical novel about Genghis Khan, probably holds a special place because it was a departure for me, a historical novel instead of sf, and because it took so much time and effort to write. Also Climb the Wind, which has pretty much dropped out of sight since its publication in the late 1990s, was another departure, an alternate history set largely in the western U.S. after the Civil War; I dedicated that novel to the memory of my father, who was a reader of Westerns, and often wish he'd been around to read it.

In addition to writing your own novels, you have edited anthologies celebrating the history of women in science fiction. What inspired you to do this? In what ways was the experience of creating these anthologies rewarding for you?

Luckily for me, I started writing and publishing science fiction when a number of other women were either beginning as sf writers or getting more attention for the work they'd been doing all along. This was in the late 1960s and early 1970s. It seemed natural to me to propose an anthology of science fiction by women to publishers – actually an anthology of sf stories by women about women. I kept proposing this to publishers for a couple of years during which I'd get responses like "Are you sure there are enough stories for a book?" (there were enough for a library and far too many for just one book) or "There isn't enough of an audience so we probably couldn't sell it" even though women were slightly over fifty percent of the population and generally buy more books than men, and maybe some men would have picked up the book, too. About the time I'd almost given up on selling this anthology, Vonda McIntyre, one of the younger women writing sf who was already making her mark in the field, informed me that she had complained to an editor at Random House's Vintage Books line about a sf anthology they'd just published that had only stories by men. The editor said to her, "Well, why don't you edit one with women?" Vonda knew I'd been sending my proposal around, so she suggested I try Vintage, and that's how the first Women of Wonder anthology came into existence. This was incredibly generous of her, as she was trying to sell an anthology of feminist sf stories at the time, but happily her project was picked up soon afterwards by Fawcett.

I feel as though I learned as much editing the Women of Wonder anthologies in the 1970s (and the two later ones I did for Harcourt Brace in the 1990s) as any reader probably learned by reading them. I knew there was a lot of interesting and extraordinary work by women in the genre, but there was even more than I realized. I also knew that I had to produce the very best anthology I possibly could, that I had to demand the best of myself and the writers. I mean, if that book had been sloppily edited and didn't do well critically or commercially, its failure would just reinforce sexist attitudes. I didn't want to screw things up for other writers!

What projects/stories are you working on currently?

I've got a novella I'd like to finish that's connected to two other long stories I've published in the past, "Common Mind," which came out in Amazing Stories in 2000 and my collection The Mountain Cage in 2002, and "Mindband," which was published by Asimov's SF in 2010. I'm also working on a novel that draws on the theme of time travel. Better not say more than that, because it's dangerous for me to talk too much about work in progress. I'm also waiting to see what if anything happens with Earthseed at Paramount although I'm not directly involved with any of that. Melissa Rosenberg, who did the scripts for the Twilight movies, is writing the screenplay and producing, but I know any movie takes time if it ever gets made at all.

Have you experienced any obstacles in your writing career because of your gender? If so, how did you overcome them? What advice would you give girls and women interested in science fiction writing?

I can't think of any particular outside obstacles, maybe because I was fortunate enough to begin writing and publishing science fiction when a growing number of other women were doing the same. That isn't to say that obstacles didn't exist, because I know there were – still are – people, not all of them male, who didn't take women writers as seriously as men or had the idea that their work wasn't "real" or "genuine" science fiction. And these attitudes persist – just a few months ago, another writer told me that as late as 1998 she had an editor tell her that her sf novel would sell better if she used only initials instead of her own obviously female first name.

In my case, the biggest obstacle I had to overcome, and still struggle with, is my own self-doubt and feeling like a failure as a writer and a human being. I am my own worst critic. Some might say that this is the kind of self-doubt inculcated in most women who grow up in a sexist culture, as I did, and there may be some truth to that. Anybody who feels like an outsider is going to wrestle with similar feelings.

As for advice to others wanting to write, I hope you don't mind if I insert an excerpt from a talk I gave last spring at my alma mater to high school-aged students in 9th through 12th grade when I was asked for my advice:

> ...now I want to talk about how somebody goes about becoming a writer. Now it would be a lot simpler to talk about how you go about preparing to become a doctor or a lawyer, just to mention two examples, because there are certain steps everybody has to take to become a doctor or lawyer, such as going to college and taking the kinds of courses law schools and medical schools expect or require you to take. But there is no one clear path to becoming a professional writer, somebody who writes stories, essays, articles, long nonfiction books, or novels and gets them published. Every writer I know has followed a different individual path. Some studied creative writing in college; some never went to college at all or else dropped out early. Some take odd jobs to support themselves while they write, some teach or work at another profession while they write, and others become hermits for long stretches of time because it's the only way they can finish anything. But almost all of them followed these rules:
>
> First, they read a lot of stuff. They read novels, stories, articles, books on any subject that interested them. They were usually compulsive readers as kids, read just about anything they could get their hands on, and have kept up the habit throughout

their lives, even if they don't read as compulsively as they used to and sometimes get too distracted by things like Facebook and smartphone apps and reality TV.

Second, they quickly learn that a writer has to write something every day. I should rephrase that: A writer has to make writing a habit that's almost as automatic as washing your face or brushing your teeth, because then you're not wasting valuable time or mental energy on deciding whether or not you're going to write. There will be days when you're just sitting there staring at a piece of paper or a laptop and will be lucky if you end up with one sentence after five hours, feeling like you've just wasted your time, but the next day might give you several pages. It may take a while before you find out which time of the day is best for you – some writers have to write first thing in the morning, while others prefer to write at night – but the more habitual it becomes, the more likely it is that you'll continue to write and actually finish a piece of work. It's much like exercise in that way; you have to keep at it to stay in shape.

Writers also manage to finish what they write. This doesn't mean you'll finish everything, or finish it right away. Sometimes you have to set something aside for a while and come back to it later, when you can more clearly see what might be holding you up from finishing the piece, but over time, writers have to finish most of what they write. Almost anybody with some writing ability can come up with a nice fragment, a few good sentences, or a great beginning to a story, but finishing what you write, and doing that again and again, establishes another habit. And if you've finished a piece of writing once, you'll have reinforcement and know you can do it again.

You also have to rewrite. Kurt Vonnegut has a great comment about rewriting, and here it is:

"Writing allows mediocre people who are patient and industrious to revise their stupidity, to edit themselves into intelligence."

I have spent most of my life trying to revise and edit myself into intelligence.

I think that about sums it up.

Lucy Taylor

Ms. Lucy Taylor is an author of horror, most notably erotic horror. Named the "Queen of Erotic Horror" by Jasmine Sailing in Cyber-Psychos AOD Issue #4, her stories are influenced by her formative years in the southern United States, resulting in a Southern Gothic flavor to her writing.

Ms. Taylor received both the Bram Stoker Award for Best First Novel and the International Horror Guild Award for Best First Novel in 1995, followed by the Deathrealm Award for Best Novel in 1996.

How were you introduced to the world of erotic horror/dark fantasy? When did you know that writing in this genre was the career for you?

I was ten or eleven the first time I read any horror stories, which I discovered in a copy of Alfred Hitchcock's Mystery Magazine. I thought the stories inside were amazing, scary, wonderful, and all these years later, I still remember them, so they made quite an impression. I already knew I wanted to be a writer, and the only thing I ever considered writing was horror. Adding 'erotic' onto it came later, of course. I started out writing non-fiction, and that included work for men's magazines of the time like Cavalier and Penthouse Forum (where I had a monthly column called "Women in Lust"). So that's how I first began writing erotica, sometimes under pseudonyms like 'Andrea Bertonelli' and 'Carla Antonelli' – I guess I always wanted to be Italian. From time to time I've written erotica without the horror angle, but I find that less appealing. For me, erotica just doesn't have the kick that erotic horror does.

When did I know this genre was the career for me? I don't know that I ever thought of it in those terms. I knew I would write, even if I had to do other things to make a living. That includes writing non-fiction, which isn't nearly as much fun as writing fiction. Horror and dark fantasy are in my blood, I guess. I had a rather dreadful childhood, a Southern Gothic childhood, unfortunately, and so writing in the horror and dark fantasy genres will always fascinate me because, in a sense, I feel I know some of those themes quite well, better, perhaps, than I wish I did.

From where do you draw inspiration for your writing?

Inspiration? Like most fiction writers, I think, I get ideas from everything around me. My personal history colors my choices, of course, but the world, to me, is a gigantic mosaic of tiny colorful bits of this and that, any one of which can become the inspiration for a story or a novel. Occasionally, I'll write something purely to express a feeling. "The Family Underwater" is a short story I wrote years ago that has been very well-received. It came to be because I was on a plane trying to contact my petsitter via the phone in the seatback in front of me with no success. I'd been trying to reach this person for days. So now I'm on a plane and she's still not picking up and my anxiety level was almost unbearable, yet there was nothing I could do. To distract myself, I tried to come up with a story that would capture not my situation, but my feelings of impotence and fury. That became "The Family Underwater."

Have you experienced any sexism in your career? If so, how did you overcome it? What are your thoughts on the way women are represented in horror and fantasy today?

For better or worse, I'm fairly oblivious about these things, and working not in an office, but at home alone, certainly helps. Life being life, sure, I've probably experienced sexism at some point; there's probably some boys' network I didn't get included in or some such, but the truth is I can't honestly tell you of a specific incident. In general, the genre writers I know, both female and male, are quite liberal in their orientation and I've always felt that male writers and editors were extremely welcoming. That said, though, I know of at least one editor who has expressed concern that an anthology series of his had more male writers than females and he's worked to rectify that, for which I commend him.

What current projects are you working on? What excites you the most?

I just finished a collection of short stories called "Fatal Journeys'" that should be out from Overlook Connection Press in 2013. Right now I'm polishing up a novel and working on a couple more short stories. What excites me most is having an idea for a story I'm just dying to write. I currently have one that's set in Niger at an archeological dig. The idea came from a dinosaur exhibit at the Royal Ontario Museum in Toronto, which I visited while at World Fantasy 2012. Now it would ordinarily never cross my mind to write a story like this, but that's the joy of it, the unexpected phrase or tidbit of information that just begs me to write a story around it.

What advice would you offer girls and women thinking about pursuing horror/fantasy writing as a career? What do you think is the greatest impediment to women's success in this genre today and how can they overcome it?

You know, I'd prefer to answer that question in more general terms. I think the greatest impediment to a woman's success in the horror genre, in writing or the arts in general, or in any career really, is the female tendency to give less attention to their own needs while devoting tremendous emotional, financial, and moral support to their mates. So basically, I'd say the biggest impediment for any woman, writer or otherwise, is that most of us aren't blessed with loving and attentive wives. We frequently have husbands/boyfriends who require or believe they require a tremendous amount of time and attention. So a man gets a helpmate and a woman, all too often, gets a 24/7 job in addition to everything else. And women tend to focus on their own needs last, so yes, of course, this would impact one's career.

Lisa Tuttle

Ms. Lisa Tuttle is an author of science fiction, fantasy, and horror. In addition, she has compiled a reference book on feminism and edited anthologies, including one that highlighted work by women and one that addressed the topic of "gender bending", i.e., rejecting normative gender roles in one's identity. Her fiction addresses many feminist issues and includes strong-willed, independent women as protagonists.

Ms. Tuttle has received multiple awards for her writing, including the John W. Campbell Award for Best New Writer, the Nebula Award for Best Short Story, and the BSFA Award for Short Fiction. She collaborated with George R. R. Martin on a novella that was nominated for a Hugo Award.

How were you introduced to the worlds of science fiction, fantasy, and horror? When did you know that writing in these genres was the career for you? What was it like to write your first novel with George R. R. Martin?

I was a big reader from as soon as I learned to read, and almost as soon as I could read, I was writing. This goes back so far into my childhood that I never feel that I made a decision about being a writer – it was something I always loved to do, and did. However, I did not assume that I would be able to make a living from writing books and stories; journalism seemed my best option for a long time. As for genre fiction, again, it is hard to pin down exactly when I "knew" this was "my" genre – ghost stories, fairy stories, fantasy, and science fiction were my favourite types of fiction from a very early age. I was lucky in that my parents owned a lot of books, and on their bookshelves were several big, fat collections of ghost and supernatural stories, as well as paperback science fiction novels. My father had a subscription to The Magazine of Fantasy and Science Fiction so I dipped in to that (attracted by the cover illustrations) when I was still too young to understand what I was reading. I do know when I became consciously a fan of science fiction – that happened when I was about 13, and met a friend from school in the public library. Looking at the books I was taking out, she asked if I'd ever read Robert Heinlein. I had not. When she showed me a book she said I was going to LOVE my heart sank at the title: Have Spacesuit, Will Travel – it sounded like a cross between a TV western (I didn't like westerns, even though – or maybe because – I lived in Texas) and some obsessive boy-engineer book about building a rocket. I thought science fiction was all about engineering and was for boys – but, thank goodness, I took my friend's advice, checked out the book – and totally fell in love with it once I had started reading. From then on, I wanted to read everything else by Robert Heinlein – and, indeed, anything and everything classified as science fiction!

Most writers probably start by imitating the books and authors they most enjoy, and so quite naturally I gravitated mostly towards writing ghost stories, science fiction, and other types of "unreal" and fantastic tales.

As to the third part of your first question, the answer to that would require an essay in itself! I have written about it at some length in my book Writing Fantasy & Science Fiction (in the "Writing Handbooks" series from A&C Black) if you are curious.

From where do you draw inspiration for your stories and characters?

Everywhere. Things people say, things I see, fragments of ideas that waft across my mind as I'm falling asleep, the great "what if...?" questions, magazine articles, news stories, life, movies, music, art, fiction...

Your stories often portray strong female characters and address issues important to women. What are your thoughts on the way women are represented in science fiction, horror, and fantasy today?

Oh, dear, this is another weighty question, and I don't think I could possibly do justice to it in an interview. I think things have changed a lot in the decades since I began writing, and nowadays women have far more images and role models and possibilities available to them. Yet there is still that impossible Hollywood ideal – even when, in books, the female characters may be overweight or nondescript in appearance, or mixed race, or disabled, somehow, if a movie is made, they turn out to be white, slender, big-breasted, heterosexual, beautiful in the most bland and socially acceptable way... which is kind of depressing. What is more encouraging is that women are no longer expected to be passive, and are very often the heroes – and villains – just as tough and competent as the old fashioned male hero.

What current projects are you working on? What excites you the most?

I'm just about to do the final (I hope!!) rewrites on a novel called "Magic Pictures." I have a small press, limited edition collection of my stories, titled "Objects in Dreams", coming out later this month. I have just finished writing an article about George R. R. Martin. I have promised to deliver three new short stories and an essay next month and have not started any of them! I am probably most excited about things I have not yet written.

Have you experienced any sexism in your career? If so, how did you overcome it? What advice would you offer girls and women thinking about pursuing science fiction, horror, or fantasy writing as a career? What do you think is the greatest impediment to women's success in these genres today and how can they overcome it?

I have encountered sexist attitudes and sexist individuals, but never of a magnitude to block or hinder my career. I began selling professionally in the 1970s, a time when women were making a big impact in science fiction – writers including Kate Wilhelm, Joanna Russ, Ursula LeGuin, and "James Tiptree, Jr." among others were very much talked about, were read, and won awards. It was quite a good time to be a woman writer. There are even more women writing in this genre now – although I do think that women are rather under-represented in both hard science fiction and in horror; a lot of the women writers I notice seem to be writing fantasy, or urban fantasy, or a kind of paranormal romance which is (personally) my least favourite sub-genre in this general field. But I don't think "sexism" can be blamed for this; presumably these authors are writing what they want to write and/or what sells. I am not aware of any women who've been told they "can't" or "should not" write a particular type of book; it's my opinion and has been my experience that although celebrities may sell books on the basis of who they are, for most writers and readers it's the story that is important. Write a good story and do your best to get it out there to the public. I don't think women face any gender-specific issues beyond the same difficulties faced by any writer in these changing times. It's unlikely to be easy, and there's no readily defined career path that fits all, but if you feel driven to write, just do it, and do your best.

Carrie Vaughn

Ms. Carrie Vaughn is a science fiction and fantasy author, best known for her urban fantasy Kitty Norville series. Not only have her Kitty books consistently ranked high on the New York Times Best Seller List, the first of the series, "Kitty and the Midnight Hour", won Romantic Times Reviewers' Choice Award for Best First Mystery.

In addition to the Kitty series, Ms. Vaughn has published a long list of short stories and other novels that have received many honorable mentions including a Hugo Award nomination. She is one of the authors for the Wild Cards anthology series.

How were you introduced to the world of fantasy and science fiction? When did you know that writing in these genres was the career for you?

My parents are big science fiction fans, so I grew up watching Star Trek, Buck Rogers, Battlestar Galactica, Wonder Woman, the Bionic Woman, and so on. My parents also gave me the books early on – Heinlein, Asimov, Clarke, all the classics. I had a horse book phase as well, and the first stories I wrote were actually horse stories. I started writing very young – I was a daydreamer, I loved books, and it seemed the most natural thing in the world to try to translate my own daydreams into stories. By junior high and high school I was firmly entrenched in science fiction and fantasy because they inspired my imagination so much and were so much fun. I started trying to get published while I was in high school, and that was really the start of my career aspirations.

What inspired you in creating Kitty Norville – her character as well as the supernatural world in which she resides?

I was inspired by other, similar stories. If there really were vampires and werewolves, they would need their own talk radio advice show because

Dr. Phil wouldn't know what to do with their problems. I needed a host for such a show, and Kitty came along. The whole thing really did start that simply. The idea ended up being pretty huge and offering endless potential for stories.

What are your thoughts on the way women are represented in science fiction and fantasy today? Do you think that things have improved for us, or are we still basically fulfilling stereotypes?

I do think things have improved. We have so many more women writers and creators, and they're writing the kind of strong, empowered characters they'd like to see. We don't have to fight for the right to create what we want, even if we still have to fight sometimes to be taken seriously. What we have to watch out for now are the unconscious stereotypes that are so pervasive we often don't recognize them – the idea that for a woman to be violent and aggressive she has to have some kind of past trauma to justify it, the assumption that the only acceptable relationship she can have is with a strong alpha male. These kinds of stereotypes are insidious because on the surface, they look like good storytelling, but you start to see these tropes so often you realize that they're actually clichés and ought to be avoided.

Tell us about your current projects. What are you working on now? What excites you the most?

I'm working on so many things, and the thing I'm most excited about changes from day to day! It's one of the most thrilling and frustrating things about being a writer; I have so many projects I want to work on and not nearly enough time for them. I'm gearing up to write the next Kitty novel, which is actually going to be about one of the secondary characters, Cormac. I'm also trying to figure out what novel to work on after that. I usually have a couple of short stories that I'm working on at any given moment as well.

Have you ever encountered any obstacles in your career because of gender prejudice? What advice would you offer girls and women thinking about pursuing fantasy/science-fiction writing as a career? What do you think is the greatest impediment to women's success in these fields today and how can they overcome it?

I haven't encountered obstacles in terms of education, learning to write, and getting published – it's a hard slog and takes a lot of time and effort to become a good enough writer to get published and gain a following no matter who you are. Where the obstacles and difficulty come is in critical response and respect. Many genres, like romance, urban fantasy, paranormal, and so on, are discounted as being not good or worthwhile – and they happen to be genres written primarily by women, and the audiences are perceived to be primarily women. (It turns out this isn't always true – I've found that urban fantasy has as many men reading it as women.) Women's writing often seems to be judged by a different standard, or categorized differently, and that can be frustrating. My response is generally to just keep doing what I want to do, write the very best books I can, and not pay too much attention to the external noise.

My advice is to write, write, write. The only person who can really stop you is you. Have great ideas and work very hard on becoming the best writer you can be. Learn how the business works, get your work out there. Study the careers of people you want to be like, and do what they do.

Chelsea Quinn Yarbro

Ms. Chelsea Quinn Yarbro is a fantasy author best known for the heroic vampire Count Saint-Germain. In 1993 she received the Fine Foundation Award for Literary Achievement, and in 1997 she was awarded the Knightly Order of the Brasov Citadel by the Transylvanian Society of Dracula. In 2003, she was named Grand Master of the World Horror Convention. In 2006, Ms. Yarbro was the first woman to be named a Living Legend by the International Horror Guild, and in 2008 she became the third woman ever to receive the Bram Stoker Lifetime Achievement Award by the Horror Writers Association (the other two being Joyce Carol Oates and Anne Rice).

How were you introduced to the world of science fiction, fantasy, and horror stories? When did you know that writing in these genres was the career for you?

I didn't start out with a genre in mind when I decided to write – I was five at the time and the concept of genre eluded me. But then, as now, I read what I liked, and when I started producing real stories (about nine or so) I wrote along the lines of what I liked to read. I always headed for the science fiction and fantasy parts of the library. In the public library, the best ones were in the grown-up section, so I went there, much to the dismay of the librarians. In my grammar school (and mind you, this was in Berkeley, but it was the end of the forties, the very period I am presently writing about) there was a girls and a boys side to the library. I used to bribe the boys a nickel for taking out books for me. By high school, I was reading a lot of plays since I thought I wanted to write plays, but about weird things, and did for a while right after college write four plays for a children's theatre company, three of which they produced and all of which were fantasies. So, to boil it down, I knew I was going to be a writer when I was five, and a couple years later decided it would have to be my profession. I didn't choose a genre or genres; they chose me. I love doing horror, although westerns are a lot more fun.

What inspired you to write your historical horror books about Count Saint-Germain? In particular, why did you choose this historical figure, and what influenced the type of vampire that you made him and the time periods in which you located him?

After reading Dracula at age fourteen, I began to wonder how a vampire could be made positive and still a vampire, and I played with that idea well into my twenties before coming up with the setting, and from the setting came Saint-Germain, who was so utterly perfect for the role. He had claimed to be so old (anywhere between 2,000 and 4,000 years) and to have been so many places, all I had to do was follow his claims. It's getting harder to do it now, because finding new places to put him consistent with what he claimed is trickier, but so far so good.

Have you experienced any prejudice in your writing career because of your gender? If so, how did you overcome it? What are your thoughts on the way women are represented in science fiction, fantasy, and horror today?

Have experienced, do experience, and no doubt, will experience, just as every other female writer has and does and will. I once called a male colleague on a really crude remark, to which he responded, "Can't you take a joke?" and I answered, "Sure – when I hear something funny." If we had not been with two other colleagues, I wouldn't have said anything. There are some wonderful exceptions out there, and I am grateful to every single one of them, but mostly, writing everything but romances is still a boys' club. There is no way to make a blanket statement about the representation of women – or men, or sports cars, or environmental misfortune, or planetary configurations, etc., etc., – but there has been a long tradition to protectivist sexism in stories with women characters in which women are not allowed to undertake something major without male protection. There are noteworthy exceptions, and some that try way too hard to sound pro female and end up with a character who is more a Boy Scout with breasts than a female. Those are often the most sad, especially when they're written by women.

What projects/stories are you working on currently?

I'm working on Saint-Germain #27, which takes place, for the most part, in western Europe from 1949-1953, and I'm beginning to think about where I go next. At present, I'm leaning toward the Khazar Empire, but we'll see. I have a period mystery novel that has not sold but I work on from time to time. I also have a science fiction novel in much the same boat. And I'm looking to get as much of my backlist into e-print as possible.

What advice would you give girls and women interested in science fiction, fantasy, and horror writing? What do you think is the greatest impediment to women's success in these fields today and how can they overcome it?

Stop thinking in terms of genre and think instead of what you like to write about, and then write about it. If you rewrite more than 7 times, you've over-written. Start something else until the cobwebs are out of your brain. If you keep revising under the assumption that tweaking this or that will make all the difference, you're kidding yourself – what you are doing is writing the life out of it. And it may mean you can't bear the thought of rejection, and if you keep making changes you won't have to submit it. That's also kidding yourself. Everyone gets rejected and all it means is no. The ego doesn't like it, but let me tell you, the last thing in the world you want is for someone to take your story who doesn't like it. That is the kiss of death. If you worry about writing bad stories, don't. Almost all of us write bad stories at the beginning. The trick is to figure out what you did wrong, and apply that knowledge to a new story, a fresh story, and keep going until you start writing good stories. As soon as your early stories stop being awful, start submitting them, and keep the stories moving. If you really are a writer, the day will come when one of the stories doesn't come back. Brava. You're over the first hurdle. Now on to the next. Conduct yourself professionally, be gracious to your fans/readers (unless they're truly nuts), work regularly, and never, never,

never, never imitate. By the way, I'd give exactly the same advice to a male.

Interviews: Comics and Manga

- Gabrielle Bell.................................p. 242
- Jennifer Camper.............................p. 244
- Alex de Campi................................p. 247
- Kelly Sue DeConnick......................p. 251
- Devin Grayson................................p. 254
- Roberta Gregory.............................p. 259
- Laura Lee Gulledge........................p. 267
- Sheila Keenan................................p. 274
- Barbara Randall Kesel...................p. 279
- Lucy Knisley..................................p. 283
- Elaine Lee......................................p. 287
- Christy Marx..................................p. 296
- Ann Nocenti...................................p. 299
- Rachel Pollack................................p. 303
- Trina Robbins.................................p. 307
- Colleen AF Venable........................p. 311

Gabrielle Bell

Ms. Gabrielle Bell is a comic book writer and illustrator, best known for her "Book of" comics and autobiographical "Lucky" series. Her work was selected for the 2007, 2009, and 2010 Best American Comics anthologies and the Yale Anthology of Graphic Fiction. Her book "Cecil and Jordan in New York" has been adapted for film.

What inspired you to begin self-publishing your "Book of" comics? Did you try to publish with major distributors and find resistance, or was there something more appealing about self-publishing?

I didn't think I was ready to publish, yet I wanted to make my own books and create my own stories on my own terms. Also, it was the thing to do for beginning indie-cartoonists.

Your award-winning "Lucky" series draws on your personal experiences and is highly relatable for many young adults. What inspired you to create this series? Can you describe the experience of creating it (e.g., was it cathartic; did you learn anything about yourself/your world from doing it)?

I've always compulsively kept a diary. When I started to do comics, I started keeping a comic diary. It took a great deal more time than a regular diary, so I wanted to turn it into something to justify all the effort. It was cathartic, on a lot of levels. To turn myself into a comic character, to create a story out of my life, helped me to look at my experiences in a more objective way, to take them less seriously, and yet, paradoxically, to value them more.

Did you experience any sexism in your efforts to publish/otherwise distribute your work? If so, how did you overcome it? If not, what do you think is responsible for the increasingly egalitarian atmosphere in comics?

Yes. A lot of male publishers and critics didn't take me seriously; I was often told I'd eventually give comics up, that maybe I'd become an illustrator or make children's books. Times have changed, but I wouldn't say they are close to egalitarian. I'd say the internet has helped a lot. Women and other minorities are able to circumvent the (still mostly white male) "gatekeepers" – publishers, critics, bloggers – by doing their own thing on their own websites and gaining their own audiences.

If I've overcome it, it's just from dogged stick-to-it-ive-ness.

Please tell us about your recent and current projects. What are you working on now? What excites you the most?

I've been doing portraits on Skype to pay the bills. I recently came out with a sort-of-memoir called The Voyeurs. I'm also intermittently working on a fictional graphic novel based on my childhood in the mountains of Northern California.

What advice would you offer girls and women thinking about pursuing comic book writing/illustrating as a career? What do you think is the greatest impediment to women's success in comics today and how can they overcome it?

I would say make sure you love it, and then stick to it. It is a difficult, misunderstood art form, but it can be very gratifying. I think the greatest impediment in women's success in comics is self-doubt.

Jennifer Camper

Ms. Jennifer Camper is a comic book writer, artist, and editor. Her work reflects on her perspective as a Lebanese-American lesbian woman. Her graphic novel subGURLZ was a 1999 Lambda Literary Award Finalist. She created, edited, and contributed to the Juicy Mother anthologies, both of which were Lambda Literary Award Finalists, and has contributed to many magazines including Ms. Magazine and Bitch.

How did you become interested in the world of comic books? Did you read them as a child, or did you only begin to love them later?

I love telling stories and writing and drawing. Making comics allows me to do all three things at the same time.

I always drew and wrote when I was a kid, sometimes on my own and sometimes with my sister and brother. Later, I started doing comics in school to entertain my friends and to make fun of school policies, teachers, and other students. Interestingly, I found that people didn't mind being ridiculed in my comics because they were so excited to see themselves in a cartoon. I also added a lot of cartoons to my school papers. I remember one teacher telling me not to do it, but later I noticed he had my cartoons hanging on the wall in his office.

I constantly read books and comics and I loved art, illustration, design, and movies. All those things contributed to my work as a cartoonist.

As a prolific comic book writer, artist, and editor, can you talk about the perspective that informs your work – how your personal experiences as a Lebanese-American lesbian woman influence you?

My comics tell the stories that I'm interested in reading. When you're not part of the mainstream heterosexual white boy world, you have to tell stories that reflect your own version of life. Otherwise, those stories will never be told. I give voice to my experience of seeing the world as an outsider.

I have a lot of opinions about everything, and I use my comics to comment on the world. Ridicule is a powerful weapon, and I sometimes use humor to make fun of things I don't agree with. But it's important to laugh at yourself, too. My work often explores how gender, sexuality, race, and class imprint characters and their actions.

But most importantly, I want to tell stories that are compelling.

What made you decide to create the two Juicy Mother anthologies? How did you decide who to enlist for them?

There are not a lot of places that publish the kinds of comics I want to read, and I thought we needed an anthology of queer comics. So I contacted all the talented cartoonists I knew and put out a call for submissions. I tried to include comics that covered a range of styles – serious, silly, sexy, political, poignant, heroic, traditional, and/or experimental. I published veteran artists and newcomers, and also comic jams.

What are your current projects? Can we anticipate a Juicy Mother 3 soon?

I'm always working on a number of projects. I like to do everything from single panel comics to long, complicated graphic stories. And I'm always doing cartoon jams with other artists. Eventually I'll compile my comics into another book. Publishing is in a confusing state now with the transition to e-books, so I'm not sure when I'll edit another anthology.

Have you experienced prejudice and/or discrimination in your work as a comic book writer/artist because of your gender and/or sexuality? What advice would you offer girls and women thinking about pursuing comic book writing, illustrating, or editing as a career? What do you think is the greatest impediment to women's success in these fields today?

There will always be people who discriminate against women or lesbians. I just laugh at them. They're missing out on the best things in life.

Because I'm mixed, most people don't know I'm half Arab. I've had experiences where people have unknowingly said horrible anti-Arab things in my face. When I bust them on their racism, they fall all over themselves trying to justify what they've said, and that's always pretty amusing.

My advice to artists is to find the strength to create their work even when they get no support. The best way to fight discrimination is to never give in to it. Get help and information from others who are working in your field, and later give help and information to those coming after you.

Take inspiration from everything around you – comics, movies, graphic design, novels, illustration, music, paintings, nature, video games – whatever you can absorb. Learn about the history of your craft and be aware of what others are doing now.

Figure out a way to make enough money to live on and still do the art you love. Sometimes you might make money from your art, and other times you'll have to make money just to support the making of your art.

It's important to love what you're doing so much that you'll do it even without getting paid or getting recognition. The longer you practice your craft, the better you'll get, so just keep at it. Always, always keep at it.

Alex de Campi

Ms. Alex de Campi is a comic book writer and author of manga. She is well-known for her mini-series Smoke, published with IDW, and Kat and Mouse, her manga series. Smoke was nominated for the Eisner Award for Best Limited Series. Ms. de Campi has also directed a number of music videos and written for other publishers including Dark Horse Comics.

How did your love of comics begin? What made you decide to pursue comic book/graphic novel writing as a career?

I grew up reading X-Men off the spinner rack in drugstores, as well as Elfquest and Asterix and stuff like that. And watching awesome and horrifically dubbed anime on the local TV stations... Star Blazers and Battle of the Planets. Then... well, then there wasn't a lot for girls to go on to once you got tired of Jean Grey rising from the dead AGAIN so I moved away from comics. Read a lot of novels, literally every bad SF/F novel produced between about 1960 and 1985, got into more literary stuff, poetry. Then about a decade ago when I was living in London a friend was moving out of his army barracks and was going to throw away this huge pile of comics. I convinced him instead to give them to me. It contained a lot of glory-days Vertigo stuff and a ton of the British SF/F serial comic magazine 2000AD. I got hooked again, and I started writing comics. My mind is so visual, and the stories I have to tell are so much about pictures more than words; it just felt natural.

What do you draw on for inspiration when writing your stories?

Oh, it usually starts with some sort of vague feeling I have, which I then build a character and a story around. Smoke/Ashes was all about how the lone male hero/vigilante idea, one man with a gun, was obsolete because of technology. I wrote a horror graphic novel that came out of being surrounded by a lot of bad, poisonous people, people who just constantly demeaned me and cut away at my confidence. So I wrote about that feeling, and it became a meditation on horror as a genre and women in horror, and a vague riff on Faust. My grindhouse series coming out from Dark Horse was just about being stupid and happy and trashy in comics again, though there is stuff in there based directly on my personal experiences... a summer-camp hazing in the seventh issue actually happened to me. Writing for me is really about starting with a definite emotion or feeling and then taking that grain of truth and then just waltzing off into the unknown with it. Coat it in a big lie and see where that takes you. But it has to be true at its heart, and parts of it have to be difficult to write because true feeling always is. Also, I think sometimes people feel there's a divide between the big, important literary stories and the fun pop-tastic ones. I sorta used to think that, too, but I increasingly realized that's not true. You have as much of an obligation to be real and honest in the poppy stories... almost more so. You can still throw in great formalistic twists, and little moments that just take the big thing and put a spin on it... the heroine does an amazing thing, saves the world maybe, but then she comes home and there's dinner to be cooked and even though everyone else has been home all day the dishes are still piled up in the sink taller than Everest and twice as dirty. Formalism, the emphasis on form and structure, is very important to me. Every time you sit down at a comic script, you must constantly be thinking whether there is a more interesting, more innovative way to visually express that page of story.

Have you experienced any sexism while pursuing your career? If so, how have you overcome it? What are your thoughts on the way women are portrayed in comics today?

Oh, I've been bullied by male co-creators, shut out by mainstream editors because they thought they were doing me a favour by hiring me and didn't like it when instead of just rolling over with gratitude I said things like, "hey, the artist you hired can't draw teenage girls", and simply not had my stories' appeal understood by the straight white guys who run certain publishing companies. But, you know, fuck 'em all. I fired the bully, quit the shitty mainstream gig, and found publishers who love and support what I do (and ironically are also straight white guys. Not all are bad!). You can't depend on "the industry" because the industry is full of shit peddled by craven idiots. All you can depend on is writing amazing stories. All you compete with is yourself. If you write enough good stories, they come to you. Sure, it's a total shitfight for like the first five years at least, because you have to get your own work out there. But once you get through that, if your stories are good enough, the readers carry you to the help you need... at the precise point you stop really needing it (but still welcome it with open arms).

Please tell us about your current projects. What excites you the most?

I'm at a weird stage right now. I'm finally finishing Ashes, which has been an 18 month saga of Kickstarter, firing artists, hiring new ones, extensive project management, marketing, pacifying, lettering, you name it. This is not to mention the two years it took me to write the damn book. I love the book; there are portions of it I am exceedingly proud of, but it needs to be over. Other than that, I'm getting a ton of help and support from Dark Horse, which is the first time a publisher's really stood behind me and said, "we believe in you", and that's just a divine situation. I have my silly grindhouse series from them, 8 issues, that I just finished writing... this was a reaction to both Ashes (a quite literary action thriller) and Margaret the Damned, which... writing Margaret the Damned was something I had to do, but it was a very rough experience because of the places I had to go in myself, the things I had to talk about. I finished writing those two books and just wanted to do something fun and stupid with a lot of kick-ass female heroines, sex, and violence. These are basically the comic books your mother warned you about. I'm doing some teen-girl stuff at the moment that's not ready to be seen yet... a really happy girls-adventure tale about things I love: rural life, sailing, comics, sci-fi... I'm also really excited for a series I'm pitching with Carla Speed McNeil, which is again starring teenagers. I love writing teens; they're such horrible, nasty, emotional creatures. I'm finishing Valentine (my fantasy webcomic), too. I can't wait to launch the Kickstarter for that. I know it sounds like I'm going in a thousand different directions at the moment and in some ways I am... but Grindhouse and Ashes are essentially done; Margaret the Damned is in limbo (no artist); No Mercy, I'm waiting for the publisher to send it to budget; and the teen books, I'm waiting on the artists to finish the promo pages (though in one case the artist is waiting on me to get back to her). So while I wait for all that, I start writing Valentine again.

What advice would you offer girls and women thinking about pursuing comic book writing as a career? What do you think is the greatest impediment to women's success in comics today and how can they overcome it?

My number one advice is: make the comics. Don't pitch things, don't spend ages trying to get publishers to notice you; just go make the comics. It's like boys. If you go running after them and always pursuing them you haven't a hope (unless they're totally skeevy). If you ignore them and are being seen to do awesome stuff, they'll be flocking to you. My number two advice: don't quit the day job. Find something that doesn't crush your brain and pays decently and gives you healthcare and benefits and doesn't come home with you at night, and write in the evenings and weekends. A reason to do this is it enables you to keep the rights in your stories, because you don't need to take up-front money from them. Work for hire is fine, but that's today's money only. The money that takes care of you in the future is the creator-owned work. My number three advice: if anyone comes up to you and warbles on about how many opportunities you have now and how wonderful it is to self-publish, punch 'em right in the eye. Because self-publishing is horrific and time-consuming. You still will have to do it, but it is not fun.

Kelly Sue DeConnick

Ms. Kelly Sue DeConnick is a prolific writer of comic books, having done work for Marvel, DC, Dark Horse, and IDW. In addition to writing comics, she adapts manga into English. She is best known for the Osborn: Evil Incarcerated mini-series and Captain Marvel, and has contributed to the anthology "Girl Comics".

How did your love of comics begin? How did you decide to pursue writing and editing comic books as a career?

My love of comics started when I was probably 8 or 9 years old, living on an Air Force base overseas. After school I stayed at a friend's house – her dad was a collector and she and I would make our way through his long boxes. Weekends meant Saturday swap meets and stacks of comics for ourselves that cost less than our allowance money. We didn't get American television and comics were everywhere. It was a simple substitution, I think.

I never decided to pursue it as a vocation, honestly. I fell into it sort of backward. My degree is in drama. I intended to become an actor, or failing that, a playwright.

As someone who has written a wide variety of female characters, what are your thoughts on the way women are represented in comics today? Which women have you most enjoyed writing and why?

The first part of that question is too broad for me to give you a good answer, I'm afraid.

Probably the woman I've most enjoyed writing (which, I'll be honest, feels like a strange distinction to make) is Helen Cobb. She's ornery and angry and imperfect and she makes me laugh.

You are also well known for adapting manga into English. How did you get into this area? What do you enjoy most about making manga accessible to English speakers?

I got my first adaptation gig because – true story – Neil Gaiman was unavailable and unaffordable and someone I think thought I might be able to parrot his voice. That was a book called Demon Diary. (Gaiman had just done the English script for Princess Mononoke, and that was the tone they wanted.)

What did I enjoy most about it? It was a fun gig – not as stressful as building comics from the ground up, but still very satisfying.

Please tell us about your recent and current projects, including your plans (to the extent that you can give us teasers!) for Avengers Assemble this spring. What excites you the most?

Oh, my. Let's see...

I've got on my plate at present: AVENGERS ASSEMBLE, CAPTAIN MARVEL, PRETTY DEADLY, and a project that I can't discuss because it hasn't been announced yet. Unfortunately I'm not in a position to be able to tell you much of anything! The timing is bad for that. Captain Marvel begins its new arc with the next issue, which will bring back an old enemy or two and put Carol in a position of having to deal with the fact that her body is failing her. Avengers Assemble, I can't even hint at until announcements are made. Pretty Deadly is a weird western I'm doing with Emma Rios that should solicit in the spring – that'll be my first creator-owned book.

And then there's the project that I can't discuss at all.

I feel really bad that that's such an unsatisfying answer! I'm sorry.

Have you experienced any sexism in your pursuit of your career? If so, how have you overcome it? What advice would you offer girls and women thinking about pursuing comic book writing/editing as a career? What do you think is the greatest impediment to women's success in comics today and how can they overcome it?

Sure, I have. Most of it is unintentional, but it still has consequences. How have I overcome it? Hm. Have I? I don't know. I guess I just don't let it in. I've got a thick skin and a hard head. I just keep going.

My advice would be not to focus on what's in your way – refine your craft. Write. Draw. Whatever it is you do or hope to do, begin it now. Regardless of your gender, making a living in an artistic pursuit is not easy. You are really only competing with yourself. Every other notion is a distraction.

There's no cabal out there trying to keep women from getting into comics. There are entrenched hiring practices that are tiring yes, but they can be overcome. If this is what you want, fight for it. No one will hire you to make comics until you've already made comics – so start making them. I know it's hard. Everything worth doing is hard. Go. Hurry.

If this is what you want to do, you can do it – don't let anyone tell you you can't.

I look forward to reading your comics.

Devin Grayson

Ms. Devin Grayson is a comic book writer who has written for DC (including Vertigo) and Marvel, as well as written novels based on comic book themes. She is well-known for writing many adventures in the Batman universe, including ones featuring Nightwing. Ms. Grayson has also worked in gaming, writing an MMO game.

How did your love of comics begin? How did you decide to pursue writing comic books as a career?

All through my childhood and teenage years, I wanted to be an actor. Growing up in the Bay Area, I was able to take advantage of many great opportunities to study at places like San Francisco's ACT, Jean Shelton Actor's Lab, and the California Shakespeare Festival. I mention this because those early lessons in character creation and scene beats became the foundation of my writing career. By the end of high school, I had shifted my focus from acting to writing, but it was all based on the same desire to explore truth through the media of fiction.

Unlike the vast majority of my peers in the comic book business, I did not grow up reading comics. They just weren't on my radar. I was an English major in college with a heavy emphasis on creative writing and had no idea that the school I attended on Annandale-on-Hudson was the real-life model for Professor Xavier's School for Gifted Youngsters until well after I'd graduated.

It wasn't until after college, while sharing a studio apartment in San Francisco and working in the research division of a large HMO by day while trying to complete a novel by night that I happened to channel surf past an episode of Batman: The Animated Series. I knew a little bit about Batman from the old Adam West series but I'd never spent any quality time with him. B:TAS was a surprisingly sophisticated cartoon, tailor-made for my generation. It was elegant, dark, and compelling and it took the psychology of the characters seriously; I was immediately hooked. Of particular interest to me was the relationship between Batman and Robin – it had never before occurred to me that Batman, who is kind of a dark, intimidating archetype, essentially raised a kid. I wanted to learn more, and I learn by writing. So I followed the characters back to their medium of origin, which of course turned out to be comic books.

Learning about comics was an amazing journey. Like any art form, comics are constantly evolving. I was immediately taken both with its rich history and with all the possibilities that were alive for its future.

Which character has been your favorite to write and why? What are your thoughts on the way women are represented in comics today?

There are two entirely separate questions, so I'm just going to answer them one at a time.

My favorite character has always been Batman. Though he is a very challenging character to write well – in addition to being reticent and guarded, he is a genius and a master detective – he is also arguably the best fictional fusion of pure archetype and unique individual ever invented. He is known and loved all around the world, and has managed to be relevant to and embraced by multiple generations. Personally, I am particularly moved by the way his heroism stems from a place of darkness; he is the ultimate tragic hero, motivated by grief and a determination to spare everyone else from having to experience it. As a writer, I am very attracted to the role that family plays in his life, and also intrigued by the price that he has had to pay to be as exceptional as he is.

As for the representation of females in contemporary comics... we're still on the wrong side of a much needed paradigm shift. There are actually fantastic female characters available in all kinds of graphic novel and comic projects, but when you say "comics" in the United States, you are still referring almost exclusively to mainstream superhero comics published by DC and Marvel. Independent, creator-owned comics, web comics, journalistic and literary comics are all light years ahead of the material produced by these two companies in terms of female readership, creators, and characters, but the industry is still measured, discussed, and – most importantly – funded by the one niche genre. There are exceptions, of course, but by and large, mainstream superhero comics do a terrible job of representing females. That's something that needs to change.

How did you decide to transition to working on video games and MMORPGs?

Well, it wasn't a transition. Most writers work in more than one medium. I write novels, comic book scripts, essays, and video game string files. Gaming, particularly RPGs, has been a part of my life for much longer than comics, but I didn't do any work in the industry until 2007 (by contrast, I believe my first comic work was published in 1997). It's not unusual as a writer to be working on two or three totally different kinds of projects at a time. What video games and comic books have in common is a format that invites the player or reader to be an active participant in the story.

Please tell us about your recent and current projects. What are you working on now? What excites you the most?

I just finished two very interesting and very different comics projects: a short story for the ongoing Womanthology project, and a contribution to the graphic novel component of the History Channel's MANKIND: The History of All of Us project. The Womanthology story was a science-fiction piece set in futuristic space and the MANKIND story was a fictionalized account of true historic events that took place in 476 CE along the series of interconnected trade routes in China now known as the Silk Road.

Currently, I'm working on a YA novel series about a contemporary young ghost hunter. One of the most exciting aspects of being a writer is getting to work on and learn about a wide variety of projects.

Have you experienced any sexism in your pursuit of your career? If so, how have you overcome it? What advice would you offer girls and women thinking about pursuing comic book writing as a career? What do you think is the greatest impediment to women's success in comics today and how can they overcome it?

The majority of the sexism I've encountered during my career has actually come from just outside of the comic book industry. Though I'm sure it was almost always well-intentioned, the coverage I've received from entertainment industry press and reviewers has consistently and relentlessly focused on my gender rather than my work. In their efforts to showcase the contributions of female comic creators, the industry press has unfortunately compounded our marginalization. It is very difficult – almost impossible – to receive attention for being anything other than a token representation of one's gender. While my male counterparts get to discuss their actual work, I am asked to discuss, over and over again, how it "feels" to be a woman in a male-dominated industry. When I'm at my best, I use these opportunities to talk about the larger cultural issue of prejudice or to call attention to the systemic sexism still at play in mainstream superhero comics. Sometimes, though, I have to admit, I just get frustrated and surly. The best way to overcome it is to befriend and stand with other females in similar circumstances, to recognize and champion one another's work and continue discussing and learning about ways to support one another.

My advice to females considering a career in comic book writing is two-fold: first, don't limit yourself to comics. Comics can be your driving passion and preferred medium, but to be successful, you're going to need a fully-rounded set of writing skills and interests. Secondly, don't let anyone tell you what you can or cannot do and don't let them define what you're doing once you accomplish it. You will need to create your own space in an industry that doesn't yet have a predetermined role for you to fill; that's both a blessing and a considerable challenge. Use everyone else's doubt and confusion to your advantage; set your own goals and rate your own progress. Supportive external validation will be rare, so build up your own network of accomplices and your own sense of self-worth. If you can't find a career ladder to climb, teach yourself to fly. And always be one of the good guys.

Roberta Gregory

Ms. Roberta Gregory is a pioneer in the world of alternative comics and the creator of the Bitchy Bitch comics, whose title character went on to stage productions and an animated cartoon. Her stories have appeared in several of the early underground women's comic anthologies including Wimmen's Comix. Ms. Gregory published Dynamite Damsels, which was the first regulation-sized comic book to be published by one woman. In 1994, she received an Inkpot Award by Comic-Con International and has received several Eisner Award nominations.

You've suggested that your father's career as a comic writer for Disney had a hand in jumpstarting your love for comics. What made you decide to go a step further and pursue comic book writing and illustrating as a career? Did your father encourage this path, or did you decide upon it independently?

We had lots of comics in the house, and I learned to read from them and also rhyming children's books that I memorized. I went on through my childhood to write and draw all manner of stories, comics, and funny novels that never got finished, but it was all good practice. My father let me use his art supplies, and I helped him write dialogue when I was high-school age. I don't really recall that much encouragement from him, especially when I started actually writing feminist comics or having a point of view different from the family – he was very politically conservative, like the rest of my family, and disapproved of most of my work. After a while I learned to just not show anything to my family members. I got some publishing opportunities in college with the women's resource center and Phil Yeh's Uncle Jam humor magazine, and then the underground comix like the Wimmen's Comix anthology, which began in 1972, I believe. When I was writing and drawing stuff on my own, I always thought most of what I was doing was too strange to ever be published, or to interest anyone else, but that may have come from growing up in a disapproving family. I think part of that is also why I self-published so much: Dynamite Damsels in 1976, Winging It in 1988 and 1998, Artistic Licentiousness throughout the 1990s, Follow Your Art in 2010. I think some of my current projects will have to go that same route, as well, but there are many more resources around these days; it is just being able to learn it all.

I don't know if I could technically call what I do a "career". I have created quite a variety of stories over the years that I really enjoy and that other folks have enjoyed, but I never really made much money from my work. I am certainly not making any right now, with much of my time and energy taken up by a 'day job.' I have always and continue to write and draw the sorts of stories that I would like to read, that nobody else seems to be doing, and will continue to do so until I am found face down on my desk someday.

Your comics include female characters with whom readers can identify and address many feminist themes. From where do you draw your inspiration for your stories and characters?

Oh, my gosh, how does someone live in the world and NOT be inspired, by friends and family and colleagues and current events and the world around us? Maybe that comes from being a creative person; born to write stories, I just process input differently than many others. When I first published the comic Dynamite Damsels, there was a saying going around that feminists had no sense of humor. I was feminist and I had what I thought was a great sense of humor, so I created a character (Frieda) who was very idealistic and kept running into obstacles but mostly overcoming them. With my Bitchy comics, I found that I saw humor in some of the unlikeliest situations, and the in-your-face drawing and dialogue was such a fun departure from the sorts of comics I was drawing at the time, which were a bit more warm and fuzzy. There was not really anything like it, comics from a woman's point of view dealing with some very specific women's issues in a rather harshly humorous manner, with a fun, rubbery art style, and stories that showed that the writer was sharing a bit of her insight with the reader. I still do not know if there is anything really like Bitchy.

As one of the pioneers in the world of female-produced comics, what sexism did you experience in the comic book industry? How did you overcome it?

Back in those days, the early 1970s, for much of society, women were at the point where we still had to "prove" that we were competent and could do the same work as men. I think a woman could not get a loan unless a male relative signed for her (was this the US or Saudi Arabia?) and flight attendants were called Stewardesses and I think they had to quit when they got married or reached the age of 40 or gained a few pounds, or something primitive of that nature, as just a few examples for our younger readers. A "career woman" was seen as a bit of a joke, and it was a big deal when Barbara Walters was a co-anchor of a TV news broadcast in 1976 because before that, women were not considered credible enough to deliver 'real' news beyond things like Hollywood gossip and homemaking tips, etc.

In my own experience, though, women were doing all sorts of things; Lyn Chevli and Joyce Farmer had their own underground comics publishing company; there were opportunities to be published in Wimmen's Comix, which was run by a women's collective (though one had to compete for limited available pages since it was a comic book that only came out perhaps once a year or so), plus there were women-run bookstores and companies like Olivia Records, which was women-only (they had a controversy early on about a transgender employee), so one could bypass much of the sexism. When Gay Comix was begun in 1980, they wanted an equal number of pages by women and men creators, and there simply were not many women creating LGBT-themed comics back then. I imagine there must have been a lot of sexism in mainstream comics, but I was not even reading those anymore.

Oh, certainly I would get a few sneering or scathing reviews, but that has pretty much happened throughout my career. Those people who read my work (and I wish there were many more) seem to react either very favorably or very negatively, if the feedback that comes my way is any indication. I basically keep chugging along. I have just a non-stop input of creative inspiration, much more than I will ever be able to produce in this lifetime, so the best way for me of coping is just to keep producing. It seems to be what I was put here to do, and I hope that there will still be people looking forward to my work, whenever I manage to get something finished.

Please tell us about your recent and current projects. What are you working on now? What excites you the most?

2012: I had a story come out in the latest Not My Small Diary recently (about my lifetime of creativity), a story in the first Graphic Canon anthology, and some reprints in Fantagraphics' No Straight Lines, but I find this very dishearteningly skimpy, to be honest, with all that I want to do.

My latest book was the self-published Follow Your Art in 2010, and I want to follow that up with a website for the many pages of travel comics I have drawn since then, and perhaps a sequel. As usual, after a recent 6 months that were so busy with non-creative business, I now have a backlog of experiences I want to draw travel comics about, though I am not sure I will actually be able to get around to them.

This year I really want to finish drawing enough True Cat Toons (the website is truecattoons.com) to make a book. I have not found a publisher for it yet, but I am looking forward to publishing it myself, to perhaps have a source of income beyond dumb day jobs. I am still collecting people's stories for it, though I have a backlog of them to draw, as well. It is really fun to do these little cat stories and I am learning how to draw cats much better than I used to. I also have a companion book,

How To Draw Cats For People Who Think They Cannot Draw, that needs to be completed, and I need to learn how to arrange text and images on a page with a computer for this one.

I am most excited about my Mother Mountain novel series, which is a spinoff from my Winging It graphic novel from the 1980s. I have been writing this off and on for over 15 years (having to drop it for many months at a time); it began as a graphic novel (part of it published in my second Winging It book though it seems to be based on quirky themes that I have been working on pretty much all my life) and morphed into words-only. I am just finishing the second installment (each book is about 130,000 words, quite a hefty amount of words) and have about half of the third (of four) books in progress. Of course, I wrote a 100-page graphic novel prequel a few years ago that I would love to draw and turn into a color web comic. I can close my eyes and visualize this in gorgeous color... I just have to design the characters and draw the story and learn more about how to do pages in color. I have not had much luck finding a publisher for this either, since it is LGBT, but not conventionally so, and sort-of fantasy but not of the urban or genre sort, and not starring the expected vampires, werewolves, pirates, zombies, wizards, or sword-slinging heroes. I had a well-respected bestselling author in our critique group who gave me glowing feedback tell me frankly that he had no idea who would want to publish it. I love this book and the characters very much, so that will hopefully become a self-published book this year, too. It would make a great e-book as well, and I am designing a web site to accompany it.

Of course, I have not forgotten Bitchy Bitch... I have been writing a new graphic novel with her over the last years, also in bits and pieces, and I would love to have the time to sit down and draw this as well, either all at once or to put on the web in installments. My goal is to have this up and running by the time of the 25th anniversary of Naughty Bits, which would be 2016. I have had to downsize and move my home office, but in the process, I came across and organized lots of my older comics that are decades out of print, and it looks like there are plenty of pages for a collection, though I would much rather have some new work published before this happens.

I have some other shorter projects, a 10-page comic with a new character I am very excited about, whom I am still designing. Writing has always been insanely easy for me, but drawing is a challenge. It takes so much constant drawing to stay in practice. I think of myself more of a writer who also draws than someone who can really balance art and writing successfully.

I realize a lot of this sounds like the ravings of some manic personality, but I sincerely want to get this all out, and more, but the challenge is to turn my days, which are now pretty chopped up with a "day job" (actually an evening and weekend job that dominates what have always been my prime creative hours), into productive enough chunks to put a dent in all this creativity. Whatever is spooning out all this wonderful inspiration seems not to realize that I come from a low income family (no big inheritances to come my way, and no well-to-do relatives to bail me out) and have needed day jobs for most of my life, because I stubbornly seem to insist on creating what I want to read, which does not happen to be bestseller material. On the other hand, it is so exciting to look at the stunning variety of very individual work that would not be in the world if I had not taken the time to create it, so really, I cannot complain. There seems to be so much to look forward to. I also have to learn a lot of techie skills that take a bit longer for someone who started out long before the age of the internet.

What advice would you offer girls and women thinking about pursuing comic book writing/illustrating as a career? What do you think is the greatest impediment to women's success in comics today and how can they overcome it?

Well, me being who I am, I want to tell young women to create work that is very unique to you. To me, the most exciting and intriguing work is something that is very honestly the work of a creative person, something that is really not like anything out there, something derived from their special life experience, colored with their unique insight, distilled from childhood dreams they did not dare share with anyone else, stuff they thought was just too wacko to interest anyone but themselves. Work I would love to stumble across on the web or on the table at Artist's Alley and just be amazed by. I want to see this work and think, "Wow!" (Hoping this does not sound too negative, I see very little of what I consider "Wow" material on the tables of comics conventions, even though I am astounded by all the skill and talent and dedication and awesome production values.)

Of course, if my experiences are any indication, I am not sure if this is really the best way to have a career in comics writing or illustrating, though younger people are already courageous with web sites and social networking and have a head start on getting work out there, so I think it is also much easier these days to get your creativity in front of those who will appreciate it. Of course, there are millions of web sites and web comics already, and there is probably work that I would just find awe-inspiring that I have just not yet happened across, so the other bit of advice is, if you can, to believe sincerely in what you are doing, and let the people who love and support your work know exactly how much you appreciate them.

Since a lot of people buy works in specific genres, I would not discourage anyone who wants to try to make a living in something more genre-specific. I have to keep reminding myself: just because the sight of most genre work makes my eyes glaze over, doesn't mean that there are not millions of readers and thousands of creators who sincerely enjoy work along those lines. (If someone is already churning out wonderful stuff that nobody else would dream of, and loving it, hopefully they are already unstoppable.) I would say, work on a little bit of everything to discover where your strengths lie and then move in that direction. To me, drawing is very labor intensive, so I would suggest gravitating toward subject matter you really enjoy, because you are going to spend a lot of time staring at those pages.

If there are any impediments these days, I believe from experience that they are mostly internal. My last bit of advice is to make the best effort to believe in the value of what you have to offer. There is nobody in the world like you, a combination of your experiences and interests and skills, and if you have something to create, nobody else is going to do it!

Laura Lee Gulledge

Ms. Laura Lee Gulledge is a graphic novel illustrator and writer. Her first graphic novel, Page by Paige, was nominated for an Eisner Award and is the only graphic novel that was nominated for the ALA Teen Top Ten 2012 list. Her second graphic novel, "Will & Whit", comes out in May. In addition, she does freelance illustration, scenic painting, and event planning, among other activities.

How did your love of graphic novels begin? What made you decide to pursue graphic novel writing and illustrating as a career?

I actually didn't read a graphic novel until 2007, so I never could have guessed I'd end up making them professionally! It was a surprising development but somehow made perfect sense. My artwork for years was only in sketchbook form, because I liked the intimacy of the format especially when compared to hanging work on a gallery wall. When I started working on loose paper, I'd hang hundreds of drawings on the wall for a show because the pieces made a stronger narrative as a whole, like I was turning the gallery wall into a book. But my work never fit into the usual categories, so every step felt like a battle. Reading a comic was such a relief, since it combined my love of narrative and books AND art. I was only familiar with capes comics growing up and never studied illustration, so I never knew about this whole other world out there.

In case you wanna know, the first one I read was Fun Home. I was struck by its honestly, because I was writing a personal blog on contemporary art at the time and was so FRUSTRATED with all the art I was seeing. Nothing said anything. But here was this girl, drawing cartoons, talking about real topics with emotional weight. Then the second book was Blankets, and that's when I decided it was the format for me. Because there was a page with no panels and no words, just a single image of two figures walking in the snow. I thought, "Wait, you can DO that?!" I started reading more.

But I'm glad I took the long way around, because I can bring my own influences to the format. I love playing with format and layout especially, since as an outsider to the form you have the benefit of not knowing all the rules (or seeing the rules but simply being willing to take more risks). In the new book "Will & Whit" there are some sections where the "panels" are loosely created using trees and ripples of water, rather than normal lines. Because I simply hate boxy panels!! I've always had a problem of not "fitting into a category" because I love experimentation, and graphic novels are the only place where I can actually mold the format to go along with my crazy ideas. Writing wise, I've never ever ever considered myself a writer. But all my art begins with writing, then thumbnails, then a final piece. So I guess part of me has been a writer the whole time; I was just choosing to distill the ideas thru art rather than translate them into written narrative.

What inspirations did you draw on when creating Page by Paige – both the story and Paige herself?

Page by Paige IS pretty much my story. Well, I merged two big stories into one. The first big story centered around my experience learning to become an artist thru a sketchbook and how the life lessons you learn on paper can spill over into your real life. I used to be a teacher, and I believe that there are many ways to do so. Page by Paige teaches how to be creative through example rather than a classroom, so the reader can take what insights they want out of it. The other big story was my move to New York. This provided more of a catalyst for why the sketchbook was so important. It amplified her feelings of loneliness. Pretty much all the things that happened in the book were based on real interactions and experiences of mine, just jumbled up differently. From making a message-in-a-bottle-tree to going to the Met my third day in New York because I didn't know anyone and wanted to see familiar faces. Paige definitely gives voice to the scared-vulnerable-artist part of my personality. My new character, Will, is more the tomboy workaholic joke-cracking part of my personality. Then the character that's on the docket next is more of my introspective loner side.

If you wanna see the inspiration for Paige, simply go to my website and check out the hundreds and hundreds of drawings! I would illustrate how I felt using myself as my own little character. I felt anxious at a party and bolted, so I drew my silhouette with a giant c-clamp tightening around my chest. I developed my own personal technique of sorta, well, self art therapy meets creative ritual I suppose. So to write the book, I pulled from perhaps 100 of my illustrations. They were like beads on a necklace, and I wrote the rest of the story around them. Will & Whit I wrote totally differently; I got to know the main character first and simply let her tell me the story.

Have you experienced any sexism while pursuing your career? If so, how have you overcome it? What are your thoughts on the way women are portrayed in comics today?

Well, there's the indie side of comics and the capes side as I call it (DC/Marvel stuff). On the indie side, there are lots of girls out there. That's where I live! I tend to avoid the capes side, because it's just not my thing. The stories they tell, the metaphors they use, the characters they present... I simply find unrelatable, but hey, I also can't get into Hemmingway so I know part of this is a gender gap thing. For example, I relate more to stories about mental/emotional strength rather than physical strength. I like to see new characters rather than the same characters over and over. Etc.

But no, I don't like how women are portrayed in mainstream comics. It creeps me out to walk around Comic Con and it's all these overly-sexualized pictures of half-naked women. But I know this is part of a bigger problem as gender roles are in a confusing state of flux right now. I think men are confused by female sexuality in general, confusing "empowered" with "hypersexual." But what can I do? Complain to fan boys? Pshaw. I think the best thing I can do is simply make BETTER COMICS. Complex characters with depth and good storytelling to show the audience a different way to do comics. In my first book there's a gay character, but I didn't flat out say it. It's implied though, so if the reader's attuned to it he or she can tell. (Because I knew she would be labeled as the "gay character" if I said it. I wanted her to be "the musician" character! And it simply never came up in conversation in the book.) In the second book I explore female competitiveness as well as finding strength thru vulnerability, since I think women are figuring out what it means to be strong in a feminine way rather than simply acting like a guy.

My frustration comes more from the fact that I can't do more to talk about sexuality and gender at this point in my career. It gets you into too much trouble, and I hate feeling censored about topics I'm passionate about. But I know it's a bigger society issue. It's the one topic I always push the envelope with. For example: I used to have a body painting business; I've produced pieces for a radio show that promoted healthy sexuality called Audiosmut (like a guide to extended orgasms!); I've held figure drawing sessions where the artists modeled nude (including me); I've spoken openly about date rape, etc. I guess I'm targeting the next wave of creators rather than the fan boys and their bizarro Catwoman covers. I mean, IMAGINE what books girls will make in 10 years now that there are all these great new graphic novels coming out of the indie side being made for them?

I guess as I'm at this point in my career, I'll keep promoting change through my conversations with people, modeling the change that needs to happen, and doing work under the radar (the radio stuff is under the name "Red Velvet," giggle).

Please tell us about your current projects. What excites you the most?

I just finished my second graphic novel, "Will & Whit," which comes out in May. I can't wait to share it with folks!! I really challenged myself to do something different than "Page by Paige," so I hope the risks pay off. I drew it really fast because I was so terrified it would be awful that I just wanted to get it over with. (I think that's called "Second Book Syndrome"?) "Will & Whit" is set in Virginia in the summertime, which was fun to draw since it reminded me of home. The main character, Wilhelmina (Will for short) is a sorta old-fashioned gal who makes lamps because she's afraid of the dark. (Her shadows in the book are alive, literally following her around.) It's the end of summer and she wants to enjoy time with her friends outside rather than hiding behind computer screens. She gets her wish in the form of a hurricane named Whitney (Whit) that knocks out the power... but it also forces her to deal with her fear of the dark. This book is about fear, strength, and dealing with change. Page by Paige felt like a story that I was telling an audience, but Will & Whit feels more like a story being told to me. I trusted my characters more, so they were able to surprise me. I didn't know where it was going. Writing makes so much more sense to me now.

I'm actually developing "Will & Whit" as a girl-powered DIY musical with my friend Lauren Larken. I'm beyond excited about this!! She's a songwriter whom I met in New York years ago, and we recently had a 6-month multi-disciplinary collaboration called "Artnership." That's when we got the idea of combining efforts to bring my story to life. The shadows could be created using shadow puppets or actors behind a screen. Smart integration of technology and simple set-design techniques rooted in my experience as a scenic artist. I could go on and on, but since it's still in the baby stages of development, I don't want to get too ahead of myself.

And I have another story I've been slowly cooking for a year now; it's called "Question Marks." Right now it's a sorta New York New Year's Eve noir-of-the-heart. I think the main character is... an animal? My imagination's been having fun with this mystery. I can't wait to have time to dive further into it, especially since I know it'll help me work through my issues about love! My art is my therapy after all. I guess it's part of the reason I work so fast; each story is a lesson I'm writing to teach myself and I can get impatient.

What advice would you offer girls and women thinking about pursuing graphic novel writing/illustrating as a career? What do you think is the greatest impediment to women's success in comics today and how can they overcome it?

Honestly, I think women and men face the same big problem in comics: making enough money to keep doing it! Jeez. Even if you are at a professional level you often still need to have side freelance or some other source of income because this is not a high-paying industry. (That's one reason I do like this industry, since it weeds out the folks who aren't passionate about the art.) But it means it can be discouraging! Heck, I wish I could make a living simply making graphic novels. But you do this because you love the art. You love the stories. So just remember that this like any other creative industry is a LIFESTYLE, not a job. It's a long game. Draw and write the stories you need to say, and don't worry about if it's marketable. Because sometimes you have to make some really bad art to clear out the way for the really good stuff. My art never fit in anywhere, but for years I told myself to keep drawing. Keep drawing. You'll figure out what to do with it later. Just keep drawing. 1000 drawings later, still keep drawing. Talk about your work with everyone, because you're your own PR agent. Creative people have to talk about themselves but you really have to do it! All it takes is one person to believe in your work, just remember that. It can feel impossible, and it sounds cheesy, but if you're making honest truthful work and believe in it (drinking your own kool-aid so to speak) then others will WANT to help you. Not everyone, but the right people. I've only gotten little tiny windows of opportunity along the way, but each one I treat super seriously. My literary agent first rejected me because my work wasn't mainstream, but then days later took me on because she couldn't stop thinking about my work. My editor was my advocate at Abrams; she really fought for my book every step of the way. Every gallery in Brooklyn rejected my work except for one, who let me put a drawing in a group show on a whim... and it was the first one sold (partly because my work was so much cheaper than anyone else's!) So you have to treat the small opportunities like big ones, cause you never know where they're gonna lead. Plant lots of seeds; all you need is for one to grow.

I've always felt that being a girl was an advantage in comics, because there are so many guys drawing similar things that it makes my work stand out from the crowd ("refreshing" is one way people have put it). But I think part of that is an underdog complex, how it's easier to make innovative things if you're not in the majority. Also I find that girls create more fun whimsical comics than a lot of the guys, perhaps because we're less married to playing by the rules when compared to the guys who grew up with comics on a pedestal. I don't think things necessarily have to be harsh and gritty and intense to be truthful, and I see a lot of that in guy's comics. I think truth can be instead presented thru something beautiful, funny, or quiet... which I see more of in girl's comics. I think the capes side of comics has gotten stale and cyclical, so perhaps it's the women who are the ones who are gonna save the day.

Sheila Keenan

Ms. Sheila Keenan is a long-time graphic novel editor and writer for children and young adults. Her work includes both fiction and nonfiction. In fall 2013, she will release Dogs of War, a historical fiction graphic novel about dogs in the military.

What made you decide to pursue graphic novel writing for children as a career?

I'm a long-time editor of fiction, nonfiction, and graphic novels for children and young people. I helped launch Scholastic Graphix in 2005 and then worked for several years at Abrams ComicArts, the comics and graphic novel imprint at the art book publisher. I recently decided to freelance to devote more time to my own writing, but I still specialize in editing graphic novels.

As an editor, I've worked with amazing artists (in alphabetical order because they are all such incredible creators; there's just no other suitable hierarchy!): Kyle Baker, Frank Cammuso, Chynna Clugston-Flores, Barry Deutsch, Amy Kim Ganter Kibuishi, Dean Haspiel, Kazu Kibuishi, Scott Morse, Ted Naifeh, Jake Parker, Greg Ruth, Raina Telgemeier, Mark Tatulli, and Jill Thompson, among others. They're who inspired me to try writing a graphic novel myself. I'm a published author of picture books, beginning readers, and nonfiction for kids, but editing graphic novels was so interesting and pleasurable that I just had to create one myself. Also, I loved witnessing the creative whirl at San Diego and New York Comic Cons and MoCCA. Artists, writers, everybody, just working hard and putting it out there. That DIY energy and determination (even if you do have a publisher) really inspires me!

What do you think is special or unique about picture books and graphic novels as a medium for storytelling?

Picture books? Always loved them! I'm sure that's partly because of childhood memories: being read to, picking one out at the library, that was all big-time fun to me.

But I came late to comics and graphic novels. I didn't read them much as a kid. Then here's what happened: this guy I worked with wanted to get my attention. So he blows up a page from a Love & Rockets comic and leaves it in my office.

It worked! We've now been married 20 years.

My husband, an artist, was a comics guy and there were piles of them and illustrated books lying around the apartment. I was now already hooked on the Hernandez Brothers, but I started checking out the rest of my husband's collection. I'll be honest: super-hero stuff doesn't draw me in as much as illustrated books and sequential narrative. (Though I did have the privilege of working on a book with the late Jerry Robinson, creator of The Joker – what a storyteller!)

When I started writing my first graphic novel, the story ran like a movie in my head, which happens when I write prose, too. But there are differences, since to create a graphic novel you have to balance text, art, and the physical limitations of the printed page. It's amazing to me that I can even think like this when I'm writing/editing graphic novels because in real life, I'm a fairly spatially challenged person: can't tell right/left quickly, have to orient myself physically to read floor plans, never can judge if a car fits in a parking spot, etc.

I think somehow the process works because, for me, graphic novels mimic the way we move through time and space. Our conscious mind is often linear, like moving from panel to panel. But we also focus in and out of the big picture/little picture; we filter words, sights, and sounds simultaneously; we break chronology when we daydream or flashback.

And that's all just like reading a graphic novel. It's a great medium for telling stories because it simulates being alive, no matter what story you're telling.

Have you experienced any sexism while pursuing your career? If so, how have you overcome it?

This is hard for me to comment on, since much of my career has been in children's book publishing, a very female-dominated industry. I do my best to promote women creators and prevent stereotyping in the books I write or edit. Clearly the huge support for a book like Womanthology shows that people want to see more work by women artists get more attention. There are so many talented women artists out there in the comics/graphic novel field that the "comic book guy" idea has got to be changing… and the more women who go into comics/graphic novel editing, the better!

Please tell us about your current projects. What excites you the most?

I'm thrilled that my graphic novel, Dogs of War, is coming out in Fall 2013 from Scholastic Graphix. It's historical fiction, three short stories in graphic format, based upon the real use of dogs in WWI, WWII, and Vietnam. It was an interesting creative challenge to get into the heads of the soldier characters I created for each of these stories, since I'm neither male nor military. Plus it was the first time I wrote (vs. edited) a graphic novel.

I also just had a picture book published, As the Crow Flies (Macmillan), which was a collaboration with my husband, Kevin Duggan. We incorporated paneling into the traditional picture book format, which I think really helped the storytelling. We're now working on another picture book about a whale rescue and will be trying to do something innovative with scale and perspective.

I've got an idea for a YA novel percolating (whales again), which will include visuals and maybe sound in an interesting way, and I've got a secret dream project, very close to my heart: a comic book series about a shadowy, high-powered global women's network. Maybe someday...

What advice would you offer girls and women thinking about pursuing comic book and graphic novel writing as a career? What do you think is the greatest impediment to women's success in comics today and how can they overcome it?

I just saw a news article this week that said that personal connections were more important than ever in helping people get jobs. Many companies were relying on suggestions/connections from their employees in looking for new hires and that just sending in resumes to HR wasn't cutting it.

In other words: everybody's got a slush pile now!

I think the comics/graphic novel world works the same way. But the good news is it's a very supportive community! So if you work hard to make connections, people will respond. Go to as many Cons/festivals/lectures as you can. Schmooze. Buy the kinds of comics/graphic novels you want to create or see published because sales are tracked by publishers when they're looking at new proposals. Talk to creators whose work you like and show them yours. If they're published, find out who their editor is. When you contact a publisher, be sure you're clear on what they publish and if your work is right for them. (Sounds obvious, but trust me, this is often overlooked!) Do a good job presenting your work: write a proposal, which should include a synopsis, address who the audience is and what works might be comparable, and have a sample attached. Include something about yourself in the proposal, especially if you have a "platform" (successful web site or blog, previously published book, etc.). Be sure you have an online presence where an editor can quickly look up your work.

Publishing is going through all kinds of changes right now, so check out traditional publishers, sure, but there are all kinds of self-publishing opportunities too, from totally DIY to Kickstarter to Amazon-sponsored. (Just read the fine print when it comes to what rights you're granting on a book and/or future books.)

I guess if you're creating comics and graphic novels (or want to), you already know this: it doesn't always start off with a bang and big bucks. It's hard work and the payoff can take a long time. But if this is what you really want to do, go for it. You will probably have to find other work to underwrite your creative adventure (to wit, I'm an author and an editor), but what the hell? Come on in, let's keep building the old-girl network!

Barbara Randall Kesel

Ms. Barbara Randall Kesel is a comic book writer and editor. She has worked for the big names in comics, including DC Comics, Marvel Comics, Crossgen, Image Comics, and Dark Horse Comics. She was a 1995 Harvey Award Nominee for Best Anthology for Instant Piano and Best Graphic Album of Previously Published Material for Hellboy: Seed Of Destruction. In 1996 she won the Best Graphic Album of Previously Published Work award for Hellboy: The Wolves of St. August. She is known for her wide variety of work including the Crossgen Chronicles, Star Wars, Supergirl and Batgirl, Comics' Greatest World, and Firestorm.

How did your love of comics begin? What made you decide to pursue comic book writing and editing as a career?

I loved superheroes: I imprinted early on the Superman TV show, the Aquaman animated show, and all the myths and fairy tales I could absorb. I wrote. I acted in my own plays. I directed anybody I could coerce. A registration glitch in high school put me into the Drama 2 class, which was kind of like "Glee" with theater geeks. We had a terrific teacher who bonded us into a little troupe of Thespians who still get together today. I followed theater to college and spent many years backstage at Cal Poly Pomona, still writing, also directing, costuming, doing a little acting, spending a lot of time in the shop, but always with a notebook, scribbling scene or character ideas.

I pretty much walked sideways into comics: escaping from a would-be kidnapper, I found myself in a used bookstore in Pomona (Pfeiffer's Books 'n' Tiques) that sold comic books. I loved comics and had picked them up from a used book store in Seabrook, TX, but could finally get them new and regularly. (You kids with your instant downloads and Amazon home delivery have NO idea how painful it was to try to chase down the conclusion to a two-part story. I only found one nearly twenty years later... Get off my lawn.) So I bought a BUNCH of back issues.

And then I realized I could actually write in to give my oh-so-useful feedback (again, no Internet, no e-mail, no instant communication gratification. I had to walk ten miles in the snow to drop my letters into a mailbox. Don't confuse me by reminding me I lived in southern California then. I'm not listening!). So I wrote about six letters before a big one responding to an editorial comment about female writers and artists... ten pages of useful advice, I'm sure.

Dick Giordano invited me to meet him at the San Diego con and offered me an editorial job. I wanted to finish off my degree, but agreed to write some Batgirl backup stories for him. (One saw print – Len took over Detective and substituted Catwoman for Batgirl. My second script was used for years as an audition piece for new artists.) Then I got my BA and realized that there weren't any theater jobs for me (I'm from the Island of Misfit Allergies, so most of the carpentry/painting/costuming work wasn't possible for me in the era before OTC antihistamines). If I did take a job with DC, that'd get me to New York and I could wander off to become the next Lanford Wilson...

I ended up enthralled by comics storytelling instead and that life took me from DC to Dark Horse to CrossGen to freelancing in between.

You are known for creating very strong female characters. Which of them is your favorite, and what is it that you love about her? What inspired you to create her?

My favorite is usually the one I'm writing at the moment. Sephie (from Meridian) probably has the top spot, but there's Dawn Granger/Dove, Grace, Andra Radiant, Meredith the vain wizard, Barbara Gordon/Batgirl, the Elsegirls, Savant, my fake daughter "L", Garrison, etc. Each was created to be a different kind of woman. I usually build a character around a specific trait or flaw or habit and invent detail from there.

You have taken a strong stance against sexism in the world of comics. Did you experience any sexism personally in your career? Was there any backlash to your creation of strong female characters? If so, how did you overcome it?

I do take a strong stance for the inclusion of vivid women characters, but I'm equally obsessive about creating specific and individualized male characters. Just "characters," no matter who they are. My theater time taught me how much the internal life of a character connects to an audience, and I have always encouraged writers and artists to consider the "role" of each character in their stories. I don't like the roles for female characters limited to "bimbo," and I don't like males limited to stereotypes either.

Girls still have it worse, though. There are a lot of people in comics who'd like to see the participation of female creators or characters limited to the Making of Sandwiches, but there are just as many who realize that women are actually also human beings.

Please tell us about your recent and current projects. What are you working on now? What excites you the most?

What's on my desk today includes a YA novel (outline's done and I'm up to all of chapter TWO!), the creative bible for a new concept I'm working on with a local producer, Digger T. Mesch, the script edits for a writer who will be self-publishing, the business plan for a new venture that I'm crossing my fingers gets funded, pieces for a patchwork quilt top, a long to-do list of the other things I'd like to bring to life, and a note that I need to find a designer to update the website I started in Tampa and kind of let lapse. And change the light bulb over the kitchen sink.

What advice would you offer girls and women thinking about pursuing comic book writing/editing as a career? What do you think is the greatest impediment to women's success in comics today and how can they overcome it?

The two greatest impediments to EVERY creator's success today are money and connectivity: more publishers want to offer creative teams less up front (or at all!) to do the most important work on a comic—making it all up!—so rates have plummeted and royalties are scarce. Luckily, self-publishing is easier than it's ever been, and the internet offers many possibilities for publishing and selling your own work, but you have to sell yourself and your work with great enthusiasm.

I would tell girls to team up when they can: it's always easier to get somebody to look at your <u>comic</u> than to look at your script and/or art pages. It's always easier for artists to break in because you can evaluate their work at a glance; writers need people with time to read their stuff. Don't be afraid to self-publish, but don't expect that you'll make your living that way. Above all else, love what you do, every line of it.

Lucy Knisley

Ms. Lucy Knisley is a comic book illustrator and author. In 2008, she published French Milk, a drawn book about her experiences living and eating in Paris with her mother. She has a web comic series called "Stop Paying Attention" as well as standalone comics and books compiling her comics. She has contributed to several anthologies, and teaches a weekly comics class at a local elementary school.

How did your love of comics begin? What made you decide to pursue comic book illustration and writing as a career? How did your focus switch from painting to comics in college?

I was a big reader as a kid, and I always loved comics. My parents weren't crazy about them, but gave in to my love for Tintin and Calvin & Hobbes and Archie. I liked to use tracing paper to copy the characters from my favorite strips. Later on, I was having difficulty choosing between a career as a writer or an artist. I don't know why it didn't really occur to me that making comics would combine both of these loves perfectly. I'd been making comics for fun, but I think I had too much fun to consider it a viable career. Careers are supposed to be serious. I went with "serious" art, but once I got to art school and was involved in the painting and drawing department, I found that I really missed storytelling and writing. It began to creep into my art in various ways, until I was doing nothing but making comics. It became my favorite way to communicate ideas, and once I was introduced to it as a way to also make money, I was hooked.

What sources do you draw on for your comics and graphic novels – the stories as well as the characters?

Because most of my work is autobiographical, it's almost entirely inspired by my own experiences, conversations with my friends, or adventures I have or hear about. I do a lot of travelogueing. I read good and horrible books, look at great and awful comics, go to movies, see plays, listen to music, eat delicious food. Inspiration is about input; what you put into your machine and how it makes that machine run.

What inspired you to create your travel journal French Milk?

I have a compulsion to create records of significant events in my life. This was a trip I shared with my mother during a time that we both were experiencing profound changes in our lives. It wasn't intended to be a book, at first, but when I got home, I saw that there was a story there, and it became a book.

What are your thoughts on how women are portrayed in comics today?

I do my best to avoid and ignore comics that perpetuate misogyny, sexism, and rape culture. There are SO MANY amazing comics out there that don't make me feel like I'm being attacked through my gender. Why would I want to read the ones that do? Occasionally they're good for a chuckle or to spread awareness, as in the case of Catwomangate, 2012, when a Guillem March cover of the Catwoman comic inspired a flood of responses about women's depictions in (specifically, superhero) comics. The conversations that were had generally needed to happen, and when such a flagrant disregard of anatomy promotes bad art in favor of sexiness, I'm offended not just as a woman, but as an artist. In general, I don't buy DC comics (a company that is guilty of a lot of bad business practices when it comes to artists and women... and costuming), and give my money to artists who deserve it. But Catwoman is a foxy lady? Comics can be sexy and still depict women in a positive way. There are tons, TONS, of great comics depicting hot women that aren't treated as objects, decoration, or victims. I love those comics. You should read those comics. Stop reading/buying/making comics that do otherwise, and they'll slowly vanish – if not from the world, at least from people's radar, one by one.

Please tell us about your current projects. What excites you the most?

This past year has been the year of the travelogue for me. I've done five travelogues of various length, about Africa, Italy, Korea, Scandinavia, and an elderly cruise ship in the Caribbean. I'm presently working on finishing another one about Oscar Wilde and a trip I took to visit geographical touchstones of his life. I've got over 600 pages of travelogue material this year, so I'm currently trying to figure out how to get it out to readers – whether to publish it en masse or dole it out. I'm talking to publishers and trying to figure out where it would be best done. I love to travel, and it makes me happy to make records of it – to write about how a place makes me think and what it looked like to me. It's a nice time capsule to have, and I enjoy sharing it with others. In the future, once I get some of these travelogues out of my system, I'll tackle some fictional stories I've had rattling around for a while.

What advice would you offer girls and women thinking about pursuing comic book writing/illustrating as a career? What do you think is the greatest impediment to women's success in comics today and how can they overcome it?

Don't allow yourself to be treated with anything but respect. I think the nerdy professional community has a tendency to automatically self-disparage. I meet so many young comic women who think that they can only behave a certain way or draw certain stories. Just do what you like, don't let yourself be too influenced by others in or out of the profession – none of us are the paragons of how to be – just draw and write what interests you and don't let the internet, readers, other creators, or critics deter you. Make work for yourself and for people who appreciate your work, and never EVER read bad reviews. They are poison. Try to give absolutely no attention to the remaining dregs of the comics industry that still roll around in their own misogyny and instead surround yourself with peers and role models who likewise shun such remnants of an eye-rolly culture of perves and jerks.

While female role models in the industry are important, as is maintaining camaraderie in the face of remaining sexism and misogyny in the industry, I look forward to an age when "women in comics" panels aren't the only panels at a show that feature women creators. Hopefully sometime soon, the exhausted "women in comics" tidal wave of do-goody separatism nonsense will have died down a bit, and it can be appreciated as a powerful and positive aspect of a creator's persona, rather than something that needs to be generalized and addressed ad nauseam as a defining characteristic of their career. By my calculations, we'll only have to be asked to do another 40 W.I.C. panels each, reiterating the problematic nature of such a panel, before a change starts to take shape. So that's good news! Hope for the future.

Elaine Lee

Ms. Elaine Lee is a science fiction writer, comic book creator, and RPG author. With regard to her work in comics, she specializes in science fiction, fantasy, and horror stories. She is best known for Vamps (with artist William Simpson, for DC/Vertigo) and Starstruck (with artist Michael Kaluta, for Heavy Metal, Marvel, and Dark Horse). She has also written short science fiction stories for magazines, theater, and collections and the computer RPG Secret of the Black Onyx.

Even before beginning your work with comics, you had been working on the science fiction play Starstruck. How did your love of sci-fi, fantasy, and horror begin?

My dad was a science fiction fan and he took me to horror movies and bought me comic books. My mother read me fairy tales. My maternal grandfather was a southern style, baptize-in-the-river preacher, so I was exposed to that biblical mythos, as well. As a child, I loved to write plays based on fantasy material, then recruit kids from my neighborhood to act them out. The picnic table in our backyard was the stage. So, I would write a play, direct it, star in it, make the costumes, and stand at the back gate, taking money for the tickets, as the audience filed in. After graduating from college with a degree in theatre, I moved to Manhattan and was hired for a running role on a soap opera. But the roles available for women were so thin in those days. And there were 11 roles for men for every female role in TV and film. I knew so many terrific young actors and about 2/3rds of them were women, so I started writing pieces for the actors I knew. They were wild talents and I wanted to write wild roles for them to play. At the same time, I was turned on to the work of European comic artists, like Moebius and Enki Bilal, through the magazine *Heavy Metal*. *Starstruck* was born out of my fascination with that work and my love of my insane actor pals. My friends and I founded a theatre company, and I went right back to doing what I loved as a kid, only with a real stage instead of a picnic table. While I was working on the *Starstruck* play, I met fantasy artist Michael Kaluta and talked him into designing our sets and costumes. The comics came after.

How did you decide to transition from television to comic books?

I'm not sure I've ever made a decision in my life. In fact, I'm not a big believer in free will. We move through life running into opportunities, or encountering obstacles, and, depending on our innate temperament, we either jump on the opportunity or we let it pass. We either attack the obstacle, or we avoid it and take another path. I was presented with the opportunity to do a comic featuring characters from the play. I love learning to do new things and was becoming a little bored with acting, so I went for it. In retrospect, it wasn't the brightest idea to quit acting just after having been nominated for an Emmy, but that's what I did, because I'm always going to do the thing that strikes my fancy or piques my curiosity, even if my wallet takes a hit. And you don't turn down working with a talent like Michael Kaluta. After that, one thing led to another.

Your resume of work is impressive and diverse – from comic books to sci-fi stories to a computer RPG, even returning to television through animated series. What is special about each of these different forms of media for telling stories?

Hmm. From a creative standpoint, I love all these forms of media equally, but some give you more freedom, purely because of the cost involved in producing the final product. Screenplays or teleplays, whether for animation or live-action, have a lot in common with comic book scripts. In the first case, you're describing action and writing dialogue to go with those descriptions. In the second, you're describing panels of still art and writing dialogue. The great thing about comics? In terms of labor, it costs the same thing to set a scene on one of Jupiter's moons as it does to set it in your back yard. Producing a comic is cheap when compared to producing a science fiction or fantasy movie or play. No expensive sets to build and the special effects are done with a pencil and pen. So, you can push all the limits without worrying too much about the budget. The medium can't be beat for telling extreme stories of all sorts.

If you're writing scripts for 3D animation, you have to think about the fact that an animator has to build every character, prop, and setting in your script, in much the same way sets, props, and costumes must be physically built for a stage play. If you're working for a small company, you can easily write a story that is too expensive to build. Traditional animation is more like a comic book script. Having a fairy fly over a forest is no more labor-intensive than having a child walk across his bedroom, and is probably less so!

When I left theatre for comics, I had to learn to be concise, as you have much less dialogue in a comic than in a play. Doing science fiction comics, you have to learn to express complex ideas in very few words. Recently, I've been adapting stories from comics and graphic novels for audio, so I'm working in the other direction, taking stories with very few words and giving the characters much more to say. In an audio script, you're still writing dialogue, but you're describing sound rather than visuals. As with comics, you can do outrageous things cheaply with audio. After all, the visuals only have to appear in the listener's mind. The thing I'm enjoying most about this work is that I'm able to give the secondary characters more space. Side characters are almost always the most fun to write.

I loved working on the RPG and spent five years doing it, first writing background and story, then game events, eventually learning to write pseudocode scripts for the events, and, finally, directing the motion capture. The art and music for the game were incredible and I had a blast working on it. But the company went under before the game came out. That sometimes happens with big projects like games or movies. There are screenwriters in Hollywood who make a very good living while never having a film released. It's happened to me only three times, once with an animated series and once with a big comics project, as well as with the game. But I loved creating the bible for the game's world and working out the huge, interactive story and would take another game job in a heartbeat, if one should come my way. (Now, my Geek Mom side comes out...) When they were teenagers, my two younger sons and some of their friends started a company that runs live-action role-playing games. I have occasionally played with them and really enjoy taking part in these big events that combine theatre, gaming, and storytelling.

It seems like I've talked a lot about the restrictions of these various forms, but that's what you must think about when you're doing collaborative writing. You're working with artists, editors, producers, and animators, and your ideas have to mesh with theirs and be fitted to the rules of the medium. From a story standpoint, writing the bible for a video game world is not much different from creating a comic book universe. But in the case of a creator-owned and controlled comic series, a writer is only limited by the talent of her artist; with a game there is so much more to consider. The only completely free medium is prose—novels and short stories—where a writer is only limited by her ability to keep her ass in the chair!

What would you say has been your favorite project so far – the one that excited you the most, or has the most lasting power for you?

Starstruck, absolutely, in all its forms. I started writing the play when I was 25 years old and have been working on *Starstruck*, on and off, and in all its incarnations, for all the years since. The play morphed into serialized comic stories, then into a graphic novel, then a comic book series. Though *Starstruck* is an adult story, we did a series of short spin-off stories for kids, *The Galactic Girl Guides*. After that, we expanded the graphic novel into another series, adding stories between the ones we had told and letting readers in on what some of the other characters had been doing. Then, in 2009, IDW began publishing a 13-issue, remastered version of those stories, with *The Galactic Girl Guides* as back-up stories, and beautiful new digitally-painted color by Lee Moyer. In 2010,

AudioComics released an audio adaptation of the play and the next year IDW did a beautiful hardback collection of the comics. This year, Michael Kaluta and I are set to begin work on a new graphic novel. And an updated version of the original play is about to be released from Broadway Play Publishing. Though I've loved doing most of the projects I've worked on, I never get tired of this universe and keep going back to it. We're putting a lot of this material online now, in the hopes that a new audience will find it.

Tell us about your current projects. What are you working on now? What excites you the most?

Working on the new *Starstruck* book, which is a lot of fun. It will be a 144-page graphic novel, 60 pages reprinted from earlier material, and 82 of them completely new story. (We may also add pages of story background and information about the multiverse.) It's sci-fi noir, both a detective story and a love story, and it's set on a huge recreation station in space. Though *Starstruck* is known for its many diverse female characters, this story centers on Harry Palmer, bartender/owner of the Sailor's Grave on Recreation Station 97. Harry is an ex-soldier of the revolution and an ex-proldier (mercenary) who is forced to turn detective in order to find the last in a line of pleasure droids. Why? Because this particular pleasure droid looks exactly like his long lost love. This is the only love story in the world of *Starstruck* and, for some reason, I gave it to a man.

I am also doing work for my company AudioComics. We produce full-cast audio adaptations of stories from comics, graphic novels, and genre fiction. After the company produced the *Starstruck* "audio movie," Bill Dufris and Lance Axt asked me to come on board as a producing partner. Right now, I'm adapting a young adult science fiction novel for audio. When I'm done with that, I'll be launching right into an adaptation of a kids' super-hero comic. As story editor, I'll be working on *Bad Planet*, *The Perhapanauts*, and *Honey West*. In 2012, we released *Honey West: Murder on Mars*, a piece I adapted from a series I wrote for Moonstone

Comics, in which Honey goes undercover to solve a murder on the set of a low-budget sci-fi film. We're continuing the series in 2013 with a story by Trina Robbins. If you're of a certain age, you may remember Honey as the blonde bombshell detective played by Ann Francis on TV in the mid-60s, but the character originated in the pulp novels by a husband and wife team who wrote under the name G. G. Fickling. Future AudioComics plans include partnering with an independent animation studio to produce motion comics, and maybe getting into doing sound for games.

So, currently, I'm doing a mix of original work, adaptation, and story editing. Then there's that 300 pages of unfinished fantasy novel that's been languishing on my hard drive, waiting for me to find time for it!

Have you ever encountered any obstacles in your career because of your gender?

Sure. But proving it is another matter. Back in the early eighties, an editor might come right out and say, "Women can't write superhero books." Discrimination these days is much more subtle than it was back when I first started working. You may be able to sense that you are being discriminated against, to know it's there, but you should always act as if it doesn't exist. I'm a big fan of "acting as if." Are you depressed? Act as if you were happy, and life will go a lot more smoothly. Is a colleague giving you problems? Act as if you couldn't care less and you stand a better chance of eventually winning him over. Thanks to social media, we are, each and every one of us, our own publicist. So we act as if we had a thriving career, in the hopes that we'll attract one. Oftentimes, we do.

What advice would you offer girls and women thinking about pursuing comic book, fantasy, or game writing as a career?

Do what you love, but know that you have little control over whether or not others will love what you do. Oprah Winfrey has done us a big disservice by promoting an idea that takes Joseph Campbell's exhortation to "follow your bliss" and adds "for if you do, you will certainly become wealthy."

I've been chasing Bliss for decades and Bliss can run like a sonuvabitch! You've got to enjoy the chase itself, as you may never receive the financial blessings Ms. Winfrey promises. It's possible you might, but you can't count on it. Maybe you find bliss in something truly odd, something that no more than a small cult of rabid fans will go for. You will be a goddess to those folks, but will never make J. K. Rowling money. When I look back over my own body of work, the projects I did for love, and that I kept control of, are the ones that still make me proud. Projects I did purely for money, and therefore had little control over, are now slightly embarrassing and, I might add, never made the promised bucks. But do what you love and you won't regret it, whether you end up living in a palace or a hobbit hole.

More advice. "There's no crying in baseball." Or in comics. Or in most geeky professions. You're probably working with men. You're certainly competing with men. Learn to take a joking insult and to give one right back. Men insult each other all the time, so you can't crumple like a wilted flower when one of them does it to you. It may even be a mark of respect, so take it as such and wear it like a badge of honor. Turn aside rude remarks or unwanted sexual interest with humor. But if it comes right down to it, no job is worth putting up with major crap. If you plant that idea firmly in your mind, and believe it, people can feel that resolve in you and you're less likely to have crap flung at you. During the time I worked in comics, I never had trouble with sexual harassment, perhaps because any guys who might engage in that behavior felt I would laugh at them. Unless I was actually interested, that is. But that's a topic for another time and place!

What do you think is the greatest impediment to women's success in these fields today and how can they overcome it?

Though it's slowly beginning to change, the audience for mainstream comics (Marvel/Disney and DC/Time-Warner) is still overwhelmingly young and male. The publishers, editors, artists, and writers are mostly male and were all comics fans before they started working in the business. They're used to living in that "no girls allowed" world and they tend to hang around with each other, doing guy things.

True story. Some years ago, Michael Kaluta and I were traveling down to Houston, Texas to sign *Starstruck* books at a comic shop. The shop owner called Michael and said, "We've never had a woman guest before. We usually take these guys to strip clubs. What do we do with her?"

These days, most comic shops have had the occasional female guest, but we are still in the minority. It can be tough to find a mentor, or to get a foot in the door. How to overcome it? Do your own thing. If you can't get a job in mainstream comics, do a web comic. Can't find a publisher who will pay you to draw or write? Publish your own book, financing the project through crowd-funding sites like Kickstarter and IndieGoGo. If I were a young woman starting out today, that's how I would do it. I believe in creating original work and keeping the rights to it.

Assuming you can get a shot at it, writing or drawing work-for-hire comics, featuring company-owned characters for a Marvel or DC, can be a good way to get your work seen by a large audience. But I wouldn't stay too long at anyplace that denied me ownership of my work. And never give the rights to an original work you've created to one of these publishers. Many "creator-owned" contracts are not what they claim to be. So, those big superhero movies that make billions for Time-Warner and Disney do not result in big paydays for the people who create the characters.

Truthfully, the old-school comic book biz is dying. Sales of monthly comics, or floppies, are down. It's all about graphic novels and web comics now, and there are lots of women doing this work. My writer son, Brennan, and artist Molly Ostertag co-created the popular web comic *Strong Female Protagonist*. They just signed an option agreement with a producer who wants to turn it into a TV show. Maybe it will happen, maybe it won't. But they own their work outright. If the producer makes money, they'll make money. In the meantime, they're planning to do a Kickstarter for a printed book as soon as they have all the pages done. That's the way to do it now.

And if you decide to sell the rights to your work, make sure you get Hollywood money, not comic book money. There's a huge difference!

Christy Marx

Ms. Christy Marx is a prolific storyteller who works in diverse areas including comic books, gaming, animation, and television. Her television credits include Babylon 5, Spiderman, Jem, and Teenage Mutant Ninja Turtles. Her game design has ranged from MMORPGs to regular RPG video games to social media games with Zynga. Her comic book credits include Sisterhood of Steel, educational manga, and work with DC Comics.

You have written for many of the TV shows with which I grew up, including Jem and Teenage Mutant Ninja Turtles, as well as the much-loved Babylon 5. How did you get into writing for TV? What made you decide that writing scripts/stories such as these was your passion?

All my life, I've been a storyteller and voracious reader. From my earliest years, I tried to tell stories by drawing them in sequential panels and I grew up obsessed with comic books. My dream was to grow up to draw comics, but I didn't quite have the artistic talent for it. Although I took stabs at creating characters and writing stories, somehow it never occurred to me that writing was a career path until I finally realized that I wasn't going to make it as an artist.

I got into writing for comics first by pitching an idea to Roy Thomas when he was editor-in-chief of Marvel Comics. Then I rather accidentally fell into writing for animation because of the comics connection. By networking with comics and animation people, I was able to cross over into live-action television. And it was my work writing in those media that got me the break to design and write videogames.

Your work is incredibly diverse, from television to comic books to video and computer games. What is unique about each medium for storytelling? What do you love most and find the most challenging about each?

I wrote a book, Writing for Animation, Comics and Games, which details the craft of these types of writing. I call them visual storytelling because each one of them presents the story in a visual manner. I love linear storytelling in comics and animation and TV. I love the challenges inherent in writing for games where the story must mesh with gameplay and allow the player to be in control. These three types of writing are also what I refer to as "shorthand" writing because there is limited space for the writing, so everything must be tight and precise.

Did you encounter any discrimination while pursuing your career because of your gender? If so, how did you overcome it?

In general, no. I was lucky enough to charge ahead in my career without stopping to consider whether I should be doing it as a woman. I only encountered one episode of sexual harassment early in my career. It had a severely negative impact because it happened to be a story editor who cut my work to shreds after I refused to go to bed with him and nearly drove me away from writing. Luckily, a far better job opportunity came along and I was able to move beyond that.

What projects are you working on now? What excites you the most?

I'm extraordinarily lucky in that I'm making a living doing things I enjoy. As a Narrative Designer at Zynga, I'm having an amazing time developing and writing social games, which is a huge new field of entertainment. There's so much to learn about it.

And I'm writing comics for DC Comics. Comics remain a deep passion of mine, so I'm enjoying that tremendously. Currently, I'm working on a series called Birds of Prey.

What advice would you offer girls and women thinking about pursuing science fiction, comic book, or game writing as a career? What do you think is the greatest impediment to women's success in these fields today?

I think the greatest impediment to anyone's success is to give up or to let someone drive you away. Women need to be aware that these careers are an option and that they have the same potential as anyone else to pursue them.

Learn what you need to know. Network. Hone your craft. Write and write and write because like anything else it takes practice. Don't let anyone tell you that you don't belong. Be thick-skinned and don't take rejection personally. These are competitive fields, so forget about being female and focus on being a writer. Be so good at what you do that no one can turn you away. Remember that success is 90% perspiration and 10% inspiration.

Ann Nocenti

Ms. Ann Nocenti is a comic book writer, journalist, editor, and filmmaker who is best known for her long run on Daredevil. Ms. Nocenti has worked with Marvel and DC and has written about several contentious political and social issues including animal rights, women's rights, alcoholism, and the role of government. She introduced the popular antagonist Typhoid Mary in the Daredevil series. Ms. Nocenti's other work includes X-Men, Spider-Man, Batman, and the Kid Eternity series at Vertigo.

How did your love of comics begin? How did you decide to pursue writing/editing comic books as a career?

I didn't have a love of comics until I started writing them. I got a job on an editorial staff, as an editor, and then started writing. It was in the course of writing them that I fell in love with them.

You have created several popular characters in your work, including Typhoid Mary. What inspires you when you are developing a new character/story?

Usually I take from my life. I think a lot of writing is unconscious; you do the mechanics of a conscious plot but what you're hoping you'll see in there is your unconscious, the things that interest you. I recently read a story that I wrote years ago. I wasn't aware that certain ideas or desires that were obsessing me at the time had made it into the comic.

I write with my morning brain; it does the mechanics. And when I'm drifting off to sleep later I'll often bolt awake; I'll have the real good stuff and write it down.

What are your thoughts on the way women are represented in comics today?

Because I don't read a lot of comics I can't answer that question. When I started out in comics there were some strong females. It's across the board; in different media, developing strong female characters came later than developing strong male ones.

There are some gender clichés that are fun to riff on for both genders; the high testosterone guy, for example. With Typhoid Mary I wasn't making a statement; I thought, what if I put all of these stereotypes into one character? Typhoid Mary the manipulator, Bloody Mary the feminist, Virgin Mary the virgin.

You have never been afraid to address important issues in your work, be it alcoholism, animal rights, or women's rights. What is it about comic books that enables frank discussion of these issues, and perhaps brings them to light in ways that simple activism can't?

I think that in a medium where you're fictionalizing a social justice issue, you think of someone like Erin Brockovich, a lot of people get drawn to the attention of an issue more than they would in journalism. It's the power of the dramatic fictional interpretation of something that hooks the heart and hooks the soul.

I remember reading way back a comic called Palestine, by Joe Sacco, which was from the viewpoint of someone in Palestine. It was aware and street-friendly; it got you into the issue in a way that journalism can't.

They're siblings of each other, fiction and journalism. I did a story on animal rights in Daredevil. I investigated the issue first; I wrote a letter to some institutions pretending to be a startup and got responses that I was able to put into the comic.

Please tell us about your recent and current projects. What are you working on now? What excites you the most?

I'm doing two books, and I'm working on both film and comics. I'm doing a film working with indigenous kids around the world. I've been teaching screenwriting for years, as well as film in Haiti. There's a group called the Indigenous Film Circle that flew people from all over the world into the Arctic Circle. I'm working with them on screenplays and am very excited about that.

As for comics, I'm working on Catwoman and Katana. Catwoman everyone knows; she's lots of sexy fun, a blast to write. She puts on her black suit and goes out; I love her.

Katana is very influenced by Japanese martial arts movies, also Chinese and Korean; they have all these deep concepts in them about justice and vengeance. I'm putting my love of that whole genre into Katana comics.

What advice would you offer girls and women thinking about pursuing comic book writing/editing as a career? What do you think is the greatest impediment to women's success in comics today and how can they overcome it?

It's an across-the-board question. The whole arts business is falling apart in terms of financial reward; it's become more of a roulette wheel, more of a craps shoot. No one should let it be daunting to them, though.

It used to be that if you created a comic, you could find someone to publish it. Film is the same; there used to be money in it. The whole paradigm of arts is shifting, with Kickstarters and crowdsourcing funding. If you're passionate and believe in it, you just have to do it. Pay attention to how the industry has changed; do a Kickstarter. Make your comic digital, online, in order to get a fan base first. The models of making art have changed radically from when I started making art. But I'm a geek; I'm a nerd; the essential core is same. You're at home being geeky and making something that comes out of your unconscious. It's just the way you take work out into the world that has changed.

Rachel Pollack

Ms. Rachel Pollack is a science fiction author, comic book writer, and expert on divinatory tarot. Her work with the tarot has been extremely influential in women's spirituality and has appeared in Neil Gaiman's work. She is known for her work on Doom Patrol with DC Comics' Vertigo imprint and for introducing themes rarely discussed in comic books, including the introduction of the transsexual character Coagula. She won the Arthur C. Clarke Award for Science Fiction for "Unquenchable Fire" and the World Fantasy Award for "Godmother Night".

Your work on Doom Patrol with Vertigo introduced many themes that are important to women but uncommonly found in comic books. What inspired you to discuss these topics through comics? How did you come to perform this work with Vertigo?

To some extent, the answers to both questions are the same. I was inspired by Grant Morrison's work on the comic. The second question first – I met the editor at a party and told him that I admired DP very much and in fact had fantasies of writing it. He said that coincidentally Grant was ending his run, and why didn't I submit a sample script. I did, and it was approved. One of the problems I had with fans, I realized much later, was that as a woman I approached the book differently than the usual model. That is, people were used to a kind of Oedipal situation, where the new writer overthrows the previous one, changing everything. This did not occur to me; I sought continuity with what had inspired me, and at the same time took it in my own direction. So I neither slavishly copied Grant nor tossed him aside. And one of the things that inspired me was his exploration of sexuality and alienation, especially the character of Dorothy. In his run, Grant hinted strongly that her powers came from menstruation, and I made that clearer, which seemed to shock some people. But more, I wanted to look at issues of shame and feelings of being different, and not good enough, which many girls (and certainly boys as well) experience.

Your influence in women's spirituality has been profound. What brought you to the Tarot and Kabbalah? When you teach seminars on the Tarot, are there any key messages you want your audiences to take home?

I came across Tarot by accident, when a friend read my cards, and was immediately smitten. I think my experience as a comics reader had something to do with it, since the images on the cards are like single panels in a comic. Through Tarot I came to Kabbalah, which I had never heard of, even though I grew up in a traditional Jewish home. By contrast, women's and Goddess spirituality was something very powerful in the feminist and counter-culture world of the 70s and 80s. So was the return of Paganism. By that I don't mean the particular practices and traditions of the modern Neo-Pagan religion, or Wicca, but the wider idea of recognizing ourselves in Goddesses and Gods, and restoring our attachment to nature, and, as with Doom Patrol, our own bodies. I wrote a book called The Body of the Goddess, looking at the origins of religion as connected to nature and the body.

With Tarot, I sometimes call my approach Loving The Image. I tell people always to return to the picture, see what you can discover there. Despite various claims, there is no official meaning of Tarot, just because the first decks were produced without explanations, and in fact, nothing was written or at least published about them until 1781. So no one owns the meanings, though there are powerful traditions. I created a deck, The Shining Tribe Tarot, and once gave a workshop on it. A woman came who loved the deck, would not use any other. But – she had never seen my book, and so had created her own meanings, many of which were opposite to mine. She was worried I would be angry at her, but I was thrilled. I also try to emphasize that Tarot is like a door – or 78 doors – to worlds of spirituality, imagination, and ancient traditions, and that this is at least as important as doing readings to find out if your boy friend loves you.

How has your spirituality informed your fantasy novels?

I would hope that it grounds them in a wider background and practical experience than is always found in fantasy. I've just finished a novel, The Child Eater, that creates its own mythology but is inspired by various magical and mythological traditions. And since my spirituality is all about people's own experiences, rather than dogma or rules created by authority, I hope my characters show how we can experience spirit in our lives.

What advice would you offer girls and women thinking about pursuing writing in fantasy, science fiction, or comics as a career? What do you think is the greatest impediment to women's success in these fields today?

The most important thing girls and women can do is believe in themselves. Men tend to put themselves forward with greater confidence. There's a joke I heard that says a lot. A woman sees a posting for a job she would love to have, and notices that it lists 5 skills or knowledges needed. She thinks, "Well, I have 4 of those, I can go off and learn the fifth, and hopefully it will still be open." A man sees the listing and thinks "Great. I've got two of those, I'm all set." Believe in your work, believe in your imagination. And most of all, keep writing. I teach in an MFA program (from Goddard College), and this is what all the faculty tell our students. The most important thing is to not write something and then stop. Something else that is important –read widely, especially older work, not just what is currently popular, and not just the kind of writing you want to do. And try to make connections with other writers. Go to conventions, join groups, meet people.

What advice would you offer girls and women seeking to explore their spirituality?

Again, read lots of different approaches, explore ancient traditions, but believe in the truth of your own spiritual feelings and intuitions. Trust that the reality of spirit is inside you, not in some priest or book. And just as with writing, find others who have similar interests – friends, groups, conventions. And have fun! Be suspicious of any spiritual tradition that says you need to suffer, and especially of any that tells you you are worthless!

Trina Robbins

Ms. Trina Robbins is a comic book writer and "herstorian", a pioneer of the underground comix movement. She is best known for the Honey West comic series, Vampirella, the anthology Wimmen's Comix, and her work on Wonder Woman. She also compiled the best of Nell Brinkley's work into a collection called "The Brinkley Girls", reprinted Tarpé Mills Miss Fury comics, paying tribute to the first female superhero by a female author, and wrote a book about Lily Renée Wilheim called "Lily Renée, Escape Artist", recognizing a woman who overcame tremendous odds to become a comic book pioneer. She has also published several volumes on the history of women in the comics industry. Ms. Robbins has received several awards, including an Inkpot Award in 1977, a 1997 Lulu of the Year award for "The Great Women Superheroes", and the 2002 John Buscema Haxtur Award for her comics published in Spain.

In previous interviews, you've stated that you have loved and been drawing comics since your early youth, inspired by the likes of Raggedy Ann, but stepped away from that passion for several years due to discouragement from your mother until East Village Other drew you back in. Is this an accurate description? Can you talk a little bit about what that process was like for you? For example, do you think your mother's discouragement was in any part gender-based, or was it more the stereotype that comics are for kids? Was the period when you were not involved with the field you loved painful for you? What about East Village Other attracted you and made you commit to comics?

Actually, I had already become interested in comics again when the Batman show started on TV, and there was a sudden interest in pop art. Then I got introduced to the new Marvel comics, with Spiderman, Doctor Strange, Thor, and that inspired me to try to draw a comic. But the comic I tried to draw didn't work, because, seeing all those superheroes, I naturally tried to draw a superhero comic, and that simply wasn't me, so I abandoned it. Then someone showed me a copy of EVO (The East Village

Other), and it featured comics I could identify with, psychedelic comics if you will, that related to my lifestyle. The one that inspired me most was a full page comic called "Gentle's Tripout," signed by "Panzika", and it was quite telling that two years later I found out that Panzika was a woman, Nancy Kalish. So, inspired by EVO's comics, I actually drew a simple 4 panel comic that was published in the L.A. Free Press before I went to NY and drew for EVO.

My mother's discouragement was never gender-based! My parents were totally permissive of my reading comics as a kid – I read everything, comics and books! – but she definitely believed that comics were for kids, and now that I was in high school I should put away childish things. No, doing without comics was not the least bit painful, because at the age of 13 I discovered science fiction, and soon was gobbling up all the sci-fi books and magazines I could find.

What were your favorite science-fiction stories? Do you think that they inspired your later work?

The writer who inspired me most has got to be Ray Bradbury. His writing is so gorgeous! But I don't think any of it inspired my later work, except that of course I have used science fiction in my comics – but so has everyone else.

As one of the pioneering women in the world of alternative comics, how did you overcome the sexism you encountered to establish yourself (both as a female comic artist and writer and as a writer of comics for women and girls)?

I overcame the sexism simply by not giving up! I'm an ornery type, so when I saw that the guys didn't want me in their books, in fact, mostly hoped I would just disappear, I knew I would NEVER disappear! Luckily, the publishers weren't part of the boys club; they just wanted to publish good comics, comics that would sell, so I did my own books, and collaborated with the only other woman in San Francisco drawing comics, Willy Mendes, and the books got published.

In addition to writing your own comics, you have also written about other female comics. Can you discuss what made you decide to become a "herstorian"?

Nobody else was writing about women cartoonists! If you read the comics histories at the time, you would find either a very cursory mention of maybe one or two women cartoonists, or none at all. (And of course all those books were written by men!) The result was that the comics publishing world suffered from a mass amnesia, believing girls and women never read and had never drawn comics. Obviously, I had to do something about that!

Tell us about your current projects. What are you working on now? What excites you the most? You were a part of the recent Womanthology: Heroic project; will you be continuing with them on the Womanthology: Space project?

I've just finished two important books: my final and definitive history of women cartoonists, "Pretty in Ink," for Fantagraphics, with much, much more art and photos and lots of new information, and a collection of the comics of Golden Age cartoonist Lily Renee. I'm always excited to discover Golden Age women cartoonists who are still with us, and to meet and speak with them and listen to their amazing stories. Last August I was in NY and took the train to Middle of Nowhere, New Jersey to meet Fran Hopper, who had drawn beautiful comics in the 1940s and was now a vibrant 90 years old – what a great experience!

Yes, I was honored to be included in the first Womanthology, and I contributed a two-page article on Lily Renee to the next one.

I continue to write graphic novels to be illustrated by other artists. I have a graphic novel series that I write for younger readers (but grownups like them, too) called "The Chicagoland Detective Agency." The illustrator, Tyler Page, gets better with each book, and #5 in the series will be out in 2013, and it's his best art yet. And I've been writing 2-part Honey West comics – two of the 2-parters are already out, and the illustrator is just finishing illustrating the 3rd 2-parter. Honey West was the first female private eye/action heroine on TV, played by the gorgeous and sultry Anne Francis, and I loved her then and love her now, so it's been fun.

What advice would you offer girls and women thinking about pursuing comic book writing/illustrating as a career? What do you think is the greatest impediment to women's success in comics today and how can they overcome it?

Well, nobody can say anymore that women don't read and/or draw comics, because there are more women drawing comics today than ever before. And there's a huge market for graphic novels out there, so nobody has to draw superheroes anymore. So the fact is, I don't think there are any impediments for a cartoonist who is willing to work hard and put a lot of time and energy into their comics.

Colleen AF Venable

Ms. Colleen AF Venable is a comic book, web comic, and graphic novel writer. She designs graphic novels for First Second Books and writes graphic novels about adorable guinea pigs and hamsters. Ms. Venable has had her photographs exhibited in seven different countries.

How did your love of comics begin? What made you decide to pursue graphic novel writing as a career?

Growing up it was a race every morning. I'd rush out of bed, run to the paper on the dining room table and frantically flip to the comics section... though if I was the loser that day there wouldn't BE a comics section since my older sister Kathleen had already taken it out! Whoever got there first got the comics. Calvin and Hobbes, The Far Side... I think of the 80s as the golden era of newspaper comics. Anything comics format that came across my eyes, I devoured it. The visual jokes, the word play, the way panels could break up the action for comedic timing; I loved regular books too, but there was something about the format of comics that grabbed me at a really early age.

There wasn't a comic book store in my village or any bookstores at all for that matter, but if I begged enough my mom would buy me an Archie or a copy of Disney Adventures in the checkout at the supermarket. I didn't read many mainstream comics when I was young, mostly because they weren't available. I didn't even step into a comic book store until my mid-20s, dissuaded by the stereotypes that girls weren't welcome and the staff would look down at me for my lack of superhero knowledge.

What really led me to a career in comics was the webcomics boom of the early 2000s. I had just finished my college degree with a focus in playwriting and was working as a receptionist with a LOT of time to surf the internet between visitors and calls. Dinosaur Comics by Ryan North and Scary Go Round by John Alison were two of the first that really grabbed me. It was like this rabbit hole, each comic linking to ten other great comics. After a few months I was following over 40 comics, all published online in a D.I.Y. fashion, most never making a single penny off of it.

I got inspired by the movement, especially after my first professionally-produced play coincided with a blizzard and our "sold out" two week run got buried under the snow. One performance only four audience members showed up. It broke my heart. The more I read comics the more I realized how easy it was to share comics. Comics didn't die the way a play did after a few performances and comics had a lot of the same elements I liked about playwriting: timing, visual comedy, and strong dialogue. In 2004 I started a webcomic named FLUFF IN BROOKLYN, a photocomic that starred stuffed animals and live actors interacting in public places all over the city. Three years later I had a small but crazy loyal following of a few hundred readers, which was nothing compared to my friends getting 150,000+ views a day. But it's not always about numbers because one of my favorite readers-turned-friend was Carol Burrell – another amazing webcomic artist; her SPQR Blues is still one of my favorites – who went on to become an editor at Graphic Universe, a comics press for kids.

What inspired you to write Guinea Pig, Pet Shop Private Eye? What do you draw on in coming up with storylines?

One night at the movies Carol was talking about books she wished existed. She mentioned something about an idea of a really young comic mystery series that took place in a pet shop. With a mouth full of popcorn, yes I am that classy, I said "Heh, how about a Guinea Pig but the g in pig falls off her sign so everyone thinks she's a P.I.?" I laughed, having no clue I just pitched a book. A few weeks later Carol wrote me a contract for the first two Guinea Pig books. I spent the next year and a half hiding under a bed telling her I was too scared to write it. Finally she got a first draft out of me, and six books later both of us couldn't be happier.

Sasspants, my guinea pig hero, was born that day at the movies, but Hamisher, her sidekick, was around way before then. Hamisher was based on a character from my webcomic, a super hyper jerboa who always means well but doesn't quite know what he's doing most of the time. And actually both Hamisher and Furboa were around WAY before either of these comics existed... because that was me growing up. Hamisher is based on me in elementary school, and Sasspants was based on my older sister Kathleen – I desperately wanted to play and be her friend and she desperately wanted me to leave her alone.

I wanted there to be an arch for the six books in the Guinea Pig series, all of the main characters growing or changing in some way, and I wanted there to be a concrete ending. I watched a LOT of Murder She Wrote growing up and I used to joke even as a kid that you should NEVER invite Angela Lansbury's character to your town because someone would die. The only plausible ending for that series was that Angela Lansbury's character was really a serial killer the whole time! I wanted the mysteries to be believable and I wanted Sasspants and Hamisher to slowly become friends and to find themselves in their little pet shop world.

Have you experienced any sexism while pursuing your career? If so, how have you overcome it? What are your thoughts on the way women are portrayed in comics today?

When it comes to the Guinea Pig books I haven't faced much gender discrimination. I think that's partially because kids' comics, in general, are thought of as a lower form of comics by many of the folks who tend towards jerk-based thought. It's okay if a woman makes a comic for kids, but HEAVEN FORBID she draw a male superhero. The stories from my female friends who work for the big two are always so shocking to me because they deal with sexism every day. Most of the time it isn't even from the publishers themselves, who – while still predominately staffed by men – have been slowly getting better over the years. The people being horrible are the fans, dissecting their art, claiming their drawings of superheroes are "too girly." I find it's often a generational thing. Comics fans and creators in their 40-50s tend to fear women in the industry.

In my own day job I've had a handful of creators who protested me designing their books because I was "a chick" and I "wouldn't get it." Once or twice it got so bad that I did a little experiment. After having a cover harshly rejected by the creator, I waited a few weeks, tweaked them ever so slightly, then had my male boss send it to them, giving the impression that he had re-designed it. Both times the creators LOVED the new version sending long paragraphs about how wonderful it was… covers they had hated just the week before. In one instance of doing this I never let the creator know I had designed it. In another instance once they found out it was me suddenly they had a list of notes for me to fix. Strangely enough it just makes me laugh now.

One thing that's been interesting for me is my character Sasspants. She's smart, gruff, and has MacGuyver-eque tendencies. Sasspants was the kind of girl hero I wanted to read about growing up! The kind I wish there were more of. Stephanie Yue, who draws the art, did an amazing job with the character design. She doesn't have long eyelashes or wear a pink bow. She doesn't have visible breasts or wear ridiculous high-heeled shoes. Because of this many readers and even reviewers just ASSUME the detective hero in the stories is a male. Very respected literary journals have written glowing reviews for the series all the while saying "he" for Sasspants. I've even had little kids come up to me and say "My librarian told me Sasspants is a girl, but I know he's a boy." Even by second grade kids have these firm lines about what men and women should be.

As for my thoughts on women being badly portrayed in comics, I say you better watch out publishers! The internet has become a powerful weapon against some of the ridiculousness in the comics industry. A perfect example is DC's revamp of Cat Woman #1 – a cover where magically her butt and boobs decide to shift around her body so they are both completely visible at the same time. The internet ERUPTED, cartoonists of both genders drawing the broke-back Cat Woman doing things like walking down the street, her butt hovering two inches above her head. Three female webcartoonists, Carly Monardo, Meredith Gran, and Kate Beaton, mocked the blatant sexism of the mainstream comics world, creating "Strong Female Characters" who fight crime in sunglasses; one even wears sunglasses as a bra, and not much else. I'm a big believer that the best way to deal with this kind of sexism is to attack it with humor. You probably won't change the mind of the people who made the problematic portrayal, but you will be able to bring it into the consciousness of the rest of the world.

Please tell us about your current projects. What excites you the most?

Stephanie and I are working on a few other projects together, again with cute small animals, because that is where our hearts lie. My first teen graphic novel comes out in two years from First Second Books and is called KISS NUMBER 8. It's a story of a girl dealing with her own gender identity after she finds out her own grandmother had left the family to live her life as a man. Strangely enough it's a comedy, but I think I look at everything in life as a comedy. Some comedies just have a bit more tears, but in the end there's humor and joy in every part of life, even the super angsty teen years.

What advice would you offer girls and women thinking about pursuing comic book and graphic novel writing as a career? What do you think is the greatest impediment to women's success in comics today and how can they overcome it?

Read like crazy! Sherman Alexie once said you should read 1,000 pages for every 1 page you write, and I truly think that's true. And don't just read comics! Read plays, read novels, get to know what types of stories make your brain glow and then read even more of those.

There are a lot of colleges that have fantastic cartooning programs, a major that didn't even exist when I was at school. Learn all the aspects, coloring, editing, even book binding. There are so many careers in comics that aren't just writing and drawing scripts. If you told me when I was eight that I could be a professional colorist when I grew up my brain would have exploded! SO COOL! Draw or write every day, and attend local indie shows. Most states have them now, from Maryland's Small Press Expo to shows like Austin's STAPLE. You'll see everything from creators just starting out, hand photocopying eight page books, to creators who have won National Book Awards. And when you feel ready don't be afraid to get a table at one of these shows and sell your own mini-comics, and don't be afraid to post your drawings online to get feedback and encouragement from your peers. The indie comics world is incredibly welcoming and encouraging. Don't worry your work isn't "good enough" to post or show. Even the greatest artists had to start somewhere. Keep creating and believing in your stories and good things will happen.

Right now so many of the creators making graphic novels and comics are women, many inspired like me by the webcomics world or by the great graphic novels that have been published over the last decade. And every year more graduate. Even those comic book stores I was so scared of when I was little are now bright friendly places with a whole lot of super smart female employees! I truly believe sexism in comics will slowly get overpowered by the sheer amount of brilliant work being made by ladies now and in the future. There will always be jerks, but just don't let those jerks ever stop you from making something you love to make. Don't let jerks rule the world.

About the Author

Jennifer Thorpe-Moscon was born and raised in Brooklyn, New York. In her youth, she loved fantasy and horror, starting with the Goosebumps series, Diana Wynne Jones, and the Twilight Zone, and continuing to authors such as Clive Barker and Anne Rice. She attended Stuyvesant High School, followed by graduating Columbia University with a dual B.A. in psychology and computer science. She received her Ph.D. from NYU in social psychology, where she also honed her skills in statistical analysis. In her spare time, she still enjoys reading, writing, and watching fantasy, science fiction, and horror, with a particular obsession for all things Doctor Who, and also participates in several roleplaying games. She lives in Brooklyn with her husband, Eric, who is a graphic designer.

Made in the USA
San Bernardino, CA
15 April 2013